Nora E

Nora Ephron

Everything Is Copy

Liz Dance

McFarland & Company, Inc., Publishers

Jefferson, North Carolina

LIBRARY OF CONGRESS CATALOGUING-IN-PUBLICATION DATA

Dance, Liz, 1954–
    Nora Ephron : everything is copy / Liz Dance.
        p.   cm.
    Includes bibliographical references and index.

    ISBN 978-0-7864-9674-7 (softcover : acid free paper) ∞
    ISBN 978-1-4766-1929-3 (ebook)

    1. Ephron, Nora.   I. Title.

PS3555.P5Z57 2015
814'.54—dc23
[B]   2015032662

BRITISH LIBRARY CATALOGUING DATA ARE AVAILABLE

Front cover: Nora Ephron (left) and Julie Kavner on the set of the 1992 film *This Is My Life* (20th Century–Fox/Photofest)

Printed in the United States of America

McFarland & Company, Inc., Publishers
    Box 611, Jefferson, North Carolina 28640
    www.mcfarlandpub.com

For David, Eli and Missy.
Because you thought I should.

Acknowledgments

My thanks go to Dr. Geoff Mayer for encouraging me in my Ephron endeavors for the past fifteen years. My thanks also to Dean Brandum for his amazing editing skills and David Ali for his unwavering support.

Table of Contents

Preface

"Everything is copy": Nora Ephron's famous quote succinctly sums up her approach to her work. Perhaps more so than anyone else, Ephron knew that, as a writer, everything that happens to you—everything you see or hear or experience—is material for your work, indeed its finest raw ingredients.

Ephron used her life as source material for her work, a claim not in dispute. However, in doing so, she also maintained authority over her life story. This was very important to Nora. She had the monopoly on what we know about her. Charlie Rose, the high-profile New York–based journalist and interviewer whose weekly interview show is aired in the United States on PBS, asked Ephron, "Who gets you?" Nora squirmed, something she rarely did, and then dismissively said she didn't bother with such things. But such things *did* bother her. Nora had control of her story, but not when she was a child. This is important. As a child, Nora's life was owned by her parents. They used her life as the basis for their most successful original works, the plays *Three's a Family* and *Take Her, She's Mine*. Ephron repeatedly claimed that having incidents from one's life used as source material in the work of others was part and parcel of growing up in a family of writers. Her own work indicates that, in fact, she was far more conflicted about the issue than she was prepared to directly acknowledge.

Ephron had a vested interest in keeping control of her story. As she writes in *Heartburn*: "If I tell the story, I control the version. ... Because if I tell the story, it doesn't hurt so much. Because if I tell the story, I can get on with it." Nora took control of her story through writing and filmmaking and, in doing so, left little room for anyone else to write an alternate version.

What does it mean when you say, "Everything is copy"? When the

1

phrase (attributed by Nora to her mother) is closely examined its implications become evident. The concerns of Nora's life were present in her work and they always had been. In 2010, it became obvious something was wrong: Nora was ill. The collection of essays published as *I Remember Nothing* is overwhelmingly dark—death and cancer surrounded her. It was a time when a number of Nora's friends were ill or had died. Nora rarely wrote about things that weren't of concern to her personally, that didn't affect her directly. The processing of personal issues and concerns had always been a function and defining characteristic of the Ephron modus operandi. Jacob Bernstein recently wrote that there were hints of his mother's ill health in her work, which has no doubt prompted others to look for clues. This book traces the genesis and form and function of this idiosyncratic Ephron credo.

Introduction:
"Everything Is Copy"

Would you go so far as to say your background [Henry and Phoebe Ephron] played no part in your entrée to that career?
No part—not remotely. Their career had ended in the '60s, and my first movie, Silkwood, *didn't come along until 1983.*—Nora Ephron[1]

Contrary to the statement above, Nora Ephron's life and experience as the child of screenwriters Henry and Phoebe Ephron does inform her work. The experience of her childhood is fundamental in the shaping of her creative voice.

Ephron was not and will not be the only writer or filmmaker to use her life as source material for her work. She was quoted as saying, "Everybody writes about their life, that's what writers do."[2] However, it is not whether all writers use incidents from their lives as material that is important. What *is* crucial is that Nora was taught to use life as raw material by her parents; there are idiosyncrasies in her work which directly link her work to that of her parents—idiosyncrasies belonging to her alone.

Over and above the external factors that provided the opportunity for Nora to pursue her career and establish herself as an artist are the circumstances of her upbringing that shape her work. As a child Nora was not only part of a family with its own unique culture, she spent time, although it would seem at times unwillingly, absorbing the craft of filmmaking:

Sometimes we used to go hang out. We certainly had been on sets growing up and had met Jimmy Stewart, and we met Fred Astaire who was in *Daddy Long Legs* [1955] which is a movie they wrote. That's kind of a divine movie. And when my father was producing *Carousel* [1956], which they did the

3

screenplay for, I remember sitting in the mix ... and they were mixing a scene in *Carousel* and watching thirty-five times as they did it over and over and over and crying every single time. I certainly knew something about making movies but I didn't really know anything about it at all.[3]

By the time she was eleven years old Nora was taking an active role in the family business, whether invited or not. Nora tells a story of how she tried to help her parents' career. What is evident from her story is that, at an early age, Nora was already evaluating the quality of the work in a field she would later enter herself.

When I was about ten or eleven, I read one of their unproduced plays and was so outraged it had never appeared on Broadway that I sent it to a famous Broadway producer. My parents were beyond embarrassed.[4]

Well before anything else, Nora Ephron was a child influenced by the life she led as Henry and Phoebe's first daughter. Without understanding her familial background it is not possible to access the core premise of Ephron's credo "everything is copy" nor is it possible to understand the full implication of that premise as it applies to her work. At its most simplified "everything is copy" can be understood to mean that "Ephron dares to draw on and barely disguise what is close to her."[5] At its most fundamental Nora Ephron's work is about herself. Nora Ephron was always in show business. She was a child of Hollywood. In a Peter Arno illustration used in the publicity package for the film adaptation of Henry and Phoebe's 1943 Broadway hit *Three's a Family*, she is the baby being held by the stork. The two people with her are fictionalized representations of her parents.

The alternate name for this book could be *Three's a Family*, such is the intimate, prolonged and ultimately unacknowledged collaboration of Henry, Phoebe and Nora. Nora was integral in the career success of her parents just as they were fundamental to her success. Had Nora not lived the life she did with her parents her artistic voice would not be what it is. Had it not been for Nora, *Three's a Family* might not have been the success it was and neither might have been Henry and Phoebe's subsequent career in Hollywood.[6]

The illustration mentioned above, a caricature drawn in the art deco style popular throughout the 1920s, 1930s and into the early 1940s, locates the film temporally and alludes to the style of their work which, like the subsequent work of their daughter, was sophisticated, dialogue driven, funny storytelling. Their characters, as with Nora's, are for the most part middle class, educated and financially comfortable. In the illustration, you see a stork in the background carrying a baby in its beak, a seated women gazing up uneasily at her husband, who looms over her, shouting, "I *told* you to put screens on the windows!" This captures the contradiction of the Ephrons' joint credo: "Always make it into a funny story, even though it was usually pretty horrible." A funny story "was our coping mechanism, our way of processing what was happening and making it survivable."[7]

On the Turner Classic Movies website, Nora Ephron is described as "one of the most prolific writers to emerge during the latter half of the 20th century." She "transitioned from successful journalist and novelist to write and direct what many consider to be among the greatest romantic comedies ever made."[8] Ephron has also been described as one of the most significant American women of recent times. She was introduced, along with journalist Gail Collins, as having a major impact on the lives of American women through her writing.[9] Such statements might seem a bit grandiose, an exaggeration, if her work is considered only in the context of her Hollywood career. A "hit and miss" director is probably how she is regarded by the contemporary film-going community.

Nora had major success as a writer/director with *Sleepless in Seattle* (1993), *Michael* (1996), *You've Got Mail* (1998) and *Julie and Julia* (2009), as well as major success as a screenwriter with *Silkwood* (1983) and *When Harry Met Sally* (1989). She suffered box-office flops as a screenwriter with *My Blue Heaven* (1990) and screenwriter/director with *This Is My Life* (1992), *Mixed Nuts* (1994), *Lucky Numbers* (2000) and *Bewitched* (2005). Her film work has been consistently described as "light romantic comedies,"[10] "ditsy romantic comedies"[11] and "shockingly conservative" in plot resolution.[12] Ephron's films, on the basis of such opinions, could be best described as popular but ultimately inconsequential.

Commenting on the outpouring of encomiums for the recently deceased screenwriter, David Rooney wrote, "Reading over those tributes, it strikes me that beyond the forgiving critical appraisals and selective memory that invariably follow a sudden celebrity death, Ephron's contribution to contemporary film culture was far more significant than her uneven output would indicate."[13] Rooney is correct in his assessment, but he misses the mark when he ascribes to Ephron the making of films that are "nostalgic throwbacks to the verbal comedies of earlier decades—grounded in chemistry, character and dialogue rather than in high concepts."

What Rooney overlooks, as do the other film critics and writers who see Ephron's films as slight and inconsequential, is Ephron's journalistic clout. She was known for her thorough, considered and incisive reporting, someone who could be provocative and outrageous. Although in this field, too, she had her critics. Of her reporting it was written: "The only investigative reporting being done was into her own spaghetti junction of neurosis."[14] Even her essays were dismissed by some as "soft, witty articles."[15] Nora's work has also been described as acerbic and deadly.

Gary Wills affords Ephron the honor of being the "wittiest journalistic headhunter of the '70s." Despite his disparaging comment on her ability as an investigative journalist, Tom Shone displayed a keen awareness and insightful understanding of humor in general and Nora's work in particular, when he wrote, "Ephron long ago realized that if you were funny, you could get away with anything."

Ephron's work is not inconsequential, nor is it slight. Her films are verbal comedies in the vein of the best "Old Hollywood" romantic comedies, typified by those starring Katharine Hepburn and Spencer Tracy. They are smart and intelligent; they are also complex, as were the best of the classic films. They hold within them the artists' secrets.

Nora was taught by her writer mother that all of life's experiences provide source material from which to write.

> "Everything is copy," she said. ... And I always realized when she said that that someday I would be able to look back on it and—maybe not write about it, but maybe work it into a nice little anecdote.[16]

When Nora transitioned from writing and journalism to screenwriting and then film directing her focus didn't change but her approach did. She had to meet the expectations of the institution of mainstream American film production, which meant she had to adapt her approach to the changed medium. Certainly her parents understood the demand of the industry; Henry wrote, "The name of the game in Hollywood ... was money,"[17] and Nora understood the way Hollywood worked for her. She was well aware of the constraints of working in the mainstream film industry, knowing that the objective of the Hollywood film industry had not altered since the time of her parents. She got work in Hollywood because, as Michael Lynton, chairman and chief executive officer of Sony Pictures is quoted as saying, "If like Nora, you have a long track record of having made money for the company" then the opportunity of more work is available.[18] However, conforming to the expectations of the institution did not prevent Nora Ephron from doing what she had always done. She continued to write about herself and her interests; to chronicle the lives of women and American culture and institutions as she had always done—with humor and from her own experience. Nora Ephron's "nice little anecdotes" formed the basis of her work. She not only managed to document her life by disguising it as fiction, she chronicled the society of which she was a part and was commercially successful while doing so. According to media reports Nora's estate was worth approximately $27 million. Her wealth was the outcome of many years of hard work and self-reliance; her ability to package her life in such a way that she could sell it to newspapers, book publishers, filmmakers, producers of plays and the people who were—and continue to be—her audience. Nora Ephron's significant contribution to contemporary art and thinking can be examined within a number of contexts: humor, genre, women in the film industry, influential women (in relation to the women's movement or as an auteur). Any of these approaches would suffice, particularly an auteurist study, but each has limitations in what could be achieved. None would completely capture the core, the essence, of Nora Ephron's work.

In consideration of looking at Nora's work from the perspective of her reputation as a humorist, comedy is its defining characteristic. She is known for her "extraordinary comic timing."[19] Prior to becoming a screenwriter Nora worked in New York for the *New York Post*, *New York* magazine and *Esquire* magazine at the height of the period, in terms of journalistic style, that became known as the time of the New Journalism.[20] This style of writing, with its blend of journalistic reporting and narrative style, suited Nora. She is renowned for her ability to "observe a social irony,"[21] often through the relating of her own experience. Ephron's writing is personal, witty, intelligent and, at times, lethal. It is a style of humor described by Valerie Grove in the following terms: "The soul of her wit is intimate revelation dipped in acid." Nora built her reputation as a journalist on being funny and she built a reputation as a humorist with an acerbic tone. Nora's wit and humor carried over to her film work. It is an expectation of a Nora Ephron film that it will be amusing and witty, often littered with her opinions delivered via the funny "one-liner."

While comedy is an integral characteristic of Nora's work it is hardly the only one. Indeed, comedy does not define her work; humor is simply a facet of her style. There is substance to the argument that Ephron's earlier career as a journalist is directly related to the style and content of her film work. However, there is a much stronger argument supporting the assertion that Nora's use of humor as both a writer and as a filmmaker is a reflection of her life experiences. Barbara Levy identifies Ephron's use of wit as a mechanism of control: "The use of wit to control both oneself and one's audience."[22] In her insightful chapter on Ephron, Levy also recognizes that it was Phoebe who gave Nora this mechanism for control,[23] thus supporting the proposition that Nora's use of wit is a result of her childhood.

A second approach to understanding Ephron's films is from the perspective of genre. She has been labeled "queen of the romantic comedy,"[24] a title earned because of the success of, in particular, *When Harry Met Sally* (writer), *Sleepless in Seattle* (writer and director) and *You've Got Mail* (writer and director). There is no question that these films have been financially successful and remain popular long after their release date. The line "I'll have what she's having" (from *When Harry Met Sally*) has become part of the contemporary lexicon[25] and *Sleepless in Seattle* is invariably shown on television to coincide with Valentine's Day.[26] The third film in the trilogy, *You've Got Mail*, although not quite as popular as the first two films, made money and completes the Ephron romantic comedies starring Meg Ryan as the female lead. These are the films that, for many, serve as an introduction to Nora Ephron.

Ephron's first romantic comedy success was *When Harry Met Sally*, which she wrote for and with director Rob Reiner. The process of writing and making this film is almost as famous as the film itself.[27] Ephron has written about the character development and that the lead male character, Harry, is somewhat based on Rob Reiner, and the lead female character, Sally, is somewhat based on herself. Because *When Harry Met Sally* is a compromise for Ephron—she did not have ultimate responsibility for the film; Rob Reiner did—and because she has documented the process of compromise it would be possible to examine this film in comparison to the other two films in the Ryan trilogy in order to identify those aspects of her romantic comedies which can be best ascribed to Ephron as a filmmaker.

An examination of Nora's work from the perspective of genre could also include a consideration of her works as part of the cycle of romantic comedies, which emerged in the late 1980s and early 1990s. Frank Krutnik writes about the return to popularity of the romantic comedy in the late 1980s and 1990s and notes that all three of the Ephron films with Meg Ryan fall into a subgenre where "many comedies invoking keynote romantic texts of the past"[28]; *When Harry Met Sally* and *Casablanca* (1942), *Sleepless in Seattle* and *An Affair to Remember* (1957), and, finally, *You've Got Mail* and *The Shop Around the Corner* (1940). But, again, this line of inquiry does not address that which is at the core of Ephron's work, that which identifies and separates her body of work from other contemporary contributors to the genre. While the three films mentioned by Krutnik successfully support his argument—that the "current cycle (of romantic comedies) persistently remobilizes the signifiers of old fashioned romance"—he wouldn't make mention of them if they didn't. Counter to Krutnik's position I would argue that what Ephron was doing was critiquing those signifiers. Her work constitutes not an apparent return to that style of romantic comedy but an examination of the relevance of those films in contemporary society or at any time in film history.

There is debate as to whether Ephron's romantic comedies are simply remakes of the films she evokes or whether she contemporizes notions of romance, allowing for the social changes that have taken place post–1970s feminism.[29] However, her body of work is not confined to that particular time or genre. Spanning 1978 to 2009, her films, at times, defy categorizing. *My Blue Heaven*, *Mixed Nuts*, *Lucky Numbers* and *This Is My Life*, for example, are not romantic comedies. Humorous certainly, but each is unique yet each is distinctly a Nora Ephron film, united by her worldview.

There is no question that to ignore genre is to ignore another significant aspect of Ephron's film work. As Mernit wrote of the development of the screenplay for *When Harry Met Sally*: "Ephron began to use the story as a means to express her experience, insights, and point of view about being single."[30] This takes us back to the personal nature of Ephron's work and the Ephron family credo, "Everything is copy."

Alternatively, Ephron's work can be approached from the perspective of a woman working in the male-dominated domain of mainstream Hollywood. This is and continues to be a topical issue. Tamara Straus, in her highly disparaging article on Ephron, comments: "Today Ephron holds the unique distinction of being a female director with two $100 million box-office hits."[31] Ephron herself spoke of the difficulty of getting films made and has said, "There's no question that it is very hard to be a woman director."[32] She has also spoken about the reluctance of the powerbrokers in Hollywood to back films that are essentially about or from a female perspective—the arena in which Ephron usually worked. The fact that Ephron beat the odds and made a successful career as a female director in Hollywood such an achievement begs the question, What are the distinguishing characteristics of an Ephron film and what marks her work as different?

The most logical framework within which to conduct an exploration of the unique nature of a filmmaker's work is to examine the body of work within the context of the filmmaker as an auteur. François Truffaut first coined the term *auteur* in his polemic "Une certain tendance du cinéma français," which appeared in the influential French film journal *Cahiers du Cinéma* in 1954. "The article was a plea for a more personal cinema,"[33] a cinema which recognized the director as having creative agency. Later, Andrew Sarris redefined Truffaut's notion of the auteur theory, turning it into an evaluative procedure for judging whether a director did fit the criteria of an auteur, criteria determined by Sarris.

Contemporary understanding is that it has now become the expectation that the filmmaker will, in some way, have a personal voice, a creative signature within her/his films. Geoff King, in his consideration of the new Hollywood, discusses the auteurist filmmaker. He writes that by the 1970s it had become an expectation of the collective unconscious of young filmmaker communities that they could and would incorporate the personal in their film work.[34] Film studies, having become part of the academic curriculum, had for the first time produced a number of the filmmakers who were film school graduates. Film directors had previously either come from the theater or had worked their way up through the film industry factory. This is the path taken by Nora's parents who began in Broadway theater and moved to Hollywood. During his Hollywood career, Henry worked as a screenwriter, then producer, and in one instance, director. Filmmakers of the 1970s, such as Martin Scorsese and Francis Ford Coppola (always referred to as auteurs), are film school graduates. As King notes, "Auteur-based approaches were internalized by many products of film schools."[35] For the first time filmmakers had come from an academic background, having studied in a relevant area. As King writes, "It is hardly surprising that they should seek to pursue forms of filmmaking that included a strong measure of personal expression in matters of both style and content."[36] Since its shift from theory to applied principle, which came about with the advent of the film school graduate and its assimilation into the collective conscious (at least for some groups of filmgoers), it is no longer possible to conceive of the film director as being anything other than auteur.[37] The collapse of the studio system where the director for the most part was seen as part of the production line of filmmaking, together with the emergence of film school graduate directors such as Martin Scorsese who have an expectation that "I get to express myself personally somehow,"[38] must lead to an expectation of the director as creative artist.

At the time of the rise of the new graduate filmmaker—the film-maker who simply expected to make films that allowed for personal expression—Nora Ephron had already established herself as a journalist and essayist who had a writing style that was characterized by a personal approach and she was writing about herself and topics of personal interest. The 1970s was a period where personal experience was recognized as artistic inspiration and personal expression had credibility as a legitimate artistic form. Journalism and filmmaking were both part of that movement.

It is of little consequence how the term *auteur* is interpreted. Whether it is an expectation of the director who "is the artist whose personality was 'written' in the film," as Truffaut asserted,[39] or as Pam Cook writes in her discussion of the director Frank Tashlin, "Every *auteur* ends up with a construction not quite like anybody else's,"[40] or as an evaluative process as asserted by Sarris, or if, ultimately, the term *auteur* is accepted in its more contemporary understanding as stated by Robert Stam, "Auteur studies now tend to see a director's work not as the expression of individual genius but rather as the site of encounter of a biography, an intertext, an institutional context and a historical moment,"[41] Ephron fits the above-stated criteria. An examination of her film work reveals a unique personality, one that is ultimately the essence of the *auteur* regardless of whose definition is found to be acceptable. "Nora Ephron" is a personality, an "élan of the soul" transposed into a filmic

11

art form. It becomes a redundant pursuit to prove Nora Ephron is an *auteur*. She "is the artist whose personality was 'written' in the film."[42] Her films are, to borrow Cook's phrase, a "construction not quite like anybody else's."[43] Nora Ephron is a "film-maker who in various ways is distinctive and noteworthy and this will inevitably involve some sense of there being qualities apparent in a range of [her] films that can ultimately be assigned to [her] creative agency."[44]

To achieve a deep understanding of Nora Ephron's work none of the identified approaches are useful; each has legitimacy as a secondary study. To examine where her work fits in relation to a study of humor, or genre, or women in the film industry, or influential women, or in relation to the women's movement, or as an auteur. But before any of those investigations can be pursued, her work must be understood. To understand the uniqueness, depth and multiple levels of meaning in Ephron's work necessitates an understanding of the artist and how her influences operate within the context of her work. It is only after the complexity of her work is fully understood that any secondary study can be conducted in an informed manner.

Concentrating on the biographical detail of Nora Ephron's life neither denies nor excludes the external factors which influenced her work. Stam's definition of the *auteur* takes into account both the institutional and historical context within which the artist worked and, of course, both of these contexts have a huge impact on the determining of one's artistic voice. However, across Nora's body of work is a consistency of style, motif, subject matter and world view that transcends historical and institutional contexts. The predominant influence on the life and work of Nora Ephron was the experience of her formative years, the experience of "growing up Ephron."[45]

1

Phoebe and Henry

You came "home" to a suit that had been waiting for you to take it up.
To some extent, "home" to the tradition of your parents...[1]

Nora Ephron, her life and her work, was informed by her experience as the daughter of playwrights and screenwriters Henry and (more particularly) Phoebe Ephron. Nora's major career choices were influenced by her parents. Her decision to become a journalist—a writer—was directly related to her being the child of writers. "I don't have any memory of telling my parents I wanted to be a journalist, but they would have been completely happy about it," Nora recalled. "They absolutely wanted us to be writers."[2]

Nora's move to a career in film, beginning as a screenwriter, was also informed by the experiences of her childhood. When Nora entered the film industry she chose the career path taken by her parents and, as they did, she began as a screenwriter, and, also as they did, she specialized in romantic comedy.

Nora discussed her formative Hollywood years on numerous occasions but rather than acknowledge the hereditary influence and familial expectation that led to her occupations, the reasons she cites, while not dispelling such a notion, omit the Ephron family association.[3] In the *Premiere* special edition focusing on women in Hollywood, Nora says it was inevitable that she would become a screenwriter. She suggests that perhaps it was "because in the 1970s everybody wrote a screenplay."[4] On another occasion Nora has been quoted as saying that the opportunity to write for film presented itself through her association with Carl Bernstein. She is also quoted as saying that her career as a screenwriter began out of necessity: "The truth is screenwriting saved me from destitution."[5]

No doubt each of her reasons has validity but it is equally plausible that Nora began to write screenplays because it was what she knew, it was what she grew up with. As much as "everybody wrote a screenplay" in the 1970s, few had experienced firsthand since childhood the process of a screenplay being written from the spark of inspiration through the act of writing to the final, finished draft.

An accomplished writer already, she could also call upon that childhood experience of the family business to help Bernstein and Woodward who, while highly regarded journalists, were neophytes in bringing a story to the screen. So familiar was this territory for the daughter of two well-established Hollywood screenwriters that it was this occupation she turned to so that she might escape the destitution she feared.

Nora's first experience of writing a screenplay echoes the experience of her mother when Phoebe and Henry wrote their first screenplay for the Hollywood film, *Bride by Mistake* (1944). Phoebe and Henry had not written material for the cinema before. Requiring inspiration and guidance, Phoebe asked her secretary to name the best screenwriter to have worked for the studio. After being told it was Norman Krasna, Phoebe instructed her secretary to gather all the Krasna scripts she could find as it was her intention "whenever we dissolve in this script or fade-out or close-shot or any other damn thing that makes screenplay, I'm going to find it in one of Norman Krasna's scripts and copy the directions out word for word."[6]

This dedication to the skill of one of the finest in the business allowed the Ephrons to construct a coherent first screenplay. Nora employed the same tactics when she worked on a redraft of the screenplay for *All the President's Men* with Carl Bernstein and Bob Woodward. Although their version was not used for the film, the process of writing the draft was significant. Nora said that she learned to write a screenplay by retyping the first draft of the script, which had been written by William Goldman. The mere act of physically replicating the original work of such a highly regarded screenwriter taught her how to construct a script.[7] Intentionally or not, Nora's actions had replicated her mother's a generation before.

Nora's background informs and provides the context, the framework for a discussion of her work. Nora's decision to become a journalist and, later, to write screenplays is not the only consequence of her having grown up in the Ephron family. The impact of being the daughter of

Henry and Phoebe Ephron is far more complex than a decision regarding career paths. This would also influence Nora's film style and genre, subject choices and her world view in general.

To understand why Nora's cinematic work is largely "intellectual, word-driven films with strong female characters,"[8] it is essential to look at the work of her parents. The Ephron home life is equally important. They were a family immersed in film, plays, literature and the fictional world they created as part of their work. The question of the blurring of the boundaries between life and art, and life informing art, and art informing life had resonance within Nora's family and, in one instance, became the basis for Henry and Phoebe's work. For the Ephrons, the imaginary and daily life co-existed. Nora's films reflect her life, and her life is reflected in her films. It is not surprising that Nora continued to investigate questions first raised by her parents when they explored the impact of film on cultural expectations in their work. Writing for the stage and screen, where the source of inspiration is one's own life, is as revealing as it is powerful.

Using life as the inspiration for art exposes not just the events of a life but the concerns, themes and emotional landscape of that life. With this in mind, an understanding of (or at least an awareness of) the complex and difficult personality who was Phoebe Ephron is fundamental to gaining an insight into the nuanced depth of Nora's work. More than anyone or anything else she was the greatest influence in Nora's early life.

Nora's world view, informed by the circumstances of her childhood, shaped her unique artistic voice. Without her particular set of circumstances Nora could not, to quote Pam Cook, "end up with a construction not quite like anybody else's."[9]

"the business"[10]

"My mother says these words at least five hundred times in the course of my growing up: 'Everything is copy.'"[11] The use of her life as the raw material for her art identifies Nora's work. She is famous for using everything (mostly)[12] in her life as the raw material for her work and for "using her own life as a prism that refracted the vagaries of how we lived then."[13]

Nora's initial fame as a writer was the result of revealing her innermost feelings. Essays such as "A Few Words About Breasts," in which Nora discusses the size of her breasts and the impact their size had on her life, showed she was fearless in disclosing aspects of herself in print.[14]

"Everything is copy" derived from the competitive newspaper trade. Through her constant use and application of the words, Phoebe's mantra came to be understood and absorbed by Nora. However, "Everything is copy" was not borne of Phoebe. It came to the Ephron family via George S. Kaufman and Moss Hart. Prior to becoming screenwriters, both Henry and Phoebe had worked in theatre in New York. Phoebe worked as secretary to theatrical producer Gilbert Miller. Henry, an almost-graduate from Cornell University,[15] first began in the theatre in 1934, working as a stage manager for playwrights George S. Kaufman and Moss Hart. Henry described these legendary writers as "extraordinary craftsmen,"[16] who were instrumental in shaping the style of what would become the Ephron writing team. They gave the Ephrons the most basic of lessons: to use life as source material for their work. It was a formula Kaufman and Hart used themselves. A case in point is the obnoxious house guest Sheridan Whiteside, the central character in their 1939 play *The Man Who Came to Dinner*. Whiteside was based on Kaufman and Hart's obnoxious, imperious, acid-tongued friend Alexander Woollcott, the renowned critic. One character in the play says of Whiteside: "He would have his own mother burned at the stake if that was the only way he could light his cigarette." While Hart was concerned with plot and structure in their theatre collaborations, "Kaufman focused on the witty, sarcastic dialogue for which he was famous."[17]

The Ephrons' own work, their most successful plays, would be based on their life and the people they knew, and, in the tradition of Kaufman, their plays became known for witty and smart dialogue. One critic wrote, "I read the script of *Three's a Family* and it's full of some of the best one-liners I've ever read."[18] Nora's early written work, like that of her parents and the Kaufman & Hart team, has been described as witty, smart and acerbic. In the 1970s, Nora proved herself to be "the wittiest journalistic headhunter" of the era.[19] Nora's early writing style, described as "intimate revelation dipped in acid,"[20] reflects her influences.

The Round Table was an elite group of journalists, editors, actors and press agents who met on a regular basis at the Algonquin Hotel in New York. The group began lunching together in June 1919 and continued to meet for approximately eight years. Contributors to hit plays, bestselling books and popular newspaper columns, the core group included Dorothy Parker, Alexander Woollcott, Robert Benchley and Edna Ferber. In total there were about two dozen members, one of the most noteworthy being George Kaufman.[21] The Round Table was revered by literary hopefuls like the Ephrons who wanted to succeed in the New York theatre. To be associated with the Algonquin Round Table denoted intellect, wit and skill as writer. Henry took great pride in one film review by Bosley Crowther, the *New York Times* critic, who according to Henry's recollection wrote of their work on *Wallflower* (1947): "Phoebe and Henry Ephron ought to stand up and take a bow for the dialogue. It is brilliant, intelligent and always interesting."[22] It is clear that in choosing to quote Crowther, words were important to Henry. To be recognized as writing intelligent and smart plays, works of the caliber of those produced by the Algonquin Round Table members, was seen as acknowledgment of their status as members of the New York literati. Even after they had settled on Southern California, the Ephrons would stay at the Algonquin Hotel when visiting New York; Henry felt it noteworthy enough to make reference to that fact when writing his memoir.[23]

Nora, like her parents, desired to be part of the Algonquin Round Table. She famously wanted to be Dorothy Parker. In her essay on her literary idol, Nora writes that all she ever wanted to be was Dorothy Parker, to go to New York, to write, to be the woman who lived by her wit; the only woman at the table. Although it is interesting to note that, in fact, Dorothy Parker wasn't the only woman at the Algonquin Round Table; in addition to the aforementioned Edna Ferber there were actresses Tallulah Bankhead, Margalo Gillmore, and Peggy Wood; women's rights activist Ruth Hale; journalists Alice Duer Miller and Jane Grant; historian Margaret Leech; and George S. Kaufman's wife, Beatrice.

Dorothy Parker was also an associate of Henry and Phoebe. She visited the Ephron home and Nora had met her as a child although Nora writes she had little memory of their meeting. On one such visit an incident occurred which led to a "first-rate Parker story." A story Phoebe first told, well before it became a story which Nora "...carried around for years." Parker was playing anagrams. She challenged her opponent when he made the word "currie." As Nora recounts the event,

"Dorothy Parker insisted there was no such spelling. A great deal of scrapping ensued. Finally, my mother said she had some curry in the kitchen and went to get it. She returned with a jar of Crosse and Black-well currie and showed it to Dorothy Parker. "What do they know?" said Parker. "Look at the way they spell Crosse.""[24]

In her essay on Parker, Nora writes that she became disillusioned with the myth of the Round Table and reluctantly gave up her fantasy of being Dorothy Parker; however, the notion of the literary table and the work of the original members was part of her upbringing and part of her being. Her reverence for Dorothy Parker has become enmeshed with the public persona of Nora Ephron.

Henry and Phoebe found success in basing their most successful original works on people and situations they knew and understood, a formula they would take with them as they moved to Hollywood and screenwriting. The practice would be continued throughout their career and would be adopted by their daughters. Nora, who honed her craft in New York, would become famous for using her life as the raw material for her work, even though her sisters Delia, Hallie and Amy have also drawn from their personal experiences to create fiction. Delia's book *Hanging Up* is a fictionalized account of the time leading up to Henry's death; Amy's novel *Cool Shades* documents some of the moments from her life; and Hallie's novel *There Was an Old Woman* is, in some respects, about her relationship with her mother.

Henry and Phoebe's first successful writing collaboration, the 1944 Broadway play *Three's a Family*, was not written until after Nora's birth. Although inspiration for the play was attributed to Phoebe's aunt Min-nie it was also inspired by Nora's birth and more importantly, dependent on her for its success. The "three" of *Three's a Family* are fictionalized versions of Henry, Phoebe and Nora. *Take Her, She's Mine*, the Ephrons' last successful play (produced on Broadway in 1961)—as with their first—was dependent on Nora for its success. Concerning a Southern Californian couple whose daughter goes east to attend school, the play is based on Nora's letters to Phoebe while she was at Wellesley College. Some of Nora's letters to her mother are quoted verbatim in the play.

Whereas her parents structured their original plays around the family unit, Nora structured her works around "the couple." One aspect of Nora's early fame was derived from being part of a couple, and one of her recurring themes is the notion of romantic love. She was initially known for her marriage to Carl Bernstein. She is even more famous for recording the demise of that relationship in her novel *Heartburn*.

Henry writes, of *Three's a Family*, that he had tried for a long time to convince Phoebe to collaborate with him on his plays, but she refused until he presented her with an idea based on her aunt Minnie. The unusual circumstances of Minnie's home life, including "her upside-down household ... was obviously a good idea for a play, at least one written in 1942."[25] Phoebe's aunt set the standard for real-life screwball comedy domestic situations. Minnie was a dentist, an educated woman with a profession at a time when few married women worked. Even more unusual, Minnie was the principal income earner in her family. She worked and provided financially for her family while her partner, a stay-at-home husband and father, ran the household and cooked and cared for the children. This unusual domestic arrangement interested Henry and he saw it as the possible basis for a play. Phoebe, who much admired her aunt, was excited by the prospect of writing a play based on her life. The madcap household—at a time when screwball comedy was popular and not long after Kaufman and Hart had won the 1937 Pulitzer Prize for drama for their play *You Can't Take It with You*, also the story of an eccentric family and how they lived during the Great Depression—was an ideal premise for a play. Nora writes that one of the stories she grew up with as a child was "how my mother's aunt Minnie became the first woman dentist in the history of the world."[26] Henry once stated that Aunt Minnie was probably the most important influence on Phoebe's life.[27]

With her agreement to collaborate with Henry in writing a play, Phoebe suggested the inclusion of a baby, a suggestion, no doubt, based on their experiences with their own newborn daughter, Nora. Phoebe believed "that play will be a hit if we put a baby in it. All the nonsense with the baby can be terribly funny, even though we don't see it that way now."[28] Her intuition was proven correct. The play was a Broadway hit, running for an impressive 497 performances. The inclusion of the baby, Nora, was instrumental in the success of *Three's a Family*. Thus, from the very start of her life Nora was an integral element of the family business. The success of *Three's a Family* opened the door for her parents to a twenty-year career in Hollywood. In their film work, Henry and Phoebe drew on their lives to solve plot problems rather than use their life as the basis for the work as they had done with *Three's a Family*. Some examples include:

- *Look for the Silver Lining* (1949), Henry and Phoebe wrote the film's opening scene based on an incident that had occurred when Henry was working in Boston as second assistant manager on George M. Cohan's *I'd Rather Be Right.*[29]
- In *The Jackpot* (1950), the daughter of the protagonist, Bill (James Stewart), in a scene where the writers needed to distract their character while he is waiting for the phone to ring, gets her head stuck in the banister railing, her vantage point of choice for watching her father. The distraction is based directly on an incident involving the Ephrons' second daughter, Delia.[30]
- For the opening scene of *Daddy Long Legs* (1955), Phoebe and Henry were struggling to show, in cinematic terms, the extreme wealth of the Fred Astaire character Jervis Pendleton III. Inspiration for the scene was drawn from Phoebe's life. When working as secretary to Gilbert Miller, Phoebe would go to Miller's New York residence to take dictation. The Miller house in New York was, in fact, the Bache Museum on Fifth Avenue. When Phoebe went there she was surrounded by the art works of Picasso, Botticelli, Vermeer, Matisse and Monet. In the film the Bache Museum becomes the Pendleton Museum. Jervis Pendleton III lives on the upper level of the museum, as had the Millers. Of finding the resolution to the issue Henry writes: "Finally it came and, as usual, out of our lives—Phoebe's this time."[31]

The Ephrons in Hollywood produced a substantial body of work and they were constantly employed but their lives figured less and less in their screenplays. In Hollywood their lives informed their work in an impersonal way, often as problem solvers. Henry and Phoebe understood that much of their work in Hollywood would be adapting the work of others and, often, it would involve working on films of minor consequence. Henry wrote that he and Phoebe wanted to be taken seriously as writers but what happened to them at Warner Bros. was that "we were stuck in the rut of being capable writers," which kept them beneath the industry's radar.

Like her parents, Nora did her fair share of adapting the work of others into successful films, *Sleepless in Seattle* being a perfect example, and also like her parents, Nora was successful in mainstream Hollywood terms. But Nora, unlike her parents, achieved recognition far beyond anything her parents ever achieved. She is famous in her own right as a filmmaker, a screenwriter and director. The changed circumstances of film production in contemporary Hollywood has allowed the creative artist behind a film to, in some instances, be as well recognized as the stars of the film. Nora has been described by Ariel Levy as "by some measures the most successful female director working in this country."[32]

Nora was well taught that the first priority of success in the film industry is to entertain and, as a consequence, make money. In meeting that priority she became adept at ensuring her work had broad appeal. However, while meeting the business obligations of the Hollywood film industry Nora continued using her life as source material and making herself a part of her films. Within Nora's commercial and financially successful films, described by Levy as "deeply comforting comedies,"[33] as with her journalism and essay writing, is her continued exploration of her own life. Nora's films are idiosyncratic and personal. The notion that they are "comforting comedies" is, to some extent, a decoy.

In many discussions of *When Harry Met Sally* (1989), it is frequently referred to as a Nora Ephron film, even though Rob Reiner is both its director and producer, while Nora was the screenwriter only. However, as Nora wrote in the prologue to the published script of *When Harry Met Sally*, Harry and Sally are, respectively, "a male character based somewhat on Rob, and a female character based somewhat on me."[34]

Ultimately, most of Nora's principal female characters are based somewhat on her. Sally (Meg Ryan) is a college graduate heading to New York to be a journalist. Sally is fanatical and precise in her ordering of food—a trait for which Nora is well known. Annie (Meg Ryan), in *Sleepless in Seattle*, is also a journalist, and Kathleen (Meg Ryan) in *You've Got Mail*, is the owner of a bookshop—Nora's first job was working at a book shop[35]—who becomes a writer. Kathleen loves Jane Austen's *Pride and Prejudice*, a favorite of both Nora and Phoebe. In one instance, *This Is My Life*, the central characters are an amalgam of Nora, Phoebe and Delia. Dottie Engels (Julie Kavner) embodies these roles while Dottie's daughters, Erica (Samantha Mathis) and Opal (Gaby Hoffman) are characters who resemble Nora and Delia as children.

Again, in relation to Rob Reiner's *When Harry Met Sally*, Nora still managed to make it as much about herself as it is about the director. She writes, "What made this movie different was that Rob had a character who would say whatever he believed, and if I disagreed, I had Sally to say it for me."[36] Nora embraced the use of her life as the raw material for her art. It is her identifier as a writer and it is the approach to art with which she was most familiar. However, it is not just the use of life experiences as raw material or the style of her work that is informed by Nora's experience as the child of Henry and Phoebe Ephron.

Nora loved and adored her mother and father. She writes of her parents that they were "the people you grew up idolizing," as a child they "have enormous power over you," and of her mother she writes, "My mother was a goddess."[37] Nora, the child, could not help but take on, absorb into her being, Phoebe's expectations of her. As Delia says of the expectations placed on Nora: "She was given dreams and ambition—to be a successful woman, a successful person, a successful writer."[38] Nora, not wishing to be part of Hollywood ("I wasn't going to work in the horrible movie business, living in horrible Beverly Hills with those horrible strawberry blond ladies. I was going back to New York")[39]—and, knowing she was expected to be a writer, decided on journalism.

Nora gives credit to her high school journalism teacher, Charles Simms, for providing her with what she describes as "this great epiphany moment for me. It was this, "Oh my God, it is about the point! It is about figuring out what the point is." And I just fell in love with journalism at that moment."[40] But her decision to become a journalist was not based solely on any particular rational logic, but a combination of things. Nora also writes that her decision to become a journalist, made prior to her epiphany moment, was probably a combination of the influence of Lois Lane, Superman's intrepid female newspaper reporter, and a book she was given one Christmas titled *A Treasury of Great Reporting*.[41]

The Ephron girls grew up in a family which valued and was influenced by literature. Both of Nora's parents, and particularly Phoebe, "were readers."[42] Books and writers were revered in the Ephron household. "*The New Yorker* arrived by mail every week along with the *Sunday New York Times* and *The Saturday Review of Literature*."[43] Phoebe had a love of Jane Austen. Her character, Elizabeth Bennet, became one of the strong women of Nora's childhood and the novel *Pride and Prejudice* is a central component in *You've Got Mail*.

It was not only books that were valued by the Ephrons. Henry, on the first page of his memoir, describes himself and Phoebe as being movie buffs long before it was fashionable, long before they went to Hollywood. The Ephron family, both professionally and privately, was immersed in film, plays, literature and the fictional world they inhabited and also created. This is reflected in the combination of factors which influenced Nora's decision to become a journalist.

Henry described moments of his life in terms of cinematic references, as did Nora. Their lives were peopled, and for Nora continued to be peopled, by both the real and the imagined—and both had influence. Henry describes one evening while he and Phoebe were on location for the filming of *Carousel*: "That night Phoebe and I sat in the porch like two characters from *Our Town*."[44] So influenced were Henry and Phoebe by theater that they chose to name their first child after a character from an Ibsen play, "We named Nora for the heroine of *A Doll's House*."[45]

Nora writes in *Heartburn*, her roman à clef, when she describes her character, Rachel Samstat, going through her husband's papers to find evidence of his affair: "I felt like a character in a trashy novel: I even knew which trashy novel I felt like a character in, which made it worse 'The Best of Everything.'"[46] Elsewhere in her novel as she recounts a visit to her house by the police, Rachel explains that she is always shocked when the police will accept a beer because "I spent so many years as a child watching Jack Webb turn down beer on *Dragnet* that I've come to believe it's practically insulting to offer a policeman even a cup of coffee."[47]

Along with giving credit to Charles Simms for providing the impetus for her decision to become a journalist, Nora has also written that Lois Lane, Brenda Starr and Hildy Johnson influenced her choice of career. Strong female characters—creations, certainly—but as Nora writes of Hildy Johnson, as played by Rosalind Russell in *His Girl Friday* (1940), she was someone she aspired to be.[48] These fictional influences reflect the Ephron family's world. Nora liked to say that her family life made her feel as though "I grew up in a sitcom"[49]; Bennetts commented, "Nora remembers her childhood as if it were a wonderful movie."[50] A very apt analogy given the place of the fictional in the daily lives of the Ephrons and in the works produced as part of the family business.

Nora said that film is "the literature of this generation and all subsequent generations."[51] She recognized the impact of the arts—theatre, film and literature—in the lives of people, including her own. The question of the blurring of the boundaries between life and art, and life informing art, and art informing life had resonance within Nora's family. It is not at all surprising that Henry, Phoebe and Nora have all used their works to discuss the impact of film on belief systems and cultural conditioning. This almost-subversive theory, on which Henry and Phoebe's first screenplay, *Always Together* (1947), is predicated, is taken up again in a more overt way, by Nora, in her screenplay for *Sleepless in Seattle*.

Always Together, as the predictable and expected romantic comedy is played out, contemplates the role of cinema in influencing the expectations of the viewing public. The film opens with Jane Barker (Joyce Reynolds) in a theater watching a movie in which a marriage breaks up because the husband is not happy being supported by his rich wife. As a result of watching the film, Jane and her boyfriend, Donn (Robert Hutton), a struggling writer of gloomy stories, argue over whether they could be happy if she were rich and he, poor. Jane is convinced as a result of the film she has seen that they could not be happy if she were the wealthier of the two. Jane and Donn marry and, through totally unexpected circumstances, Jane receives a bequest of $1 million. The marriage falters because of Jane's money or, more precisely, because of Jane's concern about the impact the money might have on her relationship with her husband. Donn soon files for divorce. In preparing the conditions of his divorce agreement, Donn demands his wife, as the wealthier of the two, pay *him* alimony. His reasoning is that if he received alimony he would have money and consequently not be dependent on his wife for financial support which, in turn, would result that Jane would no longer believe he was unhappy because he would now be independently wealthy. The film comes full circle and the marriage is saved. In order to resolve their differences, Donn has to convince Jane that he has found the solution, albeit a wacky one, to their problem. The trouble is, Jane cannot be located. At the conclusion of the film, Donn finds Jane in a movie theatre, as she was just in the opening. *Always Together* is a romantic comedy with a serious debate at its core—questioning whether cinema is an instrument of cultural conditioning and whether its impact is significant.

Always Together foreshadows *Sleepless in Seattle*, but unlike her parents' screenplay, Nora's film openly declares its subject when Becky (Rosie O'Donnell) says to Annie (Meg Ryan), "You don't want to be in love, you want to be in love in the movies." The aim with *Sleepless in Seattle*, written and directed nearly half a century after *Always Together*, was, according to Nora, "to make a movie about how movies screw up your brain about love, and then if we did a good job, we would become one of the movies that would screw up people's brains about love forever."[52] *Sleepless in Seattle* achieved its objective. Highly successful in pleasing audiences, it is in constant rotation on television and often programmed annually on Valentine's Day. Its enduring popularity ensures that it has become "one of the films that screws up people's minds about love (perhaps) forever." Where *Always Together* was a minor work in Hollywood and the question of "film as a tool of cultural conditioning" a plot device, *Sleepless in Seattle* was a major Hollywood success and the plot device of her parents' film the declared subject of Nora's major Hollywood success.

The work of both generations of writers also reflects the family's broader interest in the society and time in which they lived. Nora and Henry and Phoebe all used their material to chronicle "the vagaries of how we lived then." Although neither the veteran Ephrons nor Nora foreground contemporary social concerns, their work is always grounded within the context of the moment. As a journalist and essayist, Nora has written extensively about cultural change and society's quirks, and has done so with great relish. She has been described as the funny voice of feminism,[53] who has explored many and varied cultural institutions,[54] including having written extensively on the Fourth Estate.

Three's a Family was the first of Henry and Phoebe plays to be written against a backdrop of contemporary social concerns. The play is a domestic comedy, a "farce comedy"[55] about an eccentric family living in cramped conditions. The aftermath of the stock market collapse and the Second World War are the precipitating factors leading to the family's current domestic circumstances. The crowded conditions in the family home is the result of a poor financial investment instigated by Sam Whitaker, formerly a stockbroker, who lost all of his sister-in-law Irma's life savings in 1919 and, as a consequence, she has lived with the Whitakers ever since.

The housing shortage, caused by the war and the enlistment into the forces of most able-bodied men, results in many family homes being overcrowded as women such as the Whitakers' married daughter, Kitty, return to their families with their children. The immediate reason for

Kitty's return is a fight with her husband, but she stays on because he had just enlisted in the army. Later in the play the doctor who is called to tend to the ill baby is described as the "oldest man you ever saw,"[56] again a consequence of the war where all younger doctors are away contributing to the war effort.

While the play is set against this larger social backdrop, predominantly the narrative revolves around the lives of the family members. *Three's a Family* documents the lives of an Upper West Side middle-class New York family during the war years: the food they eat, the clothes they wear, the furniture they own, the baby furniture needed, the help they have, the taxes they pay as a consequence of the war effort, and the activities they enjoy such as outings to the movies. It is through the recording of the minutiae of their fictional daily lives that we have a comedic depiction of life as it was for these New Yorkers. Nora's film *Sleepless in Seattle* works in the same way. The story of Annie (Meg Ryan) and Sam (Tom Hanks) is precipitated by the untimely death of Sam's wife from cancer. In contemporary society, when cancer (particularly breast cancer) is very much a prominent issue, the film has an historical anchor and reflects contemporary concerns.

Other examples of Nora and her parents using their work as social chronicle include: Nora using a one-liner to comment on the nature of "the family" in contemporary society, with its high rates of divorce and remarriage. In *You've Got Mail*, Joe Fox (Tom Hanks), introducing the two small children who accompany him on a trip to Kathleen's bookshop as his aunt and his brother, declares in Nora's best ironic tone: "We are an American family!" In *Sleepless in Seattle*, Nora comments on the impact of cable television in a scene in which father and son, Sam and Jonah Baldwin (Ross Malinger) talk about sex. Jonah asks Sam if he will have sex with his girlfriend and then asks if his back will get all scratched up. This is what Jonah has learned about sex from watching cable television programs; it is a humorous moment with an enormous impact.

Henry and Phoebe's *Take Her, She's Mine* and *Howie* also serve as chronicles of their time: the advent of television, the phenomenon of the television quiz show, the place of alcohol in society, and the changing role of women are all incorporated into their comedies of the late 1950s and early 1960s. More prominently, under the guise of a romantic comedy, *Desk Set* (1957) contemplates the impact a computer will have on business and on society. This exploration is taken up again by Nora in *You've Got Mail*, wherein her romantic life is at the mercy of the home computer and, more specifically, email.[57]

Nora acquired an understanding of successful screenwriting from her parents. She adopted a style of writing specific to a type—intelligent, witty and sophisticated, and place—New York, and experience—the world of her parents, theatre and the Algonquin Round Table. She learned to draw on life for inspiration from her parents. William Goldman's script for *All the President's Men* may have been the first tool with which she practiced the art of screenwriting, but what Nora learned from her parents is immeasurable. But writing comedy was more than a consequence of type, place and professional experience for Henry and Phoebe and Nora. Humor, the art of telling a funny story, served a function in the life of the Ephron family as it would come to do in Nora's life and work. Humor allowed for a place in which to examine the emotional landscape of life and, in doing so, provided a mechanism for survival. Phoebe, in particular, used her work as a way of processing the difficult aspects of her life. Nora followed suit and continued to use her sense of humor as a way of addressing the distressing aspects of her life. It is this characteristic of the work of the Ephrons that made it unique and specific to their family, as opposed to those who use life as the raw material for art. The work produced by the Ephrons can be identified as theirs alone because it has, at its core, *their* life and *their* particular issues. The nature of Nora's upbringing, the family she grew up as part of—the expectations, particularly Phoebe's of her daughters—is of the utmost significance when considering the film career of Nora Ephron.

"Not everyone grew up in my family."[58]

There was a blurring of work and home in the Ephron family. There was not a clear division between the two spheres but home, where "everything is copy" was also very much in evidence as a "life instruction" instrumental in shaping Nora's world view, subject choice and future work. Nora's life with her parents and their lives and their work are an integral part of her biography[59] and, as such, their shared life is the conduit through which the work and preoccupations of the parents have been passed to their daughter.

It would be erroneous to assume that Nora simply watched her parents' films, took their ideas and then revamped them for her own work. It is more likely that she absorbed their work, their work practices, their beliefs and their emotional and psychological response to life events. Akin to a form of osmosis, it was part of her being and her life within the family unit. While Nora did watch and was familiar with her parents' films it is more likely it is the meshing of their lives, the entanglement and intertwining that is the relationship of parents and child which informs her work.

Henry and Phoebe recorded aspects of their life together in plays and films, and they recorded Nora's early life in two works of fiction. Henry recorded a version of his life, including the life he shared with Phoebe as a memoir, one that was hotly contested by both Nora and Delia as being somewhat inaccurate. Nora documented the significant moments and events of her life as fiction in the novel *Heartburn* and in her films and essays. One of the recurring themes of Nora's life and work is her belief that there is neither nonfiction nor fiction, only narrative.[60] This is not surprising given that from the time of her birth Nora was immersed in a type of fiction. It was at the family dinner table that Nora learned how to interweave the real and the fictional, where she learned to tell a funny story. The evening meal, the family dinner table features strongly in Nora's recollections of her childhood and frequently appears in various incarnations in her work. The nightly gathering of the family was instrumental in the shaping of Nora's world view. For Nora, as the eldest Ephron daughter, "The Ephrons' dinner table was a nightly bonanza of bon mots, with everyone vying for the title of cleverest, but the competition didn't faze Nora—probably because she won without even trying."[61]

> My mother and father raised us in a home that was full of love. I got a little more of it than the others did—I suppose the eldest child always does—and I remember so clearly their relationship: not just the working together, but their shared joy at simple things like having dinner with us, listening to us tell them about what happened in school that day, singing rounds at the table and playing charades after dinner.[62]

Nora loved the evening ritual. She writes of the joy of her home, encapsulated by her recollections of the evening meal and of feeling loved. The same dinner table and the same activities, however, are not so warmly remembered by her sisters. "Everyone used to sit around the table and you were expected to tell stories and it was really grotesque," says Delia.[63] Hallie, the third Ephron daughter," says dryly, "You had to claim your airspace ... it was a lot like the Algonquin Round Table."[64] An apt analogy given the reverence in which the Algonquin Round Table and its members were held by Henry and Phoebe and, subsequently, by Nora. When she was a journalist based in New York, she would meet with Victor Navasky, Bud Trillin and C.D.B. Bryan at the Algonquin at 6:00 p.m. on Tuesday nights "and sit around pretending to be the Algonquin Round Table" where she "of course got to be Dorothy Parker."[65]

That the dinner table ritual was so fondly remembered by Nora and with horror by her siblings calls into question the idea of a singular truth. One person's truth is not the same as another's; nor are two people's recollection of the same event. What the difference in recollections clearly exemplifies, as Leslie Bennetts succinctly states, "is the variable nature of reality in any family, given the differences in perspective among individual members."[66] The *Rashomon* Effect, the same event seen from the point of view of the various participants, is evident in the varied recollections of the Ephron daughters of their experience. Because the recollections differ, there is neither a singular nor reliable truth, only individual narratives. While Nora and Delia challenge Henry's memories, his narrative has as much validity as theirs, and all of their recollections are tempered by the emotional investment in the memory.

The significance of the family dinner table, the sharing of food and stories, is not confined to the memories of those who sat at the table. Food, a significant topic in their life, was given a prominent place in their work. Food became an identifier, a *motif*, of the work of both Nora and her parents. Nora understood the connotations food can have. She understood "food as habit, food as biography, food as metaphor, food as love" and she understood "food as food."[67] As an adult she was known for her ability as a cook. Nick Pileggi said of his wife, Nora: "You like to cook so that people will sit at a table and you can bring out all these things and everybody can talk."[68] Nora liked to re-create the atmosphere of her childhood family dinner table as she remembered it, a place of fun, love and conversation. She is famous for the quality of the catering on her film sets: "craft services [where the food is] ... on Nora's movies were always spectacular, no surprise."[69] Dinner table gatherings, the sharing of food and food itself feature prominently in *Heart-burn*, *When Harry Met Sally*, *Sleepless in Seattle*, *Michael* and, of course, in *Julie and Julia* food is one of the central characters.

Henry and Phoebe set the precedent for Nora. *Desk Set* best exemplifies how the use of food characterizes their material. Being closely based on the William Marchant play *The Desk Set*, the film can be compared to the original work. Henry and Phoebe wrote an additional scene for the film and significantly altered another. The altered scene, a key scene in which Richard Sumner (Spencer Tracy) tries to evaluate Bunny Watson's (Katharine Hepburn) intelligence by asking her questions takes place in Bunny's office in the stage version and does not involve food. The new premise has Richard inviting Bunny to lunch. She is excited at the prospect and anticipates where they might go. Ultimately, they end up on the office building's rooftop, in very cold weather, eating roast beef sandwiches and drinking take-out coffee. Food, in this instance, operates as a comic device as Bunny, shivering, dissects and eats her sandwich in a series of distinct and exaggerated steps as she tries to carry on a rather intricate conversation.

An entirely new scene, written by Henry and Phoebe, takes place in Bunny's apartment. Bunny invites Richard for dinner after they are stranded outside her apartment in a rainstorm. The scene is funny, and food is the plot device. There is much discussion about what is to be prepared and who will prepare it. Floating Island, a French dessert, is not only heartily enjoyed by Richard, who happens to be wearing Bunny's boyfriend Mike's new bathrobe when Mike arrives unexpectedly but the manner in which Bunny eats the dessert operates as both indicator of the tension of the moment and Bunny's increasing anger at Mike's jealous display. It is one of the best—and certainly funniest—scenes in that 1957 film.

In *We Thought We Could Do Anything*, one of Henry's recollections is of Phoebe working on an original story that was later called "An Apple for the Teacher." As a natural part of the relating of the anecdote, Henry writes that as Phoebe worked on the story she ate sandwiches and drank coffee. Phoebe worked through the night while Henry, using a recipe Phoebe wrote out, prepared chopped chicken liver for his wife.[70] Henry effortlessly incorporates such detail—the preparation and consumption of food—into his memoir.

Food, or, more precisely, food fashion—and the role food plays in defining an era—appears in Henry and Phoebe's work as early as 1943. In act 1 of *Three's a Family*, the Whitaker's maid and cook, Adelaide, resigns. The concern of the family is that they will miss her or, more precisely, her cooking. Irma laments the loss of "wonderful hot roast beef—wonderful cold bread-and-butter pudding."[71] Adelaide was an intrinsic part of the Whitaker household as was the cook in the Ephron household. The food itself belonged to the time. Roast beef and bread-and-butter pudding were typical fare of the war years. Food also denotes an event. In the play Irma discusses food in relation to the Thanksgiving turkey and how she may have to remove her girdle after dinner. New York audiences easily identified with this and appreciated the humor of Irma's statement. In a later scene, set at Christmas, Irma comments that she has made a "beautiful ice-box cake" for the occasion.[72] The occasion is defined by the food presented.

Take Her, She's Mine[73] reflects the early 1960s in terms of food fashion. Mollie orders lobster when she is dining at a restaurant. Mollie's father, Frank, barbeques steaks for a family dinner and Mollie works at a grungy coffee house called The Sleeping Pill while she attends school. It is at the coffee house she and a friend sing protest songs while others read poetry. It is the social scene for the latecomers to the beat generation. *Howie*, written slightly earlier in 1957 and produced a year later, defines that time in terms of the food served: canapés, including deviled eggs and coffee cake. In the play, coffee cake denotes the failure of a social situation when it is neither desired nor consumed by the visiting guests. Later, the cake reappears at the arrival of the FBI agent to the house, but is removed when the Simms family decides the agent is not welcome.

The ease with which Henry and Phoebe incorporated food into their work anticipated the way Nora would develop the same technique in her own writing. In *Heartburn*, the character Rachel describes herself as a writer of cookbooks. She describes her creations as "very personal and chatty—they're cookbooks in an almost incidental way. I write chapters about friends and relatives or trips or experiences, and work in the recipes peripherally."[74] Rachel's description of her style of writing identifies Nora as the author and inspiration for Rachel. Nora's writing style was personal and chatty, and she often included a recipe or two. Nora's final film, *Julie and Julia* (2009), celebrates food by telling the story of celebrity chef Julia Child (Meryl Streep) and the woman, Julie Powell

(Amy Adams), who spent a year of her life cooking every recipe in Child's famous cookbook *Mastering the Art of French Cooking* while recording the experience on her blog.

The Goddess

Food was not only significant in the lives of the Ephrons because of its role in a social context—the bringing together of people, be it family or friends—it is part of the biography, the emotional landscape of the family, and it connects Nora and Phoebe, both of whom "served delicious food."[75] Nora writes in *Heartburn* that Rachel's mother, Bebe Samstat (based on Phoebe), each New Year's Day threw a party to which she and her husband would invite all their friends, and Bebe would cook for everyone. Rachel also says her mother was famous for serving a baked ham along with "her casserole of lima beans and pears."[76] Nora wrote that it was not unusual to return home at night to find her mother reading cookbooks in bed. In *Heartburn*, Bebe/Phoebe has a daughter, Rachel/Nora, who is also known as a good cook.

Food came to operate as a metaphor in Nora's work. By the time Nora made *Julie and Julia*, food, and butter in particular, came to represent Phoebe. They were inextricably linked—food and Phoebe, Nora and Phoebe and food. At their nightly meal, "The plates were heated, and there were butter balls made with wooden paddles. There was an appetizer, a main course, and dessert. We thought everyone lived like this."[77] Food and Phoebe—who ensured her family had delicious food—food and laughter, food and telling stories, food and the blending of fiction with nonfiction to create a humorous narrative, food and love.

But Phoebe didn't prepare food for her family often—that was the cook's job. Phoebe cooked food for others at big, fabulous events. Similarly, Phoebe wasn't there for her daughters; she wasn't there to nurture or care for them—that was the nurse's job. She was there to give them "life lessons" and expectations.

Not a lot is known about Phoebe Ephron (née Wolkind). She is the absent voice in her biography. She is primarily known through the recollection of others, the recollections of her husband and children. Biographies of the couple generally list Phoebe as Henry's collaborator but provide little additional information about her. Barbara Levy devotes space to Phoebe in *Ladies Laughing* (1997), her book on women in comedy, but it is in the context of her as role-model for her daughters, with particular emphasis on Nora, who is the true subject of the piece.

What *is* known about Phoebe is that she was born on January 16, 1914, to Kate and Louis Wolkind, in the Bronx. According to Henry, Louis, a dress manufacturer, had been bankrupt for about the tenth time when they were setting off for Hollywood in 1944.[78] Phoebe had grown up poor. She attended James Munroe High School and, later, the New York City public university Hunter College, where she majored in English.[79] The child of immigrants, Phoebe taught her mother to read and write English; when she was only eight, she comforted her mother, Kate, through her father's extramarital affairs.[80] She was forced by family circumstances to assume adult responsibilities while still a young child. She became the parent to her parent and lived with the uncertainty of emotional distress and being poor.

As an adult, a successful career woman working in Hollywood, Phoebe continued to protect her family. When the bankrupt Louis and Kate moved to Los Angeles, pretending to be a wealthy retired couple, Phoebe maintained the lie of her parent's circumstances; at her mother's request, she kept their bankruptcy a secret. It fell to Phoebe and Henry to take care of her parents financially and it was through Phoebe and Henry's connections that Phoebe's brother, Dickie (Harold), became an artist for Walt Disney.[81] As she had done as a child, Phoebe continued to carry the burden of responsibility for her entire family. She provided for them in ways she had never been provided for herself.

Phoebe was raised to be a keeper of secrets and she learned to live in denial of what was happening around her. She learned to protect herself. Henry writes that something happened to Phoebe before they met which caused her to demand of him, "Don't you make me cry; don't you *dare* make me cry." Henry also writes that it was a long time before he learned what caused "this strange quirk in her character."[82] It is probable that what Phoebe wanted was for Henry to be faithful to her, the complete opposite of her father. It also makes sense that Henry would be coy when writing about Phoebe's "quirk," claiming to be unsure as to what caused it, given his own propensity for philandering. Regardless of the reason, whatever had happened was so painful that Phoebe did not want to give it substance by acknowledging its reality. The impact of her childhood would have major consequences for her as well as her children.

Delia, Hallie, and especially Nora have written about their mother. As Nora began her eulogy for Phoebe: "I would like to talk to you about the unusual and complicated woman who was my mother. I can't explain her to you—I don't think any of us understood her." Delia recently, at the conclusion of her essay "Why I Can't Write about My Mother," echoes Nora's words when she writes of Phoebe, "I have no idea who she was."[83]

But Delia and Nora both knew their mother—it is evident in their work. Their mother was a deeply flawed woman whose behavior significantly impacted her daughters. She was unavailable emotionally and she was incapable of providing comfort and support. Delia writes, "Feelings were not my mother's strong suit"[84]; Nora recalled that her mother "was a washout at hard core mothering; what she was good at were clever remarks that made you feel immensely sophisticated and adult and, if you thought about it at all—foolish for having wanted anything so mundane as some actual nurturing."[85] Phoebe was too damaged to be the mother they desired. Consequently, her daughters continued to search for her all their lives.

Although ungenerous in some ways, Phoebe did give something of herself to her daughters in the only way she could—through another medium. Strong, successful women, such as Dorothy Parker, Edith Head, Aunt Minnie, Elizabeth Bennet and Jo March dominated Nora's childhood and she was introduced to these remarkable women by her mother. Phoebe would go to secondhand bookstores and hunt for out-of-print and classic children's books. She would bring home the books, books she loved, and in passing these on to her daughters she was not only passing on a love of reading and literature but, as Nora chose to see it, Phoebe was passing on something of herself.[86] "She would tell me how she had identified with Jo in *Little Women* and I would go off and read *Little Women* and identify with Jo."[87] Phoebe wanted her daughters to grow up strong, to be independent of others, not to rely on others for survival and to be able to protect themselves from hurt.

Phoebe also gave her daughters a version of herself they could love and admire. She played a role. She portrayed herself as a successful career woman. In a rare interview with Maurice Zolotow for the *New York Times* Zolotow described Phoebe as not wanting to be interviewed, preferring to shun public life. However, it is clear that Phoebe used the opportunity to present herself as a successful career woman. During the interview she defined how she measured her success as a working woman. She could afford to pay for others to do that which she did not do herself, including the care of her children.

> I'll kill you, she says shyly, if you describe me coming out of the kitchen with flour on my hands and sitting down to write funny lines. I don't go into the kitchen very often except for ice cubes for a drink. We have a cook for the cooking and a nurse for the children. I've been a full time screen writer since 1943 and I put in a full day in the office. I have room 333 in the Twentieth Century–Fox writers' building.... I get to the office at 9:30 and I don't leave until 4:30. Then I go home and report on my problems and experiences to my husband, just like any career woman seeing her husband at night.[88]

Phoebe refused to be identified as a stay-at-home wife and mother. She was as a career woman, as her aunt Minnie had been and as she expected her daughters to be. Phoebe had her independence and she wanted that for her daughters, including Nora. Nora, on her mother:

> I had this very clear sense my mother led a different life from other women. She dressed differently from the other women. She was sort of stunning and had this Katharine Hepburn, offbeat tomboy look. Every day, she and my father went off to Twentieth Century–Fox, which was about three minutes from our house, in separate cars.[89]

Zolotow's interview with Phoebe reveals a woman starkly out of synch with her moment in history. She describes herself in a stereotypically male way. As noted by Levy, "As early as 1958 she refused to present herself as a mother and housewife first, who wrote plays only in her spare time."[90]

Phoebe's women, her characters, are portrayed similarly. Phoebe, with her role as a career woman and her family arrangements and from the tone of her statements, bears a striking resemblance to her character Frances from *Three's a Family*. Frances was Phoebe's ideal. She was who Phoebe desired to be, and who she became. Frances is "a successful career woman of forty-five, smartly dressed. She is used to walking into a room and taking command."[91] Although Frances is based on Phoebe's aunt Minnie it seems that Frances is an amalgam of Minnie and the woman Phoebe would become.

Nora, renowned for her control "over everything from herself and her work down to the minutiae of domestic life,"[92] inherited her mother and great aunt's characteristic determination. Like Phoebe's character Frances, Nora's female characters are fictional incarnations of herself.

They are women who have careers and they are women who determine the course of their lives, even when circumstances beyond their control force a change in direction.

By introducing strong, successful woman to her daughters and by presenting herself to the world as a career woman, independent and successful in a male-dominated society, Phoebe gave her daughters the gift of belief in one's self:

> What I think she gave us, most of all, was the sense that we could do any-thing, anything at all, that anything was possible. Being women had nothing to do with it, just as it had had nothing to do with her. That is a remarkable thing to pass on to daughters ... she could not bear being called a feminist. She merely *was*, and simply by her example, we all grew up with with [*sic*] blind faith in our abilities and destinies.[93]

Well before the advent of the Women's Movement, Phoebe, by example, taught her daughters that their lives were their own to deter-mine. She expected her daughters to be independent. She gave them a sense of the unbounded potential of self. But, as always, she did not give freely of herself. Zolotow, in his *New York Times* interview then focused on Phoebe's role as a parent:

> Mrs. Ephron does not attend meetings of the Parent-Teachers Association and she has never delved into the books of Spock and Gesell. She does not chauffeur her children about to various activities as do other suburban matrons.... She doesn't even do any gardening.[94]

Phoebe, as the Zolotow interview reveals, takes pride in her absence from the lives of her daughters. Henry, in his account of their lives, writes that Phoebe was not content with her life as a mother. Spending time with Nora as a baby and infant was not something she could sustain and, as a consequence, she became Henry's collaborator and employed a nurse to care for Nora. Phoebe's character Kitty (Frances's daughter in *Three's a Family*) does not like being at home with her child all the time either and longs to return to work.

Substantiating that which is suggested in the Zolotow interview Henry chronicles a life of physical separation from their family. Lots of nights and dinners out, parties, film-location work and out-of-town play preparation. Despite Nora's happy reminiscences of pre-dinner drinks and crudités and then riotous fun at the dinner table with humorous stories followed later by charades, there is a sense that even *that* was not as wonderful as she had chosen to remember it. Not all of the daughters remember the family activities so fondly and there is the sense that, at one level, all the storytelling had a mercenary motive, a fodder-collecting exercise for the writing team's ever-present need for new material.

As the child of the emotionally unavailable, detached and physically absent Phoebe, Nora was hurt. Over the years, when asked in interviews about her relationship with her mother, Nora variously responded how she was proud of her mother and her achievements while at the same time speaking of the neglect she felt as a child. Although in true Ephron style, she makes a joke of it. In an interview with Peter Biskind, Nora speaks about her parents' absence, how they went away to do a play, and the impact their leaving had on her. "In fact I remember it to the extent that it cost me about $20,000 to remember it even better."[95] Later, in the same interview, Ephron articulated the mixed emotions she had regarding her mother. "I was proud of her and not at all in touch with my anger that she wasn't there for me."[96] Nora, as recently as 2006, described Phoebe as an "interesting mother" and, in one of her typically acerbic and insightful comments, said, "She was a successful mother.... She had four kids who were all able to pay for their own psychoanalysis."[97] Nora also said of Phoebe: "I think she was perceived as a bad mom. And I think on some level that she enjoyed that.... But you know, it was years before I thought, 'Wait a minute! Why couldn't you have been there? You know you were a writer, you could have left the studio for half an hour. Big deal!'"[98]

Phoebe was a woman of contradictions: demanding of and distant from her children, and a strong, independent career woman who was, at the same time, greatly admired by her neglected daughters because she was "an original woman my mother—so ahead of her time (screenwriter, career woman, feminist)."[99] But even as a successful career woman, Phoebe, according to Henry, spent much of her life avoiding confrontation.[100] She was a woman in denial.

Phoebe's inability to acknowledge or feel pain—her own or anyone else's—meant that she learned to survive by changing its shape; she turned pain into a funny story, and she taught her daughters to do the same. Instead of being able to go to her mother with her pain, Nora learned to tell a funny story. A funny story—comedy—in the Ephron household served a purpose. It was the vehicle for examining, processing and ultimately controlling that which was distressing. It made that which was unmanageable manageable and it was at the evening dinner table that Nora learned to excel at telling a funny story. She was the best and brightest and, in being so, she had her mother's approval in that moment. When life at home became unbearable, Phoebe's daughters would, according to Delia, always "make it into a funny story, even though it was usually pretty horrible.... That was our coping mechanism, our way of processing what was happening and making it survivable."[101] Nora begins *Heartburn*, the fictionalized account of the breakdown of her marriage, with the following sentences: "The first day I did not think it was funny. I didn't think it was funny the third day either, but I managed to make a little joke about it."[102]

It was only by transposing the difficult into the realm of the fictional and turning it into a funny story that Phoebe could acknowledge certain aspects her life in any meaningful way. Phoebe, the successful career woman, was not able to keep her life from falling apart. Her denial of that which was too difficult to deal with in life ultimately destroyed her. It was only in her work that Phoebe found the safety to look at her life. Her play *Howie* reveals that which she otherwise denied—the secret of her adult life. Henry and Phoebe were alcoholics.[103] They lived a life unknown to all except their children. Amy Ephron describes her mother as "this sort of closet alcoholic, where her best friends didn't know she drank"; and of Henry she says, "My father was drinking, and it was horrible."[104]

Alcohol calmed Henry and Phoebe when they were upset. Its consumption defined social situations, recognized successes and a couple of cocktails or a scotch was the accepted conclusion to the working day. Alcohol was part of the daily routine in the Ephron home. Nora writes: "Every day my parents came home from work, and we all gathered in the den. My parents had drinks and there were crudités for us."[105] Henry and Phoebe lived the Hollywood life. They were caught in the fantasy of living in Hollywood. They dined out frequently; at Preston Sturges's restaurant, The Players,[106] then later they dined at Sardi's and Romanoff's.[107] They had a box at the races. They held and attended parties. They drank socially, they drank at work functions and they drank at home; alcohol was part of the fabric of their lives. While not even Phoebe's closest friends suspected she was an alcoholic, Delia writes, "My mother's drinking was so overwhelming that I didn't notice the obvious: that my dad was drinking, too."[108] There are clear indications in their work of their relationship with alcohol.

That which Phoebe denied or at least insisted be kept a secret—
"I hope you never tell anyone what happens here"[109]—is given substance
in *Howie*. Phoebe's only individual work goes some way to acknowledging her addiction. By the time Phoebe wrote *Howie* in the mid- to late-
1950s, alcohol had become a major presence in her life and the lives of
her characters. Many of the jokes and much of the discussion in the
play revolve around alcohol and, with the exception of the younger
daughter, all the major characters drink. As the play opens, Walter
Simms, the middle-aged father, in reporting the events of his day to his
wife, tells her he has had a medical checkup. He has been told he has
to lose weight and give up smoking in order to stay healthy. Conversely,
his doctor has said his drinking is fine, in fact encouraged. Walter—with
wit, an air of cynicism and a sense of irony—when asked by his wife,
Edith, what the doctor said about his consumption of alcohol responds,
"Nothing. That's all right. Apparently I can drink myself into a stupor
as long as I give up food and cigarettes."[110] This sentiment is repeated
a number of times in the first scene of *Howie*.

Phoebe had already had twenty years of drinking by the time she
wrote *Howie*. At home she was drinking a bottle of scotch a night in
her room before she would begin to terrorize her family, ranting and
raving throughout the night.[111] It is far too coincidental that a play written by her, a play in which the characters allude to the unacknowledged
effects of alcohol and then continue to drink, is not in some way an
acknowledgment of her own awareness and concern for her personal
relationship with alcohol.

The characters in *Howie* are not the only characters created by
Henry and Phoebe who drink. Drinking was a consistent part of the
lives of all their characters. From the beginning of their collaboration
their created worlds are peopled with characters who drink in significant
quantities. By the end of the second act of *Three's a Family*, everyone,
including the maid, is drinking scotch (Henry and Phoebe's drink of
choice) and continue to do so well into the third act. Drinking is so
pronounced a feature in *Three's a Family* that *Time* magazine, in its theatre round up, commented that among other things there was "some
escapist drinking by the long-suffering older folk."[112]

As Henry recounts their life together in his memoir he inadver-
tently records the progression of their alcoholism. Alcohol was part of
celebrations in their lives—the night Eleanor Roosevelt came to see

their play Henry left the theatre to have a drink himself and then he had a second drink and became very sentimental.[113] And, years later, when their screenplay for *The Jackpot* was optioned, Henry writes that they spent the night on the town wining and dining.[114]

Alcohol was not only for celebrations; it was fortification when things went wrong. Otto Preminger took Henry and Phoebe off a screenplay they had been working on so they went to a bar to console themselves with whisky.[115] Back in New York after their first not-very-successful year in Hollywood, Henry and Phoebe left the children with Phoebe's parents, booked a suite at the Algonquin, looked for apartments during the day, and wined and dined in the famous hotel at night.[116] Towards the end of their joint career, finding a drink at times became an act of desperation. Henry writes of an incident on location in Booth Bay for the filming of *Carousel*, where he and Phoebe "were dying for a drink," and "how to get a drink was the most important problem in life."[117]

Although each single incident related by Henry appears innocuous, what emerges in his recounting of their life is that alcohol was a promi-nent feature, an important detail. As alcohol increased in significance in their lives there was a parallel increase in the use of alcohol by the characters in their plays and films. Fact and fiction blurred and merged. By the time *Daddy Long Legs* appeared on screen in 1957, alcohol had become a salve to the psychological bruises of those living in close prox-imity to Jarvis Pendleton III (Fred Astaire). At the beginning of the film, when the car in which Pendleton, his business manager/personal assistant Griggs (Fred Clark) and other members of the group breaks down, Jarvis suggests Griggs should "break out the last bottle of brandy; everyone could use a drink." Later, in Paris over martinis, Jarvis suggests to Griggs and the American Ambassador Alexander Williamson (Larry Keating) that he will adopt the eighteen-year-old female orphan Julie André (Leslie Caron). Both men, rattled as they are by the implications of such a suggestion, say, "Let's have another martini." Toward the end of the film, Griggs and his associate Miss Pritchard (Thelma Ritter) have bourbon on the rocks as they contemplate what they can do about the romantic relationship developing between Jarvis and Julie. The con-cluding moment of the film, as Jarvis and Julie declare their love via dance, Miss Prichard and Griggs retire to have a drink—declaring they, too, may be beginning a relationship—a relationship alluded to via drinking references.

Perhaps subconsciously, their characters reveal Henry and Phoebe's differing response to alcohol. The more stressful the day or the potential stress of the night, the more alcohol is consumed. The Michaelson family in *Take Her, She's Mine* drink, but it is only when their eldest daughter, Mollie, returns from college and, in line with her new sophisticated image, requests a martini, of which she takes nothing but a sip. It is not a foregrounded feature in the play, but alcohol is a presence in the play. The use of alcohol by Frank Michaelson is insidious. As it was in the Ephron family, the consumption of alcohol is a normalized feature of the daily routine of the Michaelson family. In *Take Her, She's Mine*, drinking is something that happens as part of the stage direction, not as the result of the overt actions of the characters.

Three's a Family and *Take Her, She's Mine*, unlike *Howie*, are fictional works tempered by the input of Henry and what is highlighted is the difference between the realities of the writing partners. Henry was drinking, it is true, but, as Nora writes, his abuse of alcohol was far less threatening or dramatic than Phoebe's in the Ephron household. According to Nora, Henry became sentimental and emotional.[118] "My father drank too, but he was a sloppy sentimental drunk, and somehow his alcoholism was more benign."[119] Henry's involvement in the writing of the scripts tempered the tone of the play, normalized the role of alcohol in the daily lives of the characters. The plays in no way acknowledge the effects of alcohol. Unlike Phoebe, Henry did not recognize his addiction.

Alcohol abuse was Phoebe's health issue and while she was successful in hiding her alcoholism so not even her closest friends knew, in retrospect an examination of her work reveals the secret she was unable to address in her life. Similarly, by examining the works on which they collaborated it is possible to chart Phoebe and Henry's growing dependence on alcohol. The disease from which they both suffered can be identified, but only as it has been mediated through their fiction. Phoebe died on October 13, 1971, of an alcohol-related illness, at the age of fifty-seven.

Nora, like her mother, reviewed, examined and processed the events of her life through the act of transposing the real into the fictional. Nora said she was heavily in denial[120]—but some of what she was in denial about is given the space to be examined in her work. *Heartburn* being one example: this novel, a work of fiction, is where Nora safely dealt with what she has described as the most painful event of her adult life, her bitter and traumatic divorce from Carl Bernstein. By writing a novel about the breakdown of her marriage, Nora took stock of her life and more or less moved on.

Most significantly, Nora wrote about her terminal illness, the knowledge that she was dying. That which she denied in life is on full view in her work. When Frank Rich wrote of the reaction to her death on June 26, 2012, from pneumonia brought on by acute myeloid leukemia, he reported that in New York "Nora's passing prompted nearly twenty articles or blog posts in the *Times*, more than a dozen in *Newsweek/Daily Beast*, six in *The New Yorker* and multiple entries in others, including *New York*, where she had been a columnist during the magazine-writing career that first made many, including me, fall in love with her." He also wrote, "But as was also true of most print tributes to Nora, one aspect of her death was largely relegated to the memorial's cutting-room floor: the hard fact that most of those in the hall (the Alice Tully room at the Lincoln Center where her memorial was held), not to mention the legions of Nora friends, worshippers, and fans beyond it, had not known she was dying until it was too late to say good-bye."[121]

Nora had been diagnosed with myeloid leukemia six years prior, but as Frank Rich writes and has so often been reported in other articles written at the time of her death, only a select few, who were very close to her, knew. Nora's illness was her secret in life, but not in her work. Her collection of essays, *I Remember Nothing*, published in 2010, left no doubt. "Christmas Dinner" reflects on the death of Nora's best friend, Ruthie, and "The O Word" is a dark, sad contemplation on old age and death. "What I Won't Miss" and then "What I Will Miss" and the inclusion of her doctors in the Acknowledgments said it all. Understanding how she used her work, understanding what she had been taught to do by Phoebe and understanding the multiple levels of meaning she built into her work means it is there for all to know. The idiosyncrasies of the Ephron modus operandi reveal the secrets. Nora, to the end, utilized the family coping mechanism. Tell a story, and make it funny. Don't be the victim, be the hero. So Nora wrote about what she will miss when she died. She was the subject and heroine of her story. She got to tell her story *her* way. She heralded her death in her work.

Not only did Nora reveal her impending death in her final collection of essays, she also addressed the issue of her mother. Nora's essay

"The Legend" and her film *Julie and Julia* both pay homage to Phoebe. The essay and film have a very real poignancy when understood in the context of Nora being aware of her limited time. They are each an attempt at a final reconciliation with the woman who had so great an influence on her life. When Nora alluded to her terminal illness, her death, in her work and only in her work, she cemented the absolute bond between herself and Phoebe. She is her mother's daughter. Nora Ephron's work is identifiable as unique and belonging to her alone. Her art is the space she uses to record and consider her life and the world around her. It is where she tells the stories of her life. She does this because that is what she was taught to do. Above all else, Nora's early life and experiences as the child of Phoebe Ephron are fundamental to the shaping of her creative voice. The identifying characteristics of Nora's work: food, the use of life as the raw material for art, turning the painful into the comical as a survival mechanism, Nora's admiration of strong women who rely on themselves for survival and her love of literature—all of these patterns stem from her relationship with Phoebe. It is Nora's relationship with this difficult and complex woman which shaped her.

> My mother was not this smother-us-with-kisses mother, but there were virtues to the way she was. ... She was one of those very powerful people who got a great deal by not giving a huge amount. But she did give us a lot. ... And we knew what she wanted from us.[122]

Phoebe, by her own admission, was not always available to her daughters. When she was, "She ordered us around constantly."[123] She rewarded the "good behavior," but "when things weren't going well Mrs. Ephron wasn't interested."[124]

> If you went to a dance where no one wanted to dance with you, my mother was not the person to talk to about it. ... Where did I go for sympathy? I don't know where I went for sympathy. I don't think there was a whole lot of sympathy.[125]

Nora has repeatedly reflected upon her mother's behavior, mostly with an awareness of how difficult it was to have Phoebe not be there emotionally for her in moments of need. How difficult it was when Phoebe's invariable response was "Everything is copy." There were times when Nora made a statement which reveals a deep understanding of her mother, such as when she told Xan Brooks, "And if you are going to be unbelievably serious about it I suspect it was her way of saying: 'Don't come to me with so much pain.'"[126] But Nora almost always allowed her mother positive intentions in what were clearly negative and destructive ways of behaving. She could not bear to know her mother as she truly was. Nora came to believe Phoebe's response to her emotional needs was a two-edged sword. Phoebe's refusal to buy into her child's pain, her "Get on with it and get over it" attitude—the attitude she instilled in Nora—Nora believed ultimately saved her and made her career.

According to reporter Nancy Collins, Nora is "one of the most positive people I know, Nora doesn't believe in self-pity or being depressed. She's a plucky person. You pinch her and she pops back again."[127] Phoebe was exacting and not one for nurturing, she did not have a sympathetic ear—and Nora, as an adult, "doesn't like whining"[128]; she also has a reputation for being exacting. Nora "has always had a reputation for ruthlessness, but it's easy to see where it comes from: she internalized her mother's voice a long time ago."[129]

All facets of Nora's career are attributable in part to the influence of her parents. Nora's decision to become a journalist, a writer, was as her mother intended. Later, when Nora began her film career it may not have been as the result of an opportunity directly attributed to her parents—as she correctly claims, their career in Hollywood was finished twenty years before hers began—however, Nora's background, her family, the influences of her family, the exposure to their professional life and, ultimately, the influence of her mother informed Nora's life and career. Nothing was more influential than her mother's mantra: "Everything is copy." Nora writes of her parents that they were "the people you grew up idolizing ... the people they used to be have enormous power over you" and that even when her parents had changed and had become alcoholics, she "was invested in the original narrative; I was a true believer. My mother was a goddess."[130]

2

This Is My Life

Nora Ephron's off-screen life has—in some fashion or another—always been part of our public consciousness[1]

Nora has always lived in the public domain. From the time of her birth she was involved in the family business and her life has been fictionalized and chronicled, first by her parents and then by her.

The screenwriting career of Phoebe and Henry Ephron began as a consequence of the success of their play *Three's a Family*. As their first collaboration the play was deeply personal and borrowed extensively from their own life experiences for its story, characters and dialogue. *Three's a Family* also marks the beginning of Nora Ephron's life being recorded in a fictionalized form. Long before Nora became famous for cannibalizing her life, her parents were well skilled in the practice.

While Nora is not the only Ephron child to have found herself (or events from her life) fictionalized in her parents' work, she was the child who, as an adult, became most famous for continuing the family tradition. All the Ephron girls—Nora, Delia, Hallie and Amy—write, and all have used their lives as material for their work. However, it is Nora who is the most successful and most well known. When asked about her life being used as material by her parents, Nora's usual response was that, as the children of the Ephron writing team, the girls "grew up knowing it was open season.... We all understood that's what happens if you live with writers. Your life will be up for grabs."[2] Nora also remarked that part of the reason it did not bother her to have her life used in that way is that she saw it as part of her parents' biography rather than her own. However, Nora's response to having her life used by her parents as the source material for their work was not always so simple. Nora was far more conflicted in her feelings than her responses would indicate.

Nora's works are vehicles with which she continued to do that which was begun by her parents—to chronicle her life. Henry and Phoebe began the chronicle of Nora's life documenting two major milestones—her birth and her departure for college—in their plays *Three's a Family* and *Take Her, She's Mine*, respectively. When Nora became a journalist she gained fame for writing about her life. What began as a fictionalized biography in the hands of her parents became a form of fictionalized autobiography when Nora took over the task.

Heartburn, published in 1982, and the 1986 film adaptation of the novel for which Nora wrote the screenplay and her debut film as a director, *This Is My Life*, have the material of her life as the subject. *Heartburn* is a significant work because it is not just a chronicle of the breakdown of Nora's marriage to Carl Bernstein, it is a summary of her life to that point in time; it also foreshadows her future work. The themes, the ideas and opinions that identify Nora and her work appear in *Heartburn*, even some of the lines from future films are there. For fans and scholars of Nora Ephron, *Heartburn* has gained legendary status; it is the key to understanding her life and art. The novel provides an overview of Nora's life. Nora's writing style and the function of comedy in the lives of the Ephron family is explained. Nora's world view is evident and the seed of ideas for future works is present. *Heartburn* is both a précis and summation of Nora's life.

The four texts, *Three's a Family*, *Take Her, She's Mine*, *Heartburn* (both the novel and film version) and *This Is My Life*, are overtly biographical. They are clear examples of the family ethos of using life as the raw material for art, and they are works, because of the use of the specifics of their own lives, marked as idiosyncratic and unique to the Ephron family.

When Nora began to document her life she also began to re-evaluate the life she had as a child growing up with her parents. It becomes evident she had a few things to say about being the child of Henry and Phoebe Ephron.

The mother guppies eat the baby guppies as soon as they get born.[3]

This prophetic statement, made by the character Sam Whitaker in *Three's a Family*, has enormous resonance in the lives of the Ephron daughters, particularly Nora. It is unimaginable that it was merely an accident of words. Sam, as he snaps beans for the family dinner, is busily scooping the just-born guppies from the fish tank they share with their mother. If he doesn't remove them newly born they will be cannibalized by her.

Henry and Phoebe Ephron wrote *Three's a Family* for the stage in 1942. It was first performed on May 5, 1943, at the Longacre Theatre in New York. At the time of writing the play, Nora, born on May 19, 1941, was a small baby. Henry writes in his memoir that when Nora was born Phoebe gave up work to be a mother, but very soon found she could not cope. She did not want to be a full-time mother. Phoebe found the "long hours of walking the carriage around and sitting on the park bench extremely irksome," as did Henry.[4] In *Three's a Family*, Sam invites his daughter Kitty to go for a walk with him. Kitty, a new mother, is delighted and she responds to her father's invitation with "I'd love to go for a walk just once without the carriage."[5]

Kitty's reaction to motherhood reflects Phoebe's experience of life with her baby daughter Nora. The resolution of the problem of Phoebe's struggle with the demands of motherhood was found when she and Henry employed a nurse to take care of Nora every afternoon.[6] In *Three's a Family*, Sam Whitaker, baby Susan's grandfather, returns to "retirement" in order to care for his grandchild as he had previously done for his own children. In both her life and her fiction, Phoebe neither wanted nor had the responsibility of the day-to-day care of her child.

At the time when Phoebe was finding motherhood irksome, Henry convinced her to write a play with him. The play was to be based on the life of Phoebe's aunt Minnie, who worked as a dentist while her husband ran the house, cooked and cared for their children. At Phoebe's suggestion they included a baby in the play. It was Phoebe's belief that the play would be a hit if they included a baby: "All the nonsense with the baby can be terribly funny, even if we don't see it that way now."[7] Henry and Phoebe loved their children, but, fortuitously for them, earned enough money to be able to employ someone else to look after them. Phoebe's statement—that nonsense with a baby could be terribly funny in a play even if they didn't see it that way as they were experiencing it—reveals a response and attitude toward their children that would continue throughout Phoebe and Henry's lives. The Ephrons always put their careers before their children, the day-to-day responsibility associated with having children was irksome and not something they could be bothered with for any length of time.

According to *Three's a Family*, the arrival of a baby throws the life of any new parent into chaos; something many of the audience members would identify with. In Henry and Phoebe's play, the new parents, Gene and Kitty, fight, and Kitty leaves to move back with her parents, taking baby Susan with her.

The overall chaos and disruption caused by the arrival of a baby is illustrated in the play not only by the incessantly squabbling parents but by the overwhelming and overcrowding of the Whitakers' apartment with the baby paraphernalia when baby Susan, with her mother Kitty, arrives at the apartment of her grandparents Sam and Frances Whitaker on West 110th Street—this, incidentally, was the location of Henry and Phoebe's apartment in New York before they left for Hollywood. Susan's arrival is accompanied by a variety of pieces of furniture. A bathinette arrives with her and the rest of her furniture: a baby carriage, a kiddie-koop, a playpen, a white chest of drawers, a hope chest, a baby-clothes tree and an electric floor-lamp are all delivered later by two removalists. Susan's furniture, with the exception of the bathinette, takes over the Whitakers' living room as there is nowhere else for it in the small apartment. The arrival of the baby puts the lives of her parents and grandparents in disarray.

Just as the Whitakers' living room is crowded with the baby furniture, the background action of the play is crowded with the time-consuming tasks of parenting a baby: bathing, dressing, continual laundering of clothes, preparation of bottles, feeding, walking and settling the baby to sleep—"all the nonsense of having a baby." The work involved in the care of the baby is so considerable the maid quits.

There is no doubt that Phoebe was correct, the inclusion of a baby considerably broadened the play's appeal, however the universality of the subject does not detract from the very personal nature of the play. Phoebe's statement—with regard to the comedic potential of life with Nora—not only acknowledges her skill as a playwright and her ability to recognize the comedy of the human condition, it also gives voice to Henry and Phoebe's attitude to life with their baby. For Henry and Phoebe it was not a fun time; they were having a hard time as new parents.

As Henry recorded the circumstances of the writing of *Three's a Family* in his memoir, he documented the first time the Ephrons turned something that was not funny in their lives into something that was funny in their work. Henry documented how, at Phoebe's instigation, through the inclusion of the baby in the play, they used their work to process the difficult moments in their lives and, through that process, turned the trials and tribulations of having a baby into a comedy. "What seems horrible to you today can be reborn as a funny story if you work hard enough at it"[8] is the Ephron family credo; this is evidenced in operation in *Three's a Family*.

The most personal moment in the play, the moment which identifies the work as that of Henry and Phoebe, is the exchange between Kitty and her husband, Gene, in scene 1. Kitty has moved in with her parents because she had a fight with her husband. When Gene arrives to see Kitty before he leaves for the army, they discuss their argument. Gene had shaken and then thrown baby Susan in a moment of anger. Gene acknowledges it was wrong and that he has a bad temper. He explains his action was the result of tiredness caused by Susan keeping him awake. There is no humor in the scene. When Gene tries to be funny, when he responds to Kitty's "You threw her [Susan] at me" with "I knew you'd catch her. You played basketball at Hunter," Kitty's sarcastic reply "very funny," immediately removes the possibility of humor. Kitty rebukes Gene's attempt to make a joke of the situation. She does not find Gene's retort funny and this was not a funny incident for her. The moment is made personal, linked to Henry and Phoebe, when Gene makes reference to Kitty having played basketball at Hunter; Hunter College being Phoebe's university.

The moment in the play where Kitty confronts Gene with his actions is jarring, almost horrific, but gone in a flash. The farce then continues and the moment has passed. The comedy of the Ephrons has other similar moments. The scene described is pre-emptive of one in *Hanging Up*, a novel written by Nora's younger sister Delia at the time of Henry's death. The novel is a fictionalized account of her relationship with her father. In the novel and its 2000 film adaptation there is a scene in which a drunken Lou (Henry/Walter Matthau) arrives at the birthday party of his grandchild, Eve's (Delia/Meg Ryan) son. Lou is verbally abusive. He frightens the children and wrecks the party.[9] Delia did not speak to her father for several years because of such an incident.

Amy, the youngest of the Ephron daughters, describes an incident in her novel *Cool Shades*, in which the narrator's father, based on her actual father, "grabbed me by the scruff of the neck like a kitten and kicked me down the hall toward the room that I shared with my sister. 'What the fuck are you doing up this time of night?' he screamed in a drunken rage." This incident took place when the character based on Amy was five. As a teenager, Amy moved out of her family home, as did the narrator in *Cool Shades*. In Amy's novel the narrator says she always had difficulty sleeping at night as a result of her experiences as a child.[10]

The scene from *Hanging Up* and the moment in *Cool Shades* are important because they give credibility to the scene in *Three's a Family*. Henry, by his own admission, was a man with a temper. In his memoir he cites moments when he was belligerent, when in anger he tried to kick over a desk, when he was boorish and when he was ill-behaved.[11] It is plausible given Henry's personality and his behavior, documented by himself, Delia and Amy, that the moment of throwing the baby in *Three's a Family* is a moment from his life; a painful incident from his and Phoebe's life as the new parents of Nora, processed by them in the act of creating art.

The moment in *Three's a Family* is out of character with the rest of the play as are the scenes from *Hanging Up* and *Cool Shades*. The scenes described, one from *Three's a Family* and the other from *Hanging Up*, are moments when the focus of the writing is lost and changed. In Amy's novel the descriptions of moments from her childhood, lucid, clear and precise, are in stark contrast to the novel as a whole, which is rambling and vague and remote. The description of incidents from the narrator's childhood read as vivid memories. The focus in the recording of each incident has moved from being funny, in the instance of *Three's a Family* and *Hanging Up*, and from vague and languid in *Cool Shades* to being a moment of negative, painful and unresolved emotion; a moment where the magnitude of the event is so affecting that each of the writers loses sight of the transformative nature of their writing and just leaves the event raw.

After the acknowledgment of Gene having thrown the baby, the scene continues with his responding to Kitty's accusation of "You haven't even been home" with "If I haven't, it's because the house is impossible these days. You can't seem to manage anything—the baby, the meals, the house."[12] As the quarrel between the couple resolves itself, with Kitty declaring that she is new at mothering and if Gene only gave her time she, in fact, might turn out to be a good mother, the moment of horror—the revelation of Gene throwing the baby—has passed and the universal nature of the situation returns. The new parents continue to squabble for the duration of the play until each acknowledges a love for the other and their child and each admits to having a bad temper, a trait inherited by Susan.

The situation of the young married couple is both universal and personal. It is material drawn from the real-life experience of new parents Henry and Phoebe. The immediate solution for the young couple grappling with the demands of parenthood is to have their baby looked after by Kitty's parents while they leave to spend time together before Gene is shipped out. The long-term solution for Kitty is to have Sam, her father, stay home and care for Susan while she takes a job that she would love, "Nine to five-thirty—forty-five minutes for lunch."[13] The solution is familial and idiosyncratic. Phoebe's aunt Minnie worked while her husband cared for the children and ran the house, as does Sam Whitaker. Sam is also the solution to the problem with Susan. He will look after Susan while Kitty and Gene continue their life as it was before they had a child and Kitty, like Phoebe, will resume her life as an independent, working woman.

In *We Thought We Could Do Anything*, Henry writes about life with their children. He makes comments that indicate an undeniable love for them: "I taught Delia tricks, and Phoebe read to Nora all the books that she herself had read over and over again as a child."[14] He writes that Phoebe believed "the children are really the most fun of all."[15] He also reveals where the children fitted into their lives—second, after their own: "We hired a woman to come in every afternoon and do nothing but take care of Nora. Phoebe talked about going back to work,"[16] "Phoebe's mother and father took in the children. We registered at the Algonquin,"[17] "Phoebe's mother arrived to spell the [children's] nurse,"[18] "we hadn't been very much of a father and mother lately"[19] and "the four children, Phoebe and I dined together every night we were home."[20]

The Ephron parents had the same attitude toward their children as Gene and Kitty have toward Susan in their play. Nora, and then her younger sisters, were loved, as was Susan, but they all—Susan and Nora and, later, Nora's sisters—had parents who spent time with them in measured doses. As documented by Henry, the Ephron children were frequently left in the care of others while their parents worked and lived their own lives. Phoebe made a decision when Nora was an infant: she chose a life as a working woman. We know this because her alter ego Kitty made the same decision in *Three's a Family*. Kitty articulated Phoebe's desires and decisions.

Eighteen years after Henry and Phoebe's life with Nora provided the material for their first play, Nora, with her leaving home to go to school, again provided the raw material for her parents' play *Take Her, She's Mine*. While the two works chronicle, in a fictionalized form, Nora's life as the daughter of Henry and Phoebe Ephron, they differ in one very significant aspect. Nora could not, by virtue of being a baby, have any direct input into *Three's a Family*. The play was entirely written from the perspective of her parents; however, with *Take Her, She's Mine*, again written from the perspective of Henry and Phoebe, Nora directly contributed to the play. It was her letters home to her mother while she was at Wellesley that provided the material. Her letters were, at times, quoted verbatim in the play and, because of this, her views and experiences appear for the first time in public. Nora should have been credited as a co-author.

Take Her, She's Mine was first performed at the Biltmore Theatre, New York City, in December 1961. Like the earlier play chronicling life with Nora, this one was hugely popular with audiences. The play begins with the graduation from high school of Frank and Anne Michaelson's eldest daughter, Mollie. Like Nora, Mollie is described as intelligent, alert and enthusiastic. When she is handed her diploma by her high school principal she receives four awards for outstanding performance. Frank, Mollie's father, opens the play with a direct address to the audience. Frank is an emotional man, prone to crying; he is a fictionalized version of Henry, who describes himself as "a man who burst into tears at the sight of Delia being carried downstairs by her nurse."[21] Frank tells the audience, "Anyway it's quite clear that we've got a 'Brain.'"[22] Mollie has been offered places in four universities in the East. She has chosen Hawthorne College for Women. Hawthorne College is the fictional representation of Wellesley, the women's university Nora attended.

Shortly after Mollie's graduation she leaves for school. Later, Frank, still coming to grips with the fact that his daughter has left home, begins to worry: "Suppose she comes back too smart? A misfit? Somebody who makes the boys feel inferior?"[23] Nora was extremely smart, her intelligence daunting. She could easily make boys feel inferior. Frank voicing the expectations of his culture worries that Mollie's intelligence, enhanced through her attendance at a leading college, will make her too smart and, consequently, Mollie will not be marriage material. Frank's concerns, a reflection of the time in which Nora grew up, are reiterated by Nora in her commencement address to the Wellesley class of 1996. Nora spoke of her own time as a student at Wellesley as a time when a woman was not meant to have a career: "We weren't meant to have futures, we were meant to marry them," and it was a time "when you got a master's degree in teaching because it was 'something to fall back on'"[24] in the worst case scenario, where no one married you and you actually had to go to work.

Through the characters Frank and Mollie, *Take Her, She's Mine* clearly conveys the expectations placed on women within the American and most western cultures during the early 1960s. A woman must marry and she should not be perceived as too bright lest she might appear smarter than her husband. As the character Frank performs the function of mouthpiece for conventional and accepted cultural norms, Mollie, as she grapples with the same concerns, begins to question the veracity of and conflicts inherent in society's expectations of women. By doing so, Mollie foreshadows the emergence of the women's movement, a movement in which Nora will be heavily involved:

> MOLLIE: (reading Shakespeare's sonnets) Do you suppose this is all a waste? I mean, let's face it, woman's real purpose in life is marriage, children, propagate the species and all that stuff. Does it make you any more desirable as a wife because you know the meaning of a Shakespeare sonnet, or you can describe intimately the inner workings of the female frog?
>
> ADELE: (Mollie's roommate) I intend to keep it a secret. Might scare somebody away. How many articles have you read about the aggressive American female?
>
> MOLLIE: Exactly. But if they teach us this stuff, aren't we supposed to use it? And if we use it, does that make us aggressive?[25]

Mollie's letters to home document her induction into college life. The first of these letters details how "for days now I've been oriented, registered, examined—by the way, I have poor posture, but so does everyone else apparently—indexed, filed, everything but fingerprinted. I've even had my diction analyzed, and for some reason it came out New Jersey."[26] The content of Mollie's letter is confirmed as true and accurate and belonging to Nora when in her Wellesley speech Nora says: "There were posture pictures. We not only took off most of our clothes to have our posture pictures taken, we took them off without even thinking, this is weird, why are we doing this?—not only that, we had also had speech therapy—I was told I had a New Jersey accent."[27]

Mollie's letters are a documentation of the time as well as are a chronicle of Nora's life at school. Mollie attended a lecture given by Margaret Mead, during which the noted anthropologist spoke of the need for young people not to marry but experiment and, in what is probably the most quoted passage from the letters Nora wrote to her mother, Mollie writes:

> I heard Norman Thomas speak last Monday night on disarmament, which he naturally regards as absolutely necessary, and isn't the world situation just abysmal? Sometimes I think the world won't last another week—and ... here I am ... still a ... virgin.

This extract from Nora's letter to her mother appears twice in the play. Once as it is written, with confidence by Mollie, without the breaks and with the inclusion of the word "virgin"[28] and then again as it is read—with the exclusion of the word "virgin"—with dread, by her father, Frank, who clearly does not want to contemplate his daughter's sexual behavior.[29] The way the letter has been written, with confidence and in a forthright manner, is in stark contrast to how it is received by Frank. The sending and receiving of the letter cleverly articulates the two points of view in the play. Not only is the voice of Henry heard, but so is the voice of his daughter Nora.

Henry and Phoebe, as they always did, used the raw material of their life as material for *Take Her, She's Mine*. Frank is the voice of Henry, a father, at times overwhelmed and concerned for his daughter as she entered adulthood and university life. Henry, the father, is a starkly different being than the Henry of Henry and Phoebe, the playwrights who showed no compunction in using their daughter's private letters in a public context in their work.

There are other details of Nora's life included in the play. Frank tells the audience that they received a letter in which Mollie informed her family she had become engaged.[30] This is also part of Nora's biography: "During my junior year, when I was engaged for a very short period of time..."[31] and toward the conclusion of the play when Mollie has announced she is quitting college, her prospective boyfriend, Alex, berates her for her foolishness. He says she is far too bright to throw away her education. He comments that she might want to "get a job with *Time* magazine,"[32] which is a reference to Nora's chosen career as a journalist. Nora's life at school, as recorded in her letters home to her parents, is without doubt the basis for *Take Her, She's Mine*.

The play discloses more than Nora's life at that time. *Take Her, She's Mine* clearly articulates the Ephron family's "modus operandi." Mollie gives voice to how Henry and Phoebe use their work as a vehicle for processing daily life, as a way of turning even the most distressing aspects of life into a funny story. After an incident where Mollie has been attacked physically by an ardent admirer, an incident that would today be called attempted "date-rape," Frank is deeply concerned for his daughter. Mollie responds to her father's concern with:

> Oh, I'm not really marred. Takes more than that to mar me. In some ways it was kind of funny. By the time I get back to school I'll reappraise it and it'll be a hilarious story to tell the girls.[33]

In that moment, in the statement made by Mollie, is the mix that informed the work of Henry and Phoebe Ephron and the work of Nora. When Mollie says she is not marred by what has happened and that the incident will be transformed, in a very short time, from something terrible into a funny story, she is stating how the Ephrons lived and worked. Mollie is at one and the same time Mollie and Nora and the voice of Phoebe and Henry, she is nonfiction and fiction, life and art. As Mollie says, "Life isn't just one thing or another. It's a combination of things."[34]

Take Her, She's Mine was the last success of the writing team of Phoebe and Henry Ephron. As with their first success it was a play produced on Broadway and it was about their daughter Nora. Nora's life, more accurately their life with Nora, was the impetus for her parents' original work. Henry and Phoebe took Nora's life and, like the guppy mother in their first play, they "caught" her and "ate" her. Nora's life became fodder for their work.

Nora graduated from Wellesley College in 1962 and, as she had intended, moved to New York to become a journalist. Her career in journalism is an important backdrop to the continuing documentation of her life. As a journalist Nora continued to chronicle her life. But Nora's use of the material of her life as the basis for her work, her art, was fundamentally different from the approach of her parents. Phoebe and Henry, as playwrights and screenwriters during the studio-based period of Hollywood film production, could only use moments from their lives indirectly. Conversely, when Nora wrote about herself it was declared. Nora's writing from the 1970s and before acknowledged that *she* was the subject. She put herself in the piece and was able to do so because her time, the late 1960s and early 1970s, and her profession as a journalist allowed her to do so. It was the time of New Journalism, a period of journalism history when "I-centered" journalistic pieces were in fashion.[35] Nora was writing about her experiences and even when her writing dealt with other issues and other people the reader was aware that the observation was from the perspective of the writer, from Nora's perspective.

Nora claimed that she never embraced the journalistic style that became known as New Journalism. In her essay "Journalism: A Love Story," Nora pays tribute to a colleague, Joe Rabinovich, whom she believed contributed to her success as a journalist. He "kept my occasional stylistic excesses in line; he saved me from woeful idiocy when Tom Wolfe began to write for the *Herald Tribune* and I made a pathetic attempt to write exactly like him."[36] Nora may not have considered herself an exponent of New Journalism, however, recently, she had been identified as part of the movement. Garry Wills said of the time and of Nora: "That was the time of the 'new journalism,' but Tom Wolfe, presiding over the movement, did not notice that Ephron was writing some of the best reportorial prose of the era."[37]

It is of minor significance whether or not Nora is credited as an exponent of New Journalism. What *is* important is that she was working in journalism at that time. She could not help but be influenced by the movement and the movement could be nothing but advantageous for Nora. What New Journalism provided was an atmosphere where it was acceptable, even fashionable, to have the writer appear as part of the written piece. The advent of New Journalism meant that, as the writer, Nora could now openly be acknowledged as the subject, the raw material. The time of "I-centered" journalism was an ideal time for Nora.

Nora achieved great success. In a very short time she established herself as a writer to be reckoned with. In the words of Ariel Levy, "Ephron's pieces were vivid and cunning and crackling with her personality."[38] She could annihilate a reputation and make you laugh at the same time. In 1970, just eight years after she began working in journalism, a number of her reportage pieces were published as a book. The collection, *Wallflower at the Orgy*, became her first best-seller.

In 1972, Nora was hired to write a column about women for *Esquire* magazine. Her reasons, she said, were variously self-indulgent and general: "It seemed clear that American women were going through some changes; I wanted to write about them and myself."[39] New Journalism and the emerging women's movement afforded Nora the opportunity to continue in the family business; she could build and establish her reputation as a writer doing what her family had always done. She could write about herself and, as part of the process, her work operated as a prism through which to reflect the social issues of her time.

As her parents had done, Nora chronicled the society in which she lived by writing about her own life. She built a reputation and a career for herself as a journalist because she was good at what she did. Nora was intelligent and diligent and thorough. Her writing, although damning and confrontational and at times reputation-destroying, always ensured accuracy was at its core. Her opinion might not be agreed with but her argument was always sound. Perhaps the most profound comment on Nora's writing comes from John Gregory Dunne who once wrote in *Esquire*: "Nora does not compel agreement. What she does is make you shed the extraneous, the pleasant and the comforting. She makes you align the facts, marshal an argument."[40] Dunne's comment bestows seriousness to Nora's work—an attribute rarely considered by anyone else.

In 1992, Leslie Bennetts wrote: "Ephron's propensity for cannibalizing her own life didn't become a *cause celebre* until the spectacular demise of her second marriage."[41] Nora had already been married and divorced by the time she met Carl Bernstein. He was a journalist with the *Washington Post* and famous, along with his colleague Bob Woodward, for the exposure of the Watergate scandal. Carl and Nora were very high profile; he the Watergate hero and she the New York journalist and sophisticate.[42]

After the collapse of their marriage Nora wrote her only novel. From the outset she makes a clear statement that that which is about to be read is a humorous account of what was a devastating event in the life of Rachel Samstat/Nora Ephron. The opening statement declares the family coping mechanism; "I did not think it was funny the third day either, but I managed to make a joke about it"[43] and it reveals the key to understanding Nora's work. The opening lines of *Heartburn* are

Nora's words. They show Nora had taken the words spoken by Mollie—Phoebe and Henry's words—"Oh, I'm not really marred. Takes more than that to mar me. In some ways it was kind of funny. By the time I get back to school I'll reappraise it and it'll be a hilarious story to tell the girls"—from *Take Her, She's Mine*[44] and applied them to her life and her work.

Nora begins to tell a funny story about the most traumatic event of her life. By living and working by those words Nora took control of her life. She once said of her recovery from the breakup of her marriage: "I feel I was partly saved by the advice my mother gave me, which was everything is copy—'take notes.'"[45] Nora, in writing *Heartburn*, processed the pain of the collapse of her marriage.

While Nora was writing a funny story about the end of her marriage she was also revising and reassessing other aspects of her life. Nora made sure her story about the young woman Rachel Samstat, who was cheated on by her husband, was easily identifiable as hers. The name Nora gave to Rachel's husband—Mark Feldman—was, of itself, enough to establish that the story was indeed hers. Mark Feldman and Carl Bernstein are very closely connected. To understand the name of the character and the connection to Carl Bernstein is to understand the cunning and cleverness of Nora Ephron. When Carl Bernstein and Bob Woodward exposed the Watergate Scandal they had an informant they vowed never to disclose the identity of; the informant was referred to as "Deep Throat." On May 31, 2005, Mark Felt revealed himself as "Deep Throat." On the same day Nora Ephron wrote on her *Huffington Post* blog that she had guessed a long time before the identity of "Deep Throat" and had subsequently told anyone who would listen. She was mostly ignored. The joke is, she told the world from as early as 1982; more precisely, anyone who read *Heartburn* or saw the film. She called her lead male character Mark Feldman. Carl Bernstein could not do a thing about it without revealing his Watergate source.[46]

Not content to have just one covert allusion to the identity of her characters, Nora littered her novel with clues as to whose story it was. The writing style of the central character, Rachel, was recognizable as Nora's own. In describing her own unique style, Nora wrote: "As I learned the essay form, writing became harder for me. I was finding a personal style, a voice if you will, a way of writing that looked chatty and informal."[47] Rachel, a writer of cookbooks, in describing her books, explains her style: "They're very personal and chatty—they're cookbooks in an almost incidental way. I write chapters about friends or relatives or trips or experiences and work in the recipes peripherally."[48] Nora isn't immediately thought of as a writer of cookbooks until you read how Rachel constructs her recipe manuals. This is, of course, exactly what Nora did. In her "chatty and informal" style, Nora wrote essays about friends, relatives, experiences, trips and, "in an incidental way," worked in "recipes peripherally." The inclusion of recipes in what otherwise appears to be a straightforward essay is one of the distinctive characteristics of Nora's work.

Having ensured that the story she is telling is readily identified as her own, Nora is then able to use the novel to process her emotional reaction to the events of her life. The story is hers, as are the emotions expressed. The hurt and anger Rachel/Nora feels about the betrayal by her husband and the collapse of her marriage is palpable in the novel. There is no disguising the raw emotion regardless of how well Nora has fictionalized the events of her life or how funny she makes the retelling. Statements like: "It doesn't matter how smart you are if both your husbands manage to prove how dumb you are as easily as mine had"; "It is of course hideously ironic that the occasion for my total conversion to fidelity was my marriage to Mark"[49]; and "I can't stand feeling sorry for myself. I can't stand feeling like a victim, I can't stand hoping against hope. I can't stand sitting here with all this rage turning to hurt and then to tears,"[50] reveal the depth of the hurt and anger. More than any other passage

> I must write all this down, I thought. Someday I may write something that's not a cookbook, and this will all be gist for it. But I couldn't. To write it down gave it permanence, to admit that something real had happened.[51]

expresses the overwhelming magnitude of the betrayal Rachel/Nora experienced. Nora trained all her life to transform even the most painful events into something funny as a way of coping. As with the exchange between Kitty and Gene in *Three's a Family*, where they discuss Gene throwing their baby, Nora, in this passage, lets the raw emotion sit. She could not process her utter despair into anything other than what it was.

Nora had to let time pass before she could transform the breakdown of her marriage into a funny story, even if she begins that story by saying she thought of a little joke on the third day. At an evening of "Advice for Women" with Arianna Huffington in 2006, Nora told the audience she was in denial.[52] But denial was not an option for Rachel/Nora if she wrote about the end of her marriage to Mark/Carl. The Ephron-Bernstein marriage ended in 1979, and *Heartburn* was not published until 1983. Nora took a long time to be able to deal with what had happened, acknowledge that it had happened and then give it permanence. Even in 1992, when Nora was interviewed for *Vanity Fair* at the time of the release of her first film, the impact of the breakdown of her marriage to Carl Bernstein is still palpable. Leslie Bennetts, the journalist who interviewed Nora, writes of the moment when they discuss the breakup of her second marriage: "Suddenly her hands fly up to her face, which has turned in an instant from its usual paleness to a blotchy red, and her eyes brim with tears. She clamps a hand to her mouth, and I realize her lips are quivering so that she can't control them. Her eyes are wide with surprise, as no doubt are mine…. 'You see, I can't talk about it…. Even after all these years, I just can't.'"[53]

In answer to Vera's (Rachel's therapist) question: "Why do you feel you have to turn everything into a story?" Rachel responds with almost unbearable desperation:

> Because if I tell the story, I control the version.
> Because if I tell the story, I can make you laugh, and I would rather have you laugh at me than feel sorry for me.
> Because if I tell the story, it doesn't hurt so much. Because if I tell the story, I can get on with it.[54]

In writing *Heartburn*, Nora was doing exactly that which Phoebe taught her as a child. Nora was implementing the family coping mechanism—Phoebe's "expectation that all suffering be reconfigured into a funny story before it was brought to her attention"[55]—she was processing the everyday, turning it into a funny story. Even when Nora could not turn the events of her life into a funny story, she followed her mother's advice. While Nora was in denial, getting on with her life after she left Carl Bernstein, she used her work to acknowledge the devastation and pain she felt. Just as Phoebe, unable to do so in life, explored her relationship with alcohol in *Howie* and acknowledged the difficulties of her early days as a parent in *Three's a Family*, Nora explored the absolute depth of her hurt at the collapse of her marriage in *Heartburn*.

In the course of chronicling the events of the six weeks between her discovery of Mark's affair and the end of the marriage, Rachel ruminates on many topics, meandering her way from subject to subject. Of course, the experiences and opinions expressed by Rachel are also those of her alter ego Nora. Nora told Leslie Bennetts: "I have written about every thought that ever crossed my brain,"[56] and although the statement is an exaggeration of sorts, in *Heartburn* Nora provides a summary of every thought that ever crossed her brain, via her character, Rachel.

Rachel writes about her looks, her preference in men, her first marriage, being a Jew, her sister Eleanor (Delia), Lillian Hellman, her craft, Washington, food, friends, clothes, marriage, fidelity, therapy, fantasies and how films, literature and television inform her life. Many of these topics Nora had already written about in one guise or another and some thoughts and lines re-appear years later in other works. Most relevant is that Rachel also writes about her mother, father and her childhood. *Heartburn* provides Nora with the opportunity to review her childhood, to tell her version of the events of her past.

Rachel grew up in Hollywood, as did Nora, and like Nora both her parents were in the movie business. Rachel's mother, Bebe, worked in Hollywood, where she had a "flashy career,"[57] and Rachel's father, Harry, was a "character actor ... but he played the kind of characters who have no character." Bebe was not a writer like Phoebe, she was a "lady agent."[58] She was "a classic forties career woman: she had short hair and bangs, she wore suits with shoulder pads, and she talked in a gravelly voice." Nora describes her mother, Phoebe, in the following terms: "She was sort of stunning and had this Katharine Hepburn, offbeat tomboy look."[59] "She arrived in all her stylish glory. She wore her suit, and her three-inch heels, and her clip-on earrings that matched her brooch."[60]

Rachel further identifies her mother as being a "good recreational cook, but what she basically believed about cooking was that if you worked hard and prospered, someone else would do it for you."[61] Nora often wrote about Phoebe's cooking skills, how she, too, was a good recreational cook. Phoebe did not cook regularly. By her own admission, she rarely went into the kitchen: "I don't go into the kitchen very often except for ice cubes for a drink."[62] But "she served delicious food."[63] It was part of the legend of Phoebe Ephron.

Heartburn absolutely leaves no doubt as to the characters' true identities. Bebe and Harry are fictionalized versions of Phoebe and Henry. Henry and Phoebe were wealthy; they made a lot of money in Hollywood, as did Rachel's parents, Harry and Bebe, and both the fictional Harry and Bebe and the real Henry and Phoebe invested in Tampax stock. Both Phoebe and Bebe sat next to financier Bernard Baruch at either dinner or lunch, where he advised that, if investing in stock, they should buy "something people use once and then throw away."[64] Bebe and Phoebe acted on Baruch's advice and both made lots more money.

Not only did the character and her inspiration share the same life, ultimately, Phoebe and Bebe share the same death. Both women "drank and drank and drank and finally one day her stomach swelled up like a Cranshaw melon."[65] Bebe and Phoebe were each taken to the hospital, suffering from cirrhosis of the liver, and each subsequently died.

Having well and truly established Bebe's identity as being a fictionalized version of Phoebe, Nora was able to say of her mother the things she wanted to say; that she had limitations as a parent. As already noted, Nora understood that "even in the old days, my mother was a washout at hard-core mothering."[66] Phoebe was not there for Nora in a crisis, and Bebe was not there for Rachel. What Bebe and Phoebe were good at was the brittle, smart comment. Rachel writes that had her mother been alive at the time of her marriage breakup she "would probably have said something fabulously brittle like "Take Notes." (Which is exactly what Phoebe *did* say to Nora on her death bed.) Then "she would have gone into the kitchen and toasted almonds."[67] Nora said of her mother: "It was so 'Someday this will be a funny story,' ... so 'I'm having a drink and smoking a cigarette, and what else is new?'"[68]

Nora's relationship with her mother was complex. In *Heartburn*, Phoebe, the bad mother, is present. The mother who let Nora down is the mother letting Rachel down in her time of need. In subsequent films, Nora revisits her relationship with her mother but at the time of writing *Heartburn* she was still struggling with the woman of whom she would later write, "For a long time before she died, I wished my mother were dead."[69]

Harry, Rachel's father, is a much more benign character in the life of Rachel and Henry, more the sidekick to Phoebe's main act in Nora's recollection of her life, has rarely been the subject of Nora's work. Henry is the domain of Delia. *Heartburn* is one of the few times Nora wrote about her father. Dementia and mental instability had begun to mark Henry's character by the time Nora wrote her novel. When Rachel leaves Mark she goes to stay in Harry's apartment in New York. Harry arrives home and is very comforting to his distressed daughter. He organizes practical help but upsets Rachel by his words of comfort because "the dialogue was completely lifted from an obscure Dan Dailey movie he'd played a pediatrician in, and partly because he nevertheless delivered the lines so very well."[70]

Nora has said of her father: he was "very ebullient. He was full of fun and had a good time—a light source to all of us. I just loved my daddy, in the way little girls love their daddies."[71] But Henry was not all fun and light, and Nora knew it. Rachel writes of her father: "The truth is that if my father weren't my father, he would be one of the men he hates; he is incorrigibly faithless and thoroughly narcissistic, to such an extent that I tend to forget he's also capable of being a real peach."[72] Henry confirms his "love of women" when he writes of a conversation he had with Phoebe when he was considering a move into film producing. Phoebe, according to his account, was not happy about Henry's proposed shift to producing. It meant he would spend a considerable amount of time away from home without her. Phoebe was concerned about "all those actresses." "I'm sorry," she said, "but you're no saint, Henry, and, besides, you like women."[73] Nora's sister Amy confirms their father's infidelity in *Cool Shades*. In describing her parents' arguments, the narrator says: "They had the same fight for twenty-two years. It was something about my mother's father's infidelity to my mother's mother and my father's infidelity to her...." The subject of the fights between the narrator's parents in Amy's novel validates Henry's account of Phoebe's childhood, when he writes of Phoebe supporting her mother at the time of her husband's infidelity and it also validates Nora's recognition of her father's infidelity and (Henry's own admission) of being no saint and a man who loves women.

The suggestion that Henry was also a violent man, explored in the consideration of *Three's a Family*, is referenced in *Heartburn*. Rachel, after an argument with Mark in the early part of their marriage, says: "I hate it when you get angry ... it scares me. It reminds me of my father."[74] This statement, by Rachel, indicates an ongoing consequence for Nora of having grown up in the Ephron family. In writing of Harry as a man who has left lasting scars on his daughter Rachel, Nora acknowledges Henry's temper and the impact it had on her as a child. Nora confirms Henry's acknowledgment of having a temper. It gives further credibility to the depiction of Gene in *Three's a Family* as being a man with a quick temper; a man who, in a temper, threw his daughter. It further validates Delia's experience of Henry when his actions frightened her child and it adds to the picture of a man with a propensity for violence as depicted in Amy's novel *Cool Shades*. Nora used *Heartburn* to acknowledge the conflicted experience she had growing up with her father and the emotional scar that remained.

Nora also locates herself in the sibling order of her family in *Heartburn*. Rachel identifies her sister Eleanor as the daughter labeled as the "good" daughter by their father. Eleanor "is known as the Good Daughter in order to differentiate her from me."[75] Eleanor is the one who looks after their father, which is the role Delia took on from the time she was a teenager. "Caring for her father "was a way to be loved," Delia says. "My memories of being a teenager were very painful." Nora, the "smart one," and always conscious of her looks, identifies herself as "odd and interesting-looking" in *Heartburn*,[76] while Hallie was "the pretty one." Rachel only mentions one sister in *Heartburn* but, even so, quite clearly locates herself as the first child and identifies herself and her assigned position within the sibling order and her family.

Rachel/Nora also writes about having one's life cannibalized by another in the course of their work. This is a topic of particular relevance when the intent is to show how Nora, by her continued chronicling of her life in her work, has continued the established family pattern of using life as raw material. Nora's reputation as a writer was built on her employing that very concept, but, more harshly, she has been accused of cannibalizing her life for her art. Nora's propensity to write about her life became a significant obstacle in the divorce settlement between herself and Bernstein. He spent years in court after the publication of *Heartburn* trying to stop the making of the film based on the novel, wanting the final say on the screenplay. Ultimately, the conditions of their divorce prohibited Nora from ever using anything from their life together or their children for her work. *Heartburn* became the vehicle for Nora to draw attention to the hypocrisy of Bernstein's allegations of Nora using her life as the source material for her work. An example of which is Bernstein's quip: "If Nora goes to the supermarket she uses it as material for a book."[77]

In *Heartburn*, Rachel attacks Mark for cannibalizing their son's life for material for his column. "Someday Sam was going to grow up and sit down to write about his life and there wouldn't be anything left of it to write about."[78] Sam, not having anything to write about when he grew up because his father had already commandeered his life in his work, speaks to Nora's own experience at the hands of Henry and Phoebe. It also clearly highlights that Nora was not the only writer in her marriage to use their life as material for work. Nora returns to the topic of having one's life used as material for someone else's work in *This Is My Life*.

Heartburn has been described as "a long comic monologue, closer to *Portnoy's Complaint*[79] than the higher-class *Peyton Place*[80] that Mike Nichols made of the movie." In an interview with Garry Wills, Nora is quoted as saying of the film: "I have spent more sleepless nights wondering how I might have saved that movie." In response to her statement, Wills proffers that "probably she lost it the minute her first-person voice was removed from the script."[81] However, a number of factors aside from the loss of her first-person voice influenced the making of the film adaptation of *Heartburn*—most particularly the terms of her divorce. The film was not released until 1986, as it took five years to reach a divorce settlement, and when it was released it was a "severely compromised" adaptation of the novel.[82] Regardless, Nora's screenplay for and Mike Nichol's direction of the film are quite faithful to the book when allowances are made for the cinematic form and the constraints imposed by the terms of the divorce agreement. At the time of its release, the film was neither a financial nor a critical success. It does, however, capture the essence of the relationship between Mark and Rachel and, to some extent, the people on whose lives the novel and film is based, albeit in a sanitized form.

The film *Heartburn* quickly establishes the "real" identity of the central characters. In the opening sequence, Mark defines himself as "single" and Rachel defines herself as "vicious." "Single" is Mark's state of mind, not just his marital status. Throughout his relationship with Rachel he does not move beyond the mindset of a single man, a notoriously single man as was Carl Bernstein, regardless of his marital status. Rachel has a reputation for being "vicious" in her work—her writing— a reputation also enjoyed by Nora, who has been known as a "one-woman neutron bomb," because of her ability to eviscerate people in her essays.[83]

Much of the conversation Rachel has with the reader—the first-person monologue that runs throughout the novel in which she discusses her thoughts and feelings—is transformed into dialogue between characters in the film. Instead of Rachel talking about her fears associated with marrying Mark as she does in the novel, in the film Rachel delays the wedding by refusing to come out of her bedroom. While the guests and wedding party are kept waiting, Rachel has conversations with various people; her sister, Mark's best friends, her therapist, her father, and, finally, Mark. It is through these conversations that Rachel's/Nora's thoughts about marriage are transferred from the page to the screen.

The identity of the other characters, the people on whom the characters are based, is not lost in this transfer to film. They are, of course, moderated and more glamorous versions of themselves but they are not completely buried in the transition from book to film. Rachel's father, Harry, is identified as being in "the business." He tells Rachel he has had a conversation with Gene Kelly about a possible project. More than anything else his physicality identifies him as Henry Ephron.

The actor Steven Hill makes Harry immediately recognizable as Henry Ephron. Standing in a relaxed way, smiling, and with his arms across his chest, head tilted as he waits for his daughter, the bride, to appear, Harry is the physical incarnation of Henry.[84] The film also pays homage to Henry and Phoebe when Mark, as part of a scene where the couple are singing songs about babies to celebrate the news that they were going to be parents, bursts into a rendition of "My Boy Bill," the Soliloquy from *Carousel* (1956). Henry produced *Carousel*, and, with Phoebe, wrote the screenplay.

There is a passing reference to Phoebe: Rachel tells a lie about her mother being dead as an excuse for not stopping to talk with her friend Judith when Judith sees Rachel in New York unexpectedly. Rachel is caught out in her lie, but manages her way through it. It is a humorous moment in the film that's, fittingly, at Phoebe's expense. There is a further reference to Phoebe when Rachel and her father talk on his return from Atlantic City. He arrives at his apartment to find his daughter staying there after having left Mark. Rachel says to her father that she misses her mom but then, reconsidering, says: "Although let's face it, she wasn't much good at a time like this." Harry agrees with Rachel, then adds, "Yeah, I know. Although, let's face it, neither am I."

The scene is brought to a close in typical Ephron style—with a witty retort. As Harry is leaving, Rachel asks what she should do, to which Harry replies: "There is nothing you can do. If you want monogamy—marry a swan." Harry is Henry; loving and caring as Henry was but, ultimately, self-absorbed, incapable of putting aside his own concerns in order to care for his daughter and always ready with a witty, smart response to pain. This scene provides the perfect example of the Ephron family in operation: make it funny.

In the film adaptation Rachel is portrayed by Meryl Streep, with dark short hair and, later, longer dark permed hair (Nora writes of once having a disastrous perm). The usually blond Streep is not only dark haired, she is slim, flat chested and elegantly dressed. She has a long nose. She is a cinematic version of Nora. Nora paid her respects to Meryl Streep as an actress with a characteristically funny line while acknowledging *Heartburn* as being about her when she said of Streep's acting: "The true stretch, if I do say so, was playing me, in *Heartburn*."[85]

Mark/Carl is portrayed by Jack Nicholson. His character, while not necessarily unlikable in the film, is well cast. Jack Nicholson, in this role, doesn't have to be mean or self-absorbed or a womanizer or a bastard, he brings that with him as part of his film persona. The expectation is that his character will do wrong by his wife; it is a very astute piece of casting, given the constraints imposed by the terms of the divorce agreement.

Nora's significant concerns were not lost in the translation from novel to film. Rachel's musings that could have easily been discarded are still there. They form part of the detail of the film, her words and thoughts often given to other characters. While not foregrounded, their inclusion identifies them as, not only material on which to base funny or humorous moments, but, in hindsight, concerns important enough to Nora that they stay with her over time to be developed further in other works. For example: Mark, as a columnist, who uses the lives of those around him as material for his work, becomes part of a conversation at a lunch with their friends the Siegels in the film rather than part of Rachel's monologue, as it is in the novel.[86] Mark's propensity to use other people's stories as material for his column is important because it is important to Rachel because it is important to Nora. Important enough for her to make it the subject of her first film as a director, *This Is My Life*.

This Is My Life—based on Meg Wolitzer' book *This Is Your Life*, (1988)—picks up where *Heartburn* left off. In *Heartburn*, Nora writes about using life as the raw material for art. She uses her novel as a rebuttable to the claim made against her by her husband, Carl Bernstein, that she mined their life together for her work; a claim implicit in his divorce demand that she be prohibited from using anything about his children or their life together in her future work. In *Heartburn*, Nora establishes very clearly that, in fact, Mark/Carl had been guilty of the practice himself when he used their child as source material for his column. *This Is My Life*, although a contemplation of using life as the raw material for art, is quite different and more complex in its consideration of the practice. *This Is My Life* goes to the heart of Nora Ephron's life and her work. Wrapped in a narrative is a study of what it means to use someone's life as the base material for art and to have your own life used in such a way.

"I know the emotional world of this movie," Nora said of *This Is My Life*.[87] Linda Obst, the film's producer, is quoted as saying, "When I ran across Wolitzer's book I said, 'This reminds me of Nora. Sisters in a dysfunctional show-biz family, bringing each other up'"[88] and Delia has written of *This Is My Life*. "The material was perfect for us ... the material was nearly autobiographical."[89] The subjects of the film, Dottie and her daughters Opal and Erica, are Wurlitzer's creation; however, the narrative trajectory of the film takes a different turn from the book. The film takes the basic premise of the first part of Wolitzer's book then the Ephron sisters, Nora and Delia (her writing collaborator on the film) make it their own. What Nora and Delia took from the book was the relationship between the mother and the two daughters, some of the incidents in the book, and then built their own story.[90] The premise of the book became the foundation for Nora to make a film about her own experience: "It had so much resonance for me."[91] The film, in Nora's hands, became a story about "show business and about growing up in show business. It was about growing up with a parent who used your life as their material ... which was my experience growing up with my parents."[92] Nora said that when she and Delia wrote the film they also wanted to write about "when you have a dream for your parent and you are a child, it almost never crosses your mind that if that dream comes true it will cost you."[93]

The plot of *This Is My Life* is straightforward. Dottie Ingles is a single mother of two girls, working in Queens in the cosmetics department of Macy's. Dottie has always imagined herself as a stand-up comedian but has not had the opportunity to pursue her dream. Dottie and her daughters, Erica and Opal, live with their aunt Harriet, who subsequently dies, leaving Dottie her house. Dottie decides to sell the house and move to Manhattan. Using the money she made from the sale of her aunt's house, she will try to live her dream and become a comedian. Dottie does find success in both her career and her personal life, and as she pursues her dreams she knows "at the same time that she must nurture her two daughters."[94] However, as Julie Kavner, the actress who plays Dottie, says, "The focus of the movie really isn't on me, it's on Dottie's kids,"[95] and that is where it becomes personal. Nora wanted to write and direct the film because it was about things she was interested in: "One of which was the pull between being a mother and working. And using material from your life as part of your work. And sisters. And single mothers."[96] Nora was able to make *This Is My Life* her own story. She could see the situation from all angles, in all its complexity.

This Is My Life opens with Erica (Samantha Mathis), and then Dottie, addressing the audience in a voice-over; each claiming the film is about her life. Erica introduces the story. She says it is about her, then she includes her sister Opal (Gaby Hoffman), and says it is about her as well. Finally, Erica says it is also about her mother—but not completely. Dottie takes over the narration, assuming it is all about her: "You're probably wondering how all this happened to me." It is immediately evident that for the narrative to be about the life of one it must become the story of the other. At various points in the film we see the life events of each of the characters being told from each character's perspective. Julie Kavner says the film is about the sisters. Dottie is only onscreen when she is with her daughters, or they are watching her perform. But, even in her absence, Dottie, like Phoebe, is omnipotent.

Dottie, just like Phoebe, Henry and Nora, bases her comedy, her stand-up routine, on telling funny stories drawn from her life. When Dottie says in the course of the film, "Part of being an artist is using things that come from your life," and "I have to use my life to make things up," she echoes Phoebe. Dottie shares other similarities with Phoebe. Both women are "larger than life" personalities. Both are determined, and driven and indomitable in spirit, as was Nora for that matter. Dottie, early on in the film, tells her daughters how she spent one year at summer camp looking in the mirror and coming to the conclusion "this is it, you had better make the best of it," which is how she has lived her life and how Phoebe lived her life and how Nora lived her life; making the best of it and not being beaten by it. Like Phoebe, who told her girls "Everything is copy" and, among other things, "Never buy a red coat" and "Don't eat left-overs," Dottie gives her girls lessons, "life lessons" throughout the film.

Dottie, however, is not just Phoebe. As with all the characters she is a stand-alone character as well as an amalgam of others. As Dottie is leaving for the West Coast to perform she gives Erica and Opal journals telling them not to bother writing letters: "Letter writing is ridiculous, nothing ever arrives within a week and someone else ends up with what you should have, a record of your life." In that moment she is both Phoebe and Nora. Dottie is Phoebe saying, "Take notes," and she is Nora saying, "Don't write letters," look what happened to me. I wrote letters and my parents used them in *Take Her, She's Mine*. Dottie is Nora saying, "I didn't have anything to write about my own life from that time"; Dottie is Rachel when Rachel says her baby son Sam will have nothing to write about his childhood because Mark has already commandeered his life by writing about him in his column.

It is not just the lives of the characters which are intertwined in *This Is My Life*, it is also the work. When Erica makes a joke in the company of many would-be comedians at Thanksgiving dinner Dottie quickly responds, "Anything she says belongs to me." Later, Opal tells Arnold Moss (Dan Ackroyd), the agent who becomes Dottie's manager, "Dottie Ingels is a very funny person. She does an act about our aunt; Erica helped her." These quips allude to another level in the already complex relationship between mother and daughters and art and life; one which has resonance for Nora.

The question of intellectual property ownership, previously raised in relation to whether Nora should receive recognition as a co-author of *Take Her, She's Mine*, is part of the contemplation of "Everything is copy" in *This Is My Life*. The question being: are Erica's jokes Erica's or do they become Dottie's as they form part of her act? "This Is My Life" is not only the title of the film it is also the title of Dottie's comedy act. In her act Dottie claims ownership of Erica's material when she uses it without acknowledging the source. Conversely, Erica contributes to Dottie's act without recognition for her contribution. Dottie and Erica share Dottie's act. Erica and Opal's lives do not belong to them alone but to Dottie as well. Dottie says, "Our lives are all tangled up together," which was the experience of Nora and Delia.

The film also speaks to the cost to the children of their parents' success; to the ambivalence felt by Erica and Opal about their mother's success. They scream and cheer when they see her on television. She is funny and famous and their mother—they love her. And they hate her. They are devastated when Dottie tells them she is staying on in Los Angeles for work. She is leaving them for even longer in the care of others. One of Erica and Opal's ongoing grievances in *This Is My Life* is that with Dottie's success comes her absence. She is at home less and less. She misses important moments in the lives of her children. She is not there for Erica's "Kafka night" at school. She is not there for Erica to talk to when she loses her virginity.

Dottie's absence was one of the costs of her success to her children as the absence of Phoebe and Henry was one of the costs to Nora and her sisters. Nora, reacting against her experience of being left as a child, was always available for her two sons, Jacob and Max. When they were young she worked from home. She gave up journalism, in part, because it involved traveling, which she did not want to do as the mother of small children. She did not leave her children until they were older; in fact, when she was making *This Is My Life* in Toronto. Her two sons appear uncredited in the film as trees in Opal's school play. Jacob and Max were with her on weekends and holidays.

Erica, who, in the film, has an uncanny resemblance to how we might imagine Nora looked as a teenager transposed into the late 1980s to early 1990s: slim/thin, dark haired, bespectacled, book-reading, intense, intelligent, very quick with the one-liner and devastatingly, caustically funny, is profoundly affected by her relationship with her mother. Erica loves her mother, adores her and is proud of her for who she is and what she has achieved. Erica also hates Dottie. Erica hates that Dottie has not been there for her. Erica appears tough and, at times, cruel but she is loving and vulnerable and in need of her mother's nurturing care. Like Nora, Erica is underneath the "no nonsense exterior"[97] a vulnerable young woman of whom it can be said as it has been said by Alice Arlen of Nora, "I always think of that line 'She breaks like a little girl.'"[98] She is in need of her mother, as Nora, evidenced through her writing and continual return to the subject of her mother, was in need of Phoebe.

Erica is conflicted in her relationship with Dottie's work. She understands intellectually that all artists use things from their lives in their work. Erica has even helped Dottie develop her act. Erica was part of the process of turning Aunt Harriet's death into the funny story Dottie uses when performing. At the same time, however, Erica hates that she has done that and that their beloved aunt Harriet has been reduced to a joke. Erica also hates that her life has become part of her mother's life, incorporated into Dottie's act.

Erica has perfected a stand-up routine of her own which she performs at the film's climax. Her monologue brings to full force the depth of hurt and anger felt by her towards her mother. There is so much emotion in Erica's act that the scene is devastatingly painful. It has an authenticity borne of a truth. It is deeply moving and deeply felt. The monologue is a fully developed act built up over the course of the film. The act is built around the 1984 television program *Lifestyles of the Rich and Famous*, hosted by Robin Leach. Erica, as she sits watching her mother on television, becomes more and more agitated. Finally she takes a hairbrush and begins an impersonation of her mother's stand-up routine:

> ERICA (as Robin Leach, microphone in hand): Dottie tell me, where do you get your material?
>
> ERICA (as Dottie): All artists use things from their lives, Robin. And I am no exception. No.... siree! For instance, my aunt who saved me and my two girls—or are they boys? No, I believe I have girls. Now what are their names? Oh, never mind, it will come to me. My aunt, who saved me from starvation and poverty, died and the next thing you know she was a joke in my act. My daughter got all upset and the first chance I had I blabbed it on television. I use people up and I spit them out. ... This is a "Life Lesson." Everything is material.

In the moment of Erica's monologue all the hurt and the anger she feels towards her mother comes to the fore. Erica is bitter and vitriolic and devastating in her attack. Nora is quoted as having said that what is autobiographical about *This Is My Life* is "the feeling"[99] and that comes through in Erica's monologue.

If Nora believed that which she often claimed, "I don't think my parents have really invaded my privacy. But if they had, I probably wouldn't have minded that much,"[100] her art tells another truth. Within the context of the Moss article, Nora contradicts her own confidence when she says of *This Is My Life*, "I wanted to write about how ambivalent you feel about all that"[101]—that is, being written about. Her art exposes and expresses her ambivalence and her emotional response to having her life taken by her parents and used for their own purposes.

Erica's monologue operates in the same way as the conversation between Gene and Kitty in *Three's a Family*, and the response Rachel gives her therapist when she explains why she must tell the story in *Heartburn*. It is where Nora lets her work express her innermost feelings. Erica's monologue is an extremely powerful scene in the film. The scene is raw and the emotion unimpeded by humor. It is where Nora confronts in her work that which she cannot give full reign to in her life.

Of Dottie Ingels, Nora says:

> I find Dottie Ingels so moving. ... I love people like that ... indomitable ... she's a not a person who casts a cold eye on herself.... Dottie has this almost fantastic ability not to look too closely at herself and I love that about her. I like writing complicated women ... all the women I write about are flawed in one way or another—and that's what makes them interesting and, it seems to me, makes them human and real.[102]

Nora began her eulogy to Phoebe: "I would like to talk to you about the unusual and complicated woman who was my mother."[103]

This Is My Life is part of the chronicle of Nora Ephron's life. It is part of the public consciousness. With *This Is My Life* Nora examines her life: what it means to be part of a show business family. It is a film devoted to the subject of using life as the raw material for art. It is also a film devoted to single mothers, a film devoted to mothers and daughters, a film devoted to art and the artist and it is a film devoted to Phoebe Ephron and her daughters Nora and Delia.[104] It is a continuation of the process of working through the difficult in everyday life and making a funny story of it, a process started at the family dinner table when Nora was a child. Nora writes, referring to her parents before they were alcoholics: "The people they used to be have enormous power over you"[105] and she says of her family and her life as part of that family, "We very much understood in our family you can write about one another and you just can do that, but that doesn't mean when that happens everyone is thrilled about it. I have to say that. And not everyone grew up in my family so they go: Wait a minute! But writers—they just do those things."[106]

In one way or another Nora continued to chronicle her life in the public arena. The four texts examined in this chapter are a chronicle of her life. Nora is the subject at the heart of each work. The perspective alters: *Three's a Family* is about life with a new baby; Henry and Phoebe's experiences of being new parents to Nora their child. *Take Her, She's*

Mine is a combination of experiences; the same experience told from both the perspective of the parents and the child. It is a fictional documentation of Henry and Phoebe's experience of having their child leave home to go to college, and Nora's experience of being a young woman and her experience of college life. The next two, written and/or directed by Nora, are her fictionalized documentation of major events of her life. *Heartburn* (and its film adaptation) becomes the vehicle in which Nora explores her emotional response to the demise of her marriage and a place for her to write a précis of her life as the child of a Hollywood couple. Nora uses *Heartburn* to say that her mother was not able to nurture her and be emotionally available to her as a child and that her father was variously loving and full of fun and violent and a womanizer. She examines her feelings for and her understanding of the parents she grew up with. *This Is My Life* continues the process of revision and re-evaluation by Nora of her experience of growing up in the Ephron family. It is a contemplation of the notion of life as the raw material for art.

As each work is explored and connected to the next, a detailed and complex picture of the Ephron family takes shape. The emotional terrain of Nora's life is exposed and facets of her life are revealed. The constant throughout is her family: her experience of growing up in that family, the impact and residual damage. Nora, in the most direct way, continued the work begun by her parents. She continued to chronicle her life in her work as they did before her. However, in her work Nora moved beyond just simple documentation. Nora used her work to explore and examine the implications of growing up in her family and to address the difficult and painful in her life. Nora continued the family business by using her work to manage and evaluate the core values inherent in her family's credo, "Everything is copy."

3

"Recipes from other people's cookbooks"

I just clip recipes from other people's cookbooks and pass them off as my own.—Rachel Samstat[1]

"Everything is copy" does not simply mean the reworking or processing of events from life in one's work as Nora had done with *Heartburn* and *This Is My Life*. *You've Got Mail* (1998) clearly illustrates how the family credo—in its broadest application—operates in Nora's work. With this film Nora has, as the epigraph above suggests, taken bits and pieces, recipes, from other people's work and made them her own. She has collected from Ernst Lubitsch (*The Shop Around the Corner* [1940]), Jane Austen (*Pride and Prejudice*) and Henry and Phoebe Ephron (*Desk Set*); to the mix Nora added her own ingredients, threads from her life, in order to create a work that is idiosyncratic and recognizable as belonging to her.

At first glance it might appear that Nora has taken "the best of the best" for her own purposes; to gain professional mileage and commercial success by aligning her film with the work of famous literary and film artists. While to some extent this may be true there is a strong personal connection to all the recipes Nora clips from other people's cookbooks in the instance of *You've Got Mail*. Each of the components of this film is linked to her and to her life.

Ernst Lubitsch, for example, was not only the master of romantic comedy, he was directly linked to the Ephron family. Jane Austen was loved by both Phoebe and Nora, forming a strong connecting bond between the two Ephron women. Finally *Desk Set*, the last of the Katharine Hepburn/Spencer Tracy romantic comedies was adapted for the screen by Henry and Phoebe and produced by Henry. Further, both

Henry and Nora have drawn parallels between Phoebe and Miss Hepburn.

Nora used these famous (and, at the same time, personal) works to fashion a romantic comedy which has, at its core, a history of the genre. Having constructed her film around a potted history of romantic comedy she then, through the use of music—the other "narrative code"—declared the notion of romantic love to be a fantasy and the film another of the stories which inform cultural expectations—one of "the romantic and sexual fantasies that are deeply ingrained, not just in society but in literature."[2]

Within the romantic comedy framework—the story of Kathleen (Meg Ryan) and Joe (Tom Hanks)—Nora shades and colors her romantic comedy with personal interests and concerns. She documents and comments on social and cultural conditions: the dominance of the home computer and e-mail as a tool of communication. She charts the growth and ramifications of the mega bookstore. She observes the machinations of media manipulation. She includes a very personal connection to her family with the prominence she gives to letter writing and she continues to review and process her relationship with her mother.

The interconnected nature of the business and the personal, an identifier of the Ephron's work in general and Nora's work in particular, is also foregrounded in this film. *You've Got Mail* is an illustration and declaration of that belief. In conversation with Kathleen, Joe tells her that when his company put hers out of business, "It wasn't personal." Kathleen responds with: "All that means is that it wasn't personal to you. ... But it was personal to me."

The parallels between the experience of the author and her character Kathleen are overt and important. Kathleen's business, her bookshop, is personal to her. A family business, the bookshop was her mother's before it was hers. As Nora had been part of her mother's work from the time of her childhood, Kathleen worked and spent time there. Like Nora, Kathleen's business and personal lives are intertwined, inseparable and intrinsic to her being.

Towards the end of their conversation, Kathleen asks Joe: "And what's wrong with being 'personal' anyway?" to which Joe responds: "Nothing." By stating her position—that there is little separation between business and the personal—Nora declares her modus operandi. *You've Got Mail*, like almost all of her works, is both business (a film produced for commercial success) and the personal (it is crafted from elements of her life).

You've Got Mail has been described as a remake of Lubitsch's *The Shop Around the Corner*. The connection between the two films formed part of the marketing campaign for *You've Got Mail*[3] and the link between the two films is explicit within the text. The opening credits acknowledge *The Shop Around the Corner* and include Miklos Laszlo as writer. As well, the Lubitsch film is referenced within the narrative. Kathleen's children's book store is called The Shop Around the Corner and, when Joe is promoting the opening of the new Fox Books megastore, his campaign plays on the words "shop around the corner"—indicating the entrance to the Fox Books store.

The claim that *You've Got Mail* is indebted to *The Shop Around the Corner* is not in dispute. Lubitsch's film is the story of two lonely people, Klara (Margaret Sullavan) and Alfred (James Stewart), who work together in a gift shop. As work colleagues they can't stand each other but, unbeknown to the other, each is an avid letter-writer writing to an anonymous pen-pal identified only as "Dear Friend." Both Klara and Alfred fall in love with their respective pen-pal, not realizing that, in fact, they are writing to each other. *You've Got Mail* has the same romantic trajectory. Kathleen uses the salutation "Dear Friend" as she emails her anonymous friend and the circumstance of Joe's discovery of Kathleen as his email friend is almost identical to the situation in *The Shop Around the Corner*. However, there are two significant points of departure from the Lubitsch film. Where *The Shop Around the Corner* is told from the perspective of Alfred—the first of the lovers-to-be we meet—*You've Got Mail* is primarily told from Kathleen's perspective. Secondly, and most important, is the difference in the outcomes for the couples. Although Kathleen and Joe declare their love for each other at the conclusion of *You've Got Mail*, the conflict between them is left unresolved. Conversely, when Alfred and Klara are united, their differences melt away.

Lubitsch opens his film with a conversation between two men, placing the film squarely in the male domain. The film is about the lives of men, concerned as it is with the men who work at Matuscheck's store. Alfred, the central character, and the store's owner, the kindly Mr. Matuscheck (Frank Morgan), is each the subject of a major plot line. The subtle "Lubitsch Touch" in this film lies in the unacknowledged initiator of the action. Although the story is about men, the major plot lines are concerned with the reactions of men to women. Alfred is not the originator of the action but the responder. He begins writing to his pen-pal when he responds to an advertisement placed in a newspaper by a woman. Similarly, Mr. Matuscheck reacts to the discovery of his wife's infidelity not by confrontation but by attempting to commit suicide.

Of the other employees, Ferencz Vades (Joseph Schildkraut), is an opportunistic cad who deserves his comeuppance when it arrives in the form of public humiliation and the loss of his job. He is exposed as the man with whom Mrs. Matuscheck is having an affair. Pepi Katun (William Tracy) is the errand boy with aspirations to become an assistant in the shop, and Rudi (Charles Smith) replaces Pepi when he is promoted.

In comparison to the six male characters who work in Matuscheck's shop, there are only three women: Klara and another two about whom we know little. The film is set in the world of men and is about the world of men reacting to the actions of women. *You've Got Mail*, on the other hand, is predominantly, but not exclusively, about women. Nora has given narrative space to both the female and male protagonists. We are witness to Joe's epiphany moment in the elevator when he finally understands what it is he wants from a relationship. We are privy to his conversations with his father, Nelson (Dabney Colman), and his assistant, Kevin Jackson (Dave Chappelle), about relationships and his business. Joe is drawn as a good businessman and a good person, one who spends time with his young relatives and ignores the sexual advances of his father's much younger wife. He is worthy of Kathleen despite being at odds with and different from her.

While Nora gives narrative space to Joe it is Kathleen who is the central character and the story is both hers and Nora's. The film opens on Kathleen's apartment and the viewer is acquainted with her situation both initially and in greater detail. When Kathleen is allowed to love Joe it is Nora stating her opinion that as you get older, "You get smarter about what a good person is. And a good person doesn't always vote the same way you do or believe in the same religion."[4] Nancy Collins notes that Kathleen says that she could never marry a man with a boat[5] (Joe has a boat), which fits with Nora's explanation that, in fact, "'You've Got Mail' is called 'Can you fall in love with a person who isn't the right person for you after all?'"[6] This being a reflection of Nora's own experience of her marriage to Nick Pileggi—a reflection reinforced when she adds, "One thing though: I would never be stupid enough to work with my husband." It is Nora's point of view that marks *You've Got Mail* as uniquely her film.

Another way Nora marks *You've Got Mail* as a departure from Lubitsch is when she brings the film to a close without resolving the conflict between Kathleen and Joe. *You've Got Mail* ends, as any romantic comedy promises, with the uniting of the couple. They love each other despite the fact that Joe, as the owner of Fox Books, has forced Kathleen out of business. When Joe and Kathleen part for the last time before she sets off to meet and consequently discover the true identity of NY152, her chat room friend, Joe asks her to consider how it is she can forgive her Internet friend for previously standing her up and not forgive him for putting her out of business? Business and the personal are intertwined for Kathleen, and now Joe is calling her on it. Kathleen's silence implies the unresolved state of the situation. However, like Nora (with her third and successful marriage), Kathleen has become smart about what a good person is and ultimately chooses to love someone who is not right for her.

Choosing Lubitsch's film as the basis for her work Nora has not only associated her work with, and acknowledged her debt to the director of whom Kimmel writes, "Lubitsch is owed an enormous debt by every filmmaker and fan of romantic comedy,"[7] she has also reassured her audience that they will be rewarded with the outcome they desire: the "genre movies promise that their fictional events will unfold with a measure of certainty for the audience and the expected satisfactions will be provided."[8] The certainty promised in the generic identification of Nora's film as a romantic comedy assures the audience that they will have their expectations met. Boy and girl will meet, overcome the obstacles to their union and, by the end of the film, will be united. This preestablished certainty gives Nora, as the writer/director, the creative license to take her film in whatever direction she chooses, having already made assurances by inference that she will deliver the expected outcomes.

One of the uses Nora makes of the romantic comedy framework is as a vehicle with which to document and comment on contemporary social change and issues.[9]

On the Upper West Side of New York, where Nora was living at the time of making the film, small independent book stores were being forced to close because of the economic downturn and the "changing fashions in retail bookselling."[10] Around the corner from The Shop

Around the Corner, Kathleen's small independent children's bookstore, Fox Books is opening a mega book store, a fictional Barnes and Noble–type establishment.[11]

Nora uses her film as an essay of sorts. She uses the cinematic form as a vehicle for discussion and the film becomes the visual framework and the script a dialogue-based essay in Nora's hands. She sets up the argument: the "for" and the "against" of the cultural and business phenomenon "the discount book superstore."

Nora introduces the topic: the mega book retailer verses the small independent book store. We see a visual depiction of each. The Shop Around the Corner is a quaint, old-world establishment from the exterior; it is part of the color and romance of the local community. It is a place where the local children gather to hear the "book lady" read stories. As children arrive, Kathleen greets them by name. In comparison, Fox Books is huge. As Kathleen and her employees Christina (Heather Burns) and George (Steve Zahn) stand in front of the enormous gray, characterless building which occupies a city block, Kathleen says: "It has nothing to do with us. It is big, impersonal, overstocked and full of ignorant sales people." To which George responds, "But they discount!" Kathleen counters with: "But they don't provide any service. We *do*."

Kathleen's bookstore is a busy small space, interesting in its configuration with nooks and crannies and displays of much-loved children's books. There are tables and chairs and spaces for children to sit and read. There is a history and a sense of belonging to the book store that the new big impersonal Fox Books does not have. As Joe comments to his girlfriend, Patricia (Parker Posey), "They've been there forever." Within this warm, homey, elegant space, Birdie (Jean Stapleton),[12] Kathleen, Christina and George work together like a happy, squabbling family. Fox Books is huge and nondescript.

But when Kathleen visits to investigate the competition, she is overwhelmed by what she sees: comfortable chairs for reading, an inviting café, service desks and cash registers. Large signs announce 35 percent off all merchandise. The mega bookstore is a lively place where people are clearly enjoying the experience of reading. The children's section is full of children reading and talking, happy in this new and different environment. However, Kathleen is proven correct and is upset by the lack of knowledge, interest and care displayed by a staff member as he attempts to assist a customer.

The philosophical divide between each of the book sellers is articulated when George lovingly shows Joe a rare early edition of a children's book. As George points out that the illustrations are hand-tipped, Joe asks if "that's why it costs so much?" George reframes Joe's question to form the statement: "That's why it's so valuable." In this brief moment Nora succinctly observes the two polemics of the discussion. Fox Books is about cost-saving and money-making, while Kathleen and her shop are about reading, pleasure and artistic worth. One is seen only as a profit generator; the other recognizes books for their intrinsic value. As Joe says, albeit sarcastically, of his family business, Fox Books stores are simply places that sell "cheap books and legal addictive stimulants."

When asked how she, as an author, felt about the superstore trend, Nora responded: "Pretty much the way Delia and I do in the movie. The truth is they're not all good and not all bad."[13] Fox Books might be "the inventor of the superstore and the enemy to the mid-list novel. The destroyer of City Books" as Frank (Greg Kinnear), Kathleen's boyfriend, says to Joe Fox, but what Fox Books offers isn't all bad; it simply approaches the business of book retail from a different perspective. In her interview with Nancy Collins Nora goes on to describe how there was a ripple of discontent when Barnes and Noble opened on the Upper West Side but after she had visited the store, with its leather chairs and people reading and the second-floor children's department which "is like a day care center after school"[14] she, like Kathleen, thought it was amazing. It is different from the small independent retailer, but not the evil destroyer of book stores Frank describes.

Nora's response to her local Barnes and Noble, apparent in *You've Got Mail*, does not, however, lose sight of the ramifications of such trends. Kathleen is forced to close her beloved shop; Christina loses her job; Birdie retires, living on the funds from a wise investment; and George ends up running the children's book department at Fox Books, and, in doing so, improves the quality of service provided by the department. Those who work at The Shop Around the Corner are significantly affected by the advent of the new retail giant.

In *You've Got Mail* Nora has used a play on the title of Lubitsch's film to set up a discussion about the changes taking place in the book retail business. By doing so, she has continued the family business of documenting the world in traditional Ephron style. This, however, is not the only aspect of Nora's use of a Lubitsch film which references her life. She has a personal link to Lubitsch; tenuous, certainly, but in line with the family belief that everything is copy. By using a Lubitsch film as the reference point for her film she is not only acknowledging the connection they share as directors working in the romantic comedy genre, she is using something from her own life. Henry writes of his and Phoebe's first experience of Hollywood as new screenwriters: They were told Ernst Lubitsch wanted to speak with them. Henry and Phoebe met with Lubitsch and developed a story for him. He liked their work, and the Ephrons liked him. About three weeks into their working arrangement, on September 1, 1943, Lubitsch had the first of a number of heart attacks which marked the beginning of his decline. During his recovery period, the Ephrons collaborated further with him, but the script they had worked on was ultimately taken over by Otto Preminger and Henry and Phoebe were removed from the project. The story of how they, as new writers, got a lucky break from the great Ernst Lubitsch when he decided he wanted to work with them is part of the Ephron family story, as is the joke made at their expense by other writers they were working with at the time of Lubitsch's heart attack. Henry writes that they were devastated by the news of Lubitsch's illness and stayed out of the public eye for almost a week. When Henry and Phoebe finally went to the Warner Bros.' commissary to have lunch, the screenwriter F. Hugh Herbert said: "Well, well, how are the writers who gave Lubitsch a heart attack?"[15]

To the Lubitsch framework Nora adds a further layer in the construction of her film when she includes Jane Austen's much-loved novel *Pride and Prejudice* to the mix. By association with an earlier work—an essay—Nora acknowledges what she believes to be the heritage of romantic comedies such as *The Shop Around the Corner*, *You've Got Mail* and *Desk Set* and declares the fantasy of such works. In doing so, she makes *You've Got Mail* a more complex film.

Jane Austen's *Pride and Prejudice* was one of Nora's favorite books.[16] She read it annually and wrote of the plot and the dialogue "which characterizes Elizabeth and Mr. Darcy's relationship ... has been imitated in thousands of novels that have been written since and dozens of movies."[17] *You've Got Mail* is one of those films. It is a film about "two strong-willed people—one of them rich, the other not [who] meet and take an instant dislike to each other."[18]

Nora, as she did with *The Shop Around the Corner*, declares her clipping of this recipe in the narrative. When Kathleen is to meet her e-mail friend (at the real Café Lalo), she arranges to be identified by the book and rose she has with her. It is the same form of identification used in *The Shop Around the Corner* but, instead of *Anna Karenina*,[19] Kathleen is carrying a copy of *Pride and Prejudice*. When Joe speaks with Kathleen in the café he says to her, "I'll bet you read that book every year," a claim both Nora and Kathleen make. Kathleen had unknowingly discussed her favorite book with Joe when she wrote to her unidentified email friend, writing that she has "read *Pride and Prejudice* about two hundred times." She relates how she gets "lost in the language" and how she is "always in agony over whether Elizabeth and Mr. Darcy are really going to get together." Nora wrote the same thing in her 1980 essay "A Few Words About Elizabeth Bennet." She also wrote:

> *Pride and Prejudice* is one of the greatest romantic comedies ever written ... and in many ways it is the forerunner of a genre it was instrumental in creating.[20]

Nora identifies the genre, she exposes the construct and most significantly she reveals the fantasy of such stories. As she wrote of *Pride and Prejudice*: "What a lovely fantasy this plot is!"[21]

Nora, always an astute filmmaker and thinker, knew the films she made such as *Sleepless in Seattle* and *You've Got Mail* would become part of the literature "that would screw up people's brains about love forever,"[22] but she did not deceive her audience. Despite comments such as those written by Dinitia Smith, who says of this film, "Like many of her other films, 'You've Got Mail' can be shamelessly sentimental,"[23] Nora does not allow her audience to believe in the story she tells. Frank Krutnik writes that with *You've Got Mail* Nora espouses a "romantic idealism"[24]; however, Nora did not believe the stories that form the basic romantic comedy narrative to be reflective of real life, and she made sure her audience knew this. She was not sentimental about love, nor did she believe in the fantasy of romance.[25] Delia said of Nora: "I know for sure she is not sentimental ... she kept believing in love [even after her marriage to Carl Bernstein]. But romantic—I just don't know about romantic."[26]

There are references in her work which allows the viewer to understand that Nora knew her stories are lovely fantasies. Not content with references which demand a knowledge of her other works, Nora inserted clues as to the nature of the story she was telling and for this she used music. Music is an important narrative code in *all* of Nora's work, a point that should never be underestimated. In other fields of endeavor, such as her plays *Imaginary Friends* and *Lucky Guy*, music is a prominent feature, with many of the characters singing, and music being integral to the plot development. In an online Yahoo discussion at the time of the release of *Lucky Numbers* Nora said, "When you do a movie, first you write it in words, and then you get to write it again in pictures, and then it's almost as if you get to write it again in music."[27]

In the opening sequence as the title *You've Got Mail* appears in red on the screen there is a brief moment when the refrain from "Over the Rainbow"[28] can just be discerned. The easy-to-miss moment of music in the cacophony of computer sounds tells the movie audience through the song's association with the film *The Wizard of Oz* (1939) that this story is a fantasy. "Over the Rainbow" is not a love song; it is a song about dreams and fantasy. At the film's conclusion, as Kathleen waits for her email friend to meet her in Riverside Park and where she subsequently discovers it is Joe she is waiting for, "Over the Rainbow" is foregrounded. The music, the song, becomes the dominant narrative code. Nora uses it to make a clear statement that this ending is the dream—the fantasy conclusion to stories like *You've Got Mail*.

The next layer Nora builds into her film, the third recipe she takes from someone else's cookbook and passes off as her own is her parents' film *Desk Set*. One of the functions of *Desk Set* is to work as the linchpin to secure the connection between *The Shop Around the Corner* and *You've Got Mail*. It is the connection that moves Nora's film beyond being a mere reworking of the Lubitsch film and it is the springboard for Nora to jump into another of the subjects of her film—the impact of the computer in contemporary society.

Desk Set is not part of the acknowledged framework of *You've Got Mail*. Unlike *The Shop Around the Corner* and *Pride and Prejudice*, Nora does not declare this layer of construction in the narrative. It is not until the two Ephron films are placed side by side that the similarity becomes obvious. Letter-writing is a personal motif which denotes the two films, *Desk Set* and *You've Got Mail* as the work of the Ephrons and it is the conceit that connects *The Shop Around the Corner*, *You've Got Mail and Desk Set*. Alfred and Klara write anonymously to each other. Joe and Kathleen email each other anonymously, and in *Desk Set* the art of letter-writing is central to one of the pivotal moments in the development of the relationship between the two main characters, Bunny Watson (Katharine Hepburn) and Richard Sumner (Spencer Tracy). In all three films the couple falls in love via written communication.

As already discussed, Henry and Phoebe and Nora included references to the art of letter-writing in their respective works, indicative of the Ephron voice and experience. This theme, in fact, was one of the ways Henry and Phoebe signaled their work—separated it from that of the playwright, William Marchant, who wrote the original play *The Desk Set*. In Act II of the Marchant play Bunny joins the old lady[29] who, in her youth, was the model for the Federal Broadcasting icon (Federal Broadcasting being the name of the fictional television network where the action of the story takes place). They are on the balcony looking down at the Christmas party taking place below. Bunny turns to the old lady and asks, "Is this your first Mediterranean cruise?"[30] This moment, when Bunny is pretending to be on a cruise ship, is very brief in the play. As she says her lines there is a fade-out and the scene is not developed. Henry and Phoebe altered the scene. In their screenplay it is Bunny and Richard who are on the balcony. Bunny opens the scene with the same line of dialogue, to which Richard responds that, yes, it is his first trip as well, but he asks her not to tell anybody as he is the ship's captain. Richard plays her game of pretend. He plays with her. They then retire to their deckchairs—they sit between two book shelves—and Bunny begins a personal conversation by asking, "Tell me, Skipper—don't you like women?"[31]

The conversation quickly develops, with Richard telling Bunny about Caroline, a model he used to date. When he was sent to Greenland during the war she wrote him dozens of letters, all of which covered topics in which he had no interest. As a consequence of Caroline's uninteresting letters, Richard lost interest in her. The scene is funny and gentle and the first declaration of Richard's romantic interest in Bunny. He declares his feelings when, at the scene's end, as Bunny is standing up to leave, Richard takes her hand lightly and looking directly at her, says, "I'll bet you write wonderful letters."

This scene, written by Phoebe and Henry, has the hallmark of their work and their lives. The two components of the scene—Bunny and Richard's conversation about letter writing and their pretending together—identify the scene as their creation. That Bunny and Richard should pretend to be on a cruise fits with the Ephron mindset—the family who played charades together and told stories. However, it is not the imagining which links the three films, but letter-writing. The inclusion of letter-writing as a signifier of romance in *Desk Set* and as a theme of *You've Got Mail* connects the two films to the Ephrons. Letter writing features strongly in their family story. Phoebe, particularly, was a prolific letter writer. Henry's memoir records several incidents in which Phoebe wrote letters: the morning they got the news Lubitsch had had a heart attack[32]; when she was at a health farm doing research for a script[33]; and, most famously, when Nora was away at school. Nora responded with equal eloquence: "They were both gifted letter writers."[34] Nora was indeed grateful to her mother for teaching her how to write. Phoebe insisted Nora write to her before she would write back and she told Nora the best way to learn to write was to write "a letter to your mother and tear off the salutation."[35] A great deal of Nora's eulogy to her mother is about letter writing. Nora speaks of how Phoebe wrote fantastic letters—funny, informative, gossipy letters. Letters Nora's friends loved. They "would laugh and listen, utterly rapt at the sophistication of it all."[36] It is not surprising that, given the opportunity, two of Phoebe's daughters, Nora and Delia, would write a screenplay about letter writing; it is in their blood, part of their heritage.[37]

The scene which bridges the generational jump from *Desk Set* to *You've Got Mail* is where Joe, at a meeting with his father, Nelson, and grandfather (Schuyler John Randolph)—the three generations of Fox men who own the Fox Books chain of mega book stores—discuss the proposed new store set to open in the Upper West Side of Manhattan. Joe mentions The Shop Around the Corner, the children's book store that is currently one of Fox Books' competitors. Joe's grandfather knows the store and remembers its former owner, Cecelia Kelly, Kathleen's mother. He tells Joe that Cecelia was a lovely woman: "I think we might have had a date once or maybe we just exchanged letters." He describes Cecelia as having beautiful penmanship and goes on to say that she was enchanting. When Richard Sumner looks at Bunny Watson in the book shelves of the reference department and comments that she would be a wonderful letter writer, "enchanting" is how he sees her. Bunny Watson and Kathleen's mother, Cecelia, are related: they are both fictional images of Phoebe Ephron, the former created by Henry and Phoebe, and the latter by Nora.

The changing nature of communication is one of the subjects of Nora's work. Nora chronicles this in her essay "The Six Stages of E-mail."[38] The first stage, she identifies, is "Infatuation."[39] Initially, Nora loved it: "I just got e-mail! I can't believe it! It's so great."[40] She even asks, "Who said letter writing was dead?"[41] Nora aligns email with letter writing: "I'm writing letters like crazy for the first time in years"[42] but then she begins to reassess the phenomenon and the disillusion begins with "Stage Two: Classification." In this stage, Nora begins to re-evaluate her experience of email: "E-mail isn't letter writing at all."[43] And from there on Nora's love affair with email wanes. "The Six Stages of E-mail" was published in 2007; *You've Got Mail* was released in 1998. *You've Got Mail* falls into Stage One of Nora's "Six Stages of E-mail," with an overlap into Stage Two.

In *You've Got Mail* letter writing is a dying art, one that belongs to the previous generations—Joe's grandfather and Kathleen's mother both wrote letters—and a reflection of contemporary life where letter writing has largely been replaced by email.[44] Joe and Kathleen write emails to each other. Their emails are almost poetic at times, with stories of a butterfly on the subway who, Kathleen imagines, is going to buy a hat at Bloomingdales. Joe, in his exaltation of autumn, writes of a bouquet of pencils. Their emails are the love letters of the contemporary age. Instead of writing letters to a post box as in *The Shop Around the Corner*, or exchanging letters as Joe's grandfather and Kathleen's mother, Cecelia, did, Kathleen and Joe meet in an over-30s online chat room.

The opening moments of *You've Got Mail* and *Desk Set* identifies one as the companion piece to the other and announces the shared subject of the films: the introduction and consequence of computers in contemporary society. As Mernit notes in his writing on the romantic comedy, a title can be important. In the case of *You've Got Mail* and *Desk Set*, the title "suggests more than a general story."[45]

There is no doubt that *You've Got Mail* is a relative of *Desk Set*. Both films begin, before and during the credits, in a strikingly similar fashion. Both films are about computers and their uses. *Desk Set* foregrounds business machines, computers, and identifies the computer company IBM, while *You've Got Mail* begins as a computer screen and identifies the Internet provider America on Line. The opening moments of *Desk Set* reveal the subject of the film: the modern business world, more precisely, the *machinery* of the modern business world. *Desk Set* begins simultaneously with jaunty music—a cacophony of business sounds—and a striking visual. The background, used as a floor, is a highly stylized Mondrianesque graphic design. Piet Mondrian is closely associated with New York, where he moved to in 1940. His "Broadway Boogie Woogie," a graphic representation of the busy and bustling New York, is one of his most renowned works. Nora has cited his artwork "Broadway Boogie Woogie" as one of her inspirations.[46] Mondrian's art represents New York in the late 1950s as the epicenter of the modern world. The sense of hustle and bustle, the modern world of business, is reinforced through the use of the musical score written by Cyril J. Mockridge, which is a bright musical mess of typewriters and business machines; productivity associated with an office.

On the "Mondrian" floor sits a number of business machines—computers, filing cabinets, desks, and printers—all gray and all stylized, like houses on a Monopoly board. A very modern design organized to reflect the floor on which they are sitting. The camera moves in, focusing on the central machine, a large machine reminiscent of a dot matrix printer, the IBM logo clearly and centrally located. The camera moves into the IBM logo and holds for two to three seconds before moving up and moving in to the printing page on which appear the film credits. After the credits the establishing shot is of the Rockefeller Center forecourt and the statue of Prometheus. The camera then tracks up the skyscraper that was the home of RCA to the fictional Federal Broadcasting Company.

The opening sequence of *You've Got Mail* does more than reveal the subject of the film—it declares it heritage. The film begins while the Warner Bros. sepia-colored panning shot of the studio roof tops is still onscreen. The background noise, as in *Desk Set*, reveals the film's subject. What is heard is the readily identifiable sound of a computer being turned on. As the screen image moves from the roof tops of the Warner Studios onto the Warner logo the screen transforms into a computer screen and the Warner logo moves to the left-hand corner. The credits begin as the blue computer screen—icons down the right hand side; the last icon belonging to America Online (AOL)—is activated via the cursor so as to connect to the Internet. The screen changes to black and an animated cyberspace fills the screen. The world appears in cyberspace and then New York is visible in the cyberspace world. As the name *You've Got Mail* appears in red, the dial-up of the computer connecting to the Internet can be heard. A computer-aided design of New York replaces the cyberspace image. Then, in a series of gradient steps that pre-empt Google Earth by at least six years, the model of New York moves into greater detail until it stops at the middle window of an upper-story apartment in a brownstone on the Upper West Side. A click of the cursor transforms the computer image to a "real" image, and the camera goes through the window into the living room of the apartment. A personal computer is apparent and central in the scene. The camera tracks through the apartment, coming to rest on a sleeping woman.

From the very start, before the viewer would register that the film proper has begun, the sound indicates that computers are central to the story; seconds later, it becomes clear that the Internet service provider America Online is specifically part of the story. The opening, a cyberspace shot establishes that the film is set in New York; more specifically, the Upper West Side—an area of New York known for its cultural diversity and intellectual and literary life.[47] It is also where Nora lived until rising rental costs forced her to move. It is where her parents lived. Nora had a strong connection to this New York neighborhood. "I had to explain the West Side to the actors.... When I was in college, the West Side was the intellectual capital of the world."[48]

If there is any doubt that *You've Got Mail* is something of an updating of *Desk Set* and the state of computers in the lives of people living in New York, the opening dialogue of *You've Got Mail* removes it.

As the camera focuses on the sleeping woman, Kathleen, out of shot a muffled noise can be heard. Walking towards the Kathleen is a man, Frank, carrying a folded newspaper. He says to Kathleen, who by this stage is awake, "This is amazing, listen to this, the entire workforce of West Virginia had to have Solitaire removed from their computers because they hadn't done any work in six weeks."[49] The bridge between computers in the workplace and in the home has been crossed. Instead of an aid to productivity as envisaged by Richard Sumner when he invented Emmerac in *Desk Set*, now, in *You've Got Mail*, computers have become a time waster and have been linked with a decrease in productivity.

Where Henry and Phoebe's film focused on the introduction of computers into the workplace—Bunny Watson arrives to work late, but she tells her assistants that at 9:00 a.m. she had already been to IBM to see a demonstration of the "new electronic brain"—the establishing scene at the beginning of *You've Got Mail* contextualizes computers in the workplace in 1998. Frank, to Kathleen, continues, "Do you know what this is—what we are seeing here? It's the end of western civilization as we know it!" The changes to which Frank is referring began with those depicted in *Desk Set* and are continuing with those depicted in *You've Got Mail*. The domain of this film is not computers in the workplace but computers in the home. As Frank finishes dressing he waves his arm in the vicinity of the computer and says, "You think this machine is your friend, but it's not!" He then leaves for work. So the discussion about the impact of computers that was begun in Henry and Phoebe's film is set to continue in Nora's.

As earlier stated, *Desk Set* is an adaptation of William Marchant's play *The Desk Set*. The play had a very successful Broadway run, opening at the Broadhurst Theatre on October 24, 1955, and closing after 297 performances on July 7, 1956.[50] Henry and Phoebe wrote the screen adaptation, and Henry was the film's producer. Marchant's three-act play is a dark comedy, examining the concerns and fears generated by the introduction of computers into the workplace. Fears of unemployment and redundancy in the face of this innovation inform the play. When the play was adapted to film by the Ephrons they put a greater emphasis on the romance but did not lose sight of the more serious concerns. As they had done with *Three's a Family*, in which the war and subsequent housing shortage provided the backdrop for the play, the love story of *Desk Set* is set against the technological advances and social implications of the introduction of computers in the workplace.

As the narrative begins in *Desk Set* it is quickly established that, in Payroll, there have been redundancies, a computer has replaced the people. Mrs. Loucheimer—a character never seen—the Payroll stalwart, handed in her resignation on Tuesday. The women from the Reference Department, where the action takes place—Peg Costello (Joan Blondell), Sylvia Blair (Dina Merrill) and Ruthie Saylor (Sue Randall) and head of the department Bunny Watson—are concerned that they, too, are about to be replaced by a computer. The computer, Emmerac, was designed and patented by Richard Sumner. Sylvia has consulted the union with regards to her rights in case she should lose her job when computers are introduced, a most unusual action to be taken by a woman in the 1950s.

The changes taking place in *You've Got Mail* are also technological. Home computers and email are the new technologies in Nora's film. By now computers are well installed in business, the latest generation of Emmeracs are everywhere. Computers are not only part of the business domain but also the personal lives of people. Email is the new form of communication, the alternative to writing and posting letters.

Technological advancement and the changing nature of mass communication, the subject of *You've Got Mail*, is foreshadowed at the end of *Desk Set* when Richard asks Bunny to ask Emmy (Emmerac, the computer) a question. The question being "Should Bunny Watson marry Richard Sumner?" This penultimate moment in *Desk Set*, when the computer operates as the communicator between the (at this stage) undeclared lovers heralds the possibility of *You've Got Mail*. Emmy is the first computer-based dating service, the first chat room.

In the final moments of *Desk Set* Bunny says to Richard that Emmy will always come before her; Richard says, no, that's not true. He then allows Bunny to cause Emmy to have a meltdown to prove he loves Bunny more, but the love of his invention is too great and he immediately borrows a hairpin from Bunny to fix the computer. Bunny accepts that she will share Richard with the computer, which she will also embrace; she even does so literally. Richard and Bunny kiss for the first time, nestled close to the computer.

By the time we meet Kathleen in *You've Got Mail* she is in love with her computer. She has embraced the cyber world and has a secret love affair with it (and via it). She only goes on-line when she is alone, in secret, when her boyfriend, Frank, is not around. Frank, however, is not as convinced about the wonders of the computer; he is a self-declared Luddite and lover of typewriters and warns of the evil of computers. Regardless of Frank's disapproval, Kathleen loves her laptop and e-mail even more so.

You've Got Mail focuses on both the wonder of, and the limitations associated with, email; the film is not just a one-sided celebration of the home computer and its applications. The ethical issues associated with the use of email are raised and there are various discussions on the dangers of cyberspace. Questions which, incidentally, still remain unanswered, such as: who is the person you are conversing with in the cyber chat room, and are they who they say they are? Kathleen asks Christina about the etiquette of online relationships. For example, can you have an affair with someone online? When Christine responds by asking Kathleen if she has had sex online, Kathleen is shocked. Cybersex, Christina tells Kathleen, informing her of the etiquette associated with this activity, is something you don't do—the other party won't respect you. It seems the age-old dating rules apply despite the new medium!

All these questions challenge the notion of positive and safe communication via email and chat-room meetings. Kathleen and Joe conduct their online relationship with a strict adherence to complete anonymity.

In each of the Ephron films the romantic comedy provides a vehicle for the examination of some of the broad issues associated with the new computer technologies. Neither film offers a solution to computers. Both use humor to foreground the fears and problems associated with the new technologies—unemployment, fear of being made obsolete by the new machine (*Desk Set*), the invasion of privacy, Internet stalkers and the ethical issues around email/chat room-based relationships (*You've Got Mail*). Both films accept the value of the computer as a useful tool in business. Bunny comes to see the value of the computer as an aid to research, and Kathleen has a computer in her bookshop to help her operate her business. Both films acknowledge the success (or lack thereof) of the computer is dependent on how it is used, and each film recognizes the technology's limitations. Emmerac is not as fast as Bunny in certain circumstances, and Bunny can anticipate the incorrect answers Emmerac will provide because the information it is fed is not specific enough. In *You've Got Mail* the computer has not proven to be the boon to business it was first envisaged as being, nor does it replace the human relationship. Kathleen must meet her on-line friend face to face. The chat-room relationship is not complete in and of itself.

Both *You've Got Mail* and *Desk Set* are chronicles of their time, each an artist's impression of the moment of significant cultural change. *Desk Set* is a documentation of the beginning of the massive changes the introduction of the computer brought to the business world. *You've Got Mail* documents the way mass communication has experienced major change with the advent of the home computer for personal use and its allied applications, including email.

There are other characteristics which further illustrate the connection of *Desk Set* and *You've Got Mail*. The circumstances of the romance: each film a romantic comedy in which the male and female protagonists fall in love with the assistance of a computer. Each is New York–based, set against a background of technological change. In terms of age and romantic experience Nora's couple is more closely associated with *Desk Set* than *The Shop Around the Corner*. The Henry Ephron–produced film was the last of the Hepburn/Tracy romantic comedies and the stars' ages marked *Desk Set* as quite different as a romantic comedy.[51] Hepburn was fifty years of age and Tracy fifty-seven when the film went into production. While Kathleen and Joe aren't in their fifties, nor are they young; they meet in an over-30s chat room. Romantic comedy is usually the story of young love but in this instance, in the hands of the Ephron family, romantic comedy is more the domain of the older couple. Middle-aged romance is a feature of Nora's work. All Nora's romantic couples are older and have had previous relationships.[52]

Point-of-view further links the two films. It is expected that *You've Got Mail* would be told from a female perspective. Nora became famous as an essayist who wrote about women.[53] As Valarie Groves wrote of her, "She is renowned for exposing women's lives."[54] However, watching *Desk Set* one cannot help but be struck by the female-centeredness of the film. Both *Desk Set* and *You've Got Mail*, unlike *The Shop Around the Corner*, are set in the world of women. *Desk Set* is set in the realm of women and is about women created in Phoebe's image. Men are part of the world but women are clearly the subject. *Desk Set* is the story of the women who work in the Reference Department of a major broadcasting corporation. Henry, the co-creator of that world, as already documented, loved women and was happy in the company of women. Phoebe, intelligent and independent, was a career woman used to being in charge. Her role model, her aunt Minnie, was a career woman. Phoebe and Henry write their women characters as intelligent and assertive. The characterization of Bunny is one of the ways in which Henry and Phoebe's screenplay differs from the play on which it is based.

In Marchant's play, Bunny Watson marries Abe Cutler (played by Gig Young in the film version). She has been waiting the past seven years for him to ask her to marry him. In the Phoebe and Henry version Bunny does not marry Abe—she decides not to wait for him. Bunny becomes the assertive woman in her personal life that she is in her professional life. She begins a relationship with Richard Sumner who, unlike the Abe Cutler character who is self-centered and takes Bunny for granted, is a man who loves and admires and respects Bunny for her intelligence and uniqueness. Bunny has all the traits admired by the Ephrons.

Desk Set's Reference Department is the "brain" of the organization and it is staffed exclusively by women—women who are drawn with an obvious affection. They are very smart, intelligent, funny women who have careers and relationships (or at least desire a relationship, as in the case of Peg). They want everything. They love clothes; Bunny has a dress from Bonwit's on approval, and Ruthie is quietly negotiating the purchase of a "black velvet strapless with a puce scarf." These women have not been drawn as one-dimensional characters; they are rounded people. Women Phoebe would approve of—they are like her—and they are the type of women Henry loves.

Henry's hand is also evident in the creation of the Spencer Tracy version of the character Richard Sumner. Like Henry, Richard admires and loves women. When Richard moves into the world of women, the Reference Department, he does so with respect, affection and care. He takes a phone message for Ruthie with regard to the "black strapless velvet" with a wry sense of amusement but no disrespect. He admires and ultimately loves Bunny Watson for her intellect and personality. With gentle laughter in his voice, Richard suggests "a drink" to cure the hiccupping, tipsy secretary.

Conversely, Richard differentiates and separates himself from the accouterments of powerful men. He is not interested in displaying his importance even though he is very important. He has no regard for the enormous space and grandeur of the office of the head of the network, Mr. Azae. He refuses when he is offered a similar space. He is not interested in the world of men—he prefers women.

Similarly, *You've Got Mail* is set in the world of women, but with a glimpse of the unsatisfying world of men without women. Nora had already established, with *When Harry Met Sally* and *Sleepless in Seattle*, that she was not concerned only with women. She regularly gives space and narrative time to men, but without losing the female focus.[55] This is quite different perspective from that found in *Desk Set*, where the women are drawn with respect, and the men, with the exception of Richard, are depicted as self-centered and, at times, buffoons.

The Fox men: Joe, his father Nelson and his grandfather Schuyler, are three generations of men with a history of unsuccessful relationships. When they are without women they live on their boats. Their world is somewhat like the Legal Department in *Desk Set*; however, Nora provides a glimpse of that world whereas the broadcasting corporation's male world is quite separate from the world of women and largely unexplored. *Desk Set* is about how women order their world and how their world is different from the world of men. When the women set off for the Christmas party in "Legal" they take their own champagne. Earlier in the scene Bunny gives Kenny (Sammy Ogg), the messenger boy, his gift from the department. Bunny asks Kenny if Legal have given him anything. He replies they haven't. Bunny then tells him what to do in order to get Legal to give him a gift. The plan worked last year; it will work again this year for him.

Women know things in the Ephron world. They know men won't think to provide champagne for the women at the Christmas party; they know how to get men to remember to give presents and to memorize the names of Santa's reindeer. Even Richard Sumner, the intelligence behind the development of the new computer, does not have the breadth of knowledge the women in "Reference" have. Left alone to answer the constant requests for information, he fails miserably. On the other hand, Peg is the Reference Department's baseball expert. She knows more than "women's information"; she does not need to consult reference books to know baseball details.

Peg is the most senior of the reference assistants. She is a single woman who would like a relationship with a man, but would rather be lonely than settle for less than she desires. Sylvia and Ruthie, the other two women in Reference are young, independent women. All are intelligent, love their work and value being independent. All are very concerned about the impact the introduction of a computer into their department might have on them. Sylvia has waited a long time to get the job and she does not plan to lose it without a fight. Ruthie is a fresh-faced new recruit, eager to work and learn. She also wants to be good at what she does. The fact that the "brain" of the organization is run by women is typical of the Ephron perspective—often wry and slightly askew—and not in line with conventional thinking of the time. Nora's world of women has its antecedents in the creation of her parents. In *Desk Set*, because Henry had greater creative control as screenwriter and producer, the female characters are drawn as he and Phoebe would have intended—in Phoebe's image. Katharine Hepburn, of course, being a movie star most often associated with roles as strong, independent and unusual women, is ideal as Bunny. From the time of their first meeting Henry drew a comparison between Phoebe, his then wife-to-be, and Katharine Hepburn.[56]

Kathleen's bookshop, as with the Reference Department in *Desk Set*, is staffed predominantly by women. Nora, however, has included one "gentle" man. The women span almost three generations. Birdie, the bookkeeper, is a friend of Kathleen's mother, Cecelia. Kathleen is a woman in her thirties, and Christina is a university student. Birdie is independently wealthy and intimates that at some time she had a passionate love affair with Spain's General Franco. Kathleen is a business woman with her own bookshop and an impeccable reputation in the book business. Christina is a young woman who is supporting herself while she goes to school. George is the quiet, often morose, male counterpart in the bookstore. He is the monitor of male reaction to the female world.

What *Desk Set* illustrates is the family position on the role and rights and (virtual) obligation of women. Nora and her women are as much, if not more, a product of her family circumstances as they are historical time.

Nora has long been associated with the women's movement. She began writing for *Esquire* magazine in the 1970s because she wanted to write about women and herself. But never one to gloss over issues, Nora wrote about the factional feuding within the movement,[57] which incurred much criticism. She was seen by some as disloyal to the cause or, alternatively, as the "least threatening female observer."[58]

According to Linda Obst, Nora once said to me, "Give it up. You're never gonna marry a rich guy. That's not who you are. Women like us are gonna make it ourselves."[59] While this statement can be understood in terms of these women being part of the post-feminist era Nora's belief that women are responsible for themselves and their lives and that women are to be respected and admired on their merits, came about because it is part of the Ephron family ethos.

The women in *Desk Set* and *You've Got Mail* have succeeded and will continue to succeed in their own right, not because they marry well, if at all. They are women who simply know they can do whatever they want. It is part of their life, not the result of a movement that was yet to happen, as in the case of the *Desk Set* female characters. None of these women fit neatly into a "feminist model" of modern womanhood. They are more complex, more flawed and more rounded. They are informed by Henry and Phoebe and they reflect the expectations Nora's parents held for her, and in Nora's film her more complex view of the life of women in her culture.

You've Got Mail—multi-faceted and complex—is, in the most obvious way, a film about the book trade. But it is more than that. Books, particularly children's books, were important to Nora. They were one of the significant connections Nora had to her mother and it is one of the ways *You've Got Mail* becomes uniquely her work rather than simply a romantic comedy told against the backdrop of a bookshop. The film pays homage to Phoebe.[60] She is the unseen presence dominating the film.

Cecilia is referenced throughout *You've Got Mail*. Schuyler Fox, Joe's grandfather, knew Cecilia. He remembers her because of her penmanship and her bookshop. There is no mention of a husband to Cecilia, or father to Kathleen. There is just Cecilia: independent, business woman and mother. This is Cecilia's connection to Phoebe. It is these traits which connect her to Bunny and to Phoebe. Instead of the film being set in the bookshelves of the Reference Department as in *Desk Set*, *You've Got Mail* has moved forward a generation and into a book store. Bunny loves books. She has a personal collection of rare and valuable books stored on the top bookshelf in her office. Kathleen's store, formerly owned by her mother, is a small, intimate bookshop with a section of rare and valuable books—possibly the books Bunny stored high on her bookshelves. Cecilia, who could have been Bunny, has left her legacy, her love of books, her penmanship and her enchanting personality and her independence to her daughter, Nora's creation, Kathleen Kelly. Phoebe Ephron, Bunny Watson, Cecilia Kelly, Kathleen Kelly and Nora Ephron are all related through their love of books. Kathleen's recollection of her childhood is closely linked to books and her mother's bookstore. Nora's happy recollections of her childhood are linked to books and her mother. Nora has written about and spoken about her mother many times but always within the same parameters: the good Phoebe and the bad Phoebe. Phoebe was, as already discussed, a withholding parent. She was difficult, demanding and absent from the everyday lives of her children. She prided herself on being a career woman. The one consistently positive attribute Nora ascribes her mother is her love of reading and books.

The often recalled story of Phoebe is of her bringing to Nora and her sisters found copies of books she herself had read as a child. Phoebe would scour second-hand book stores to find wonderful books to share with her daughters.[61] Phoebe taught Nora to read at an early age. It was a shared activity for mother and daughter and it was a positive experience, an activity that gave them both great joy. A bond between mother and daughter so tightly held and treasured by Nora that even as an adult she kept the books from her childhood, from her mother. "Visiting Nora's apartment recently, I was surprised to see many of the *Oz* books we grew up with, lining a shelf in her bright living room. I took one down and, sure enough, there was my mother's name, printed in block letters on the flyleaf."[62]

Nora, in speaking about the gift of a love of books and reading her mother gave her, writes, "It was as if she were giving us a part of herself."[63] For the type of woman Phoebe was, the parent she was, this gift was one of the few instances of Phoebe giving anything of herself to her children, and it was cherished by Nora. And because Nora was a quick learner, she was rewarded by having her mother's approval. Everything connected to books and reading in Nora's childhood is positive and loving. The memory of the time Nora shared with her mother, the love shared through books, is what is captured in Kathleen's bookshop. The lighting is soft and warm, the people gentle and convivial. The shop has the feel of a home full of love. Twinkling lights, iconic children's books, a poster of Eloise[64]—the ultimate New York child, not unlike Nora, who had a killer wit and was left in the care of nanny while her mother led a glamorous show business life—is frequently evident in the background. The reading to children by Kathleen, the coming and going of customers who have strong associations with the store and the people who work there, George, Christina, Birdie and Kathleen, operate as a family, of sorts. They know about each other's lives, they bicker—George leaves to go to the nut shop when the women get boring—and they support one another, as instanced when Kathleen was "stood up" by her email friend. Ultimately, they share a love and knowledge of the books, and it is the books, the store, which unites them. The place, Kathleen's store, the memory of the books from her childhood and Cecilia's ghostly presence are evocative of Phoebe and her relationship with Nora. Kathleen, her bookshop and the people who work there connects to Bunny with her family of women, the women with whom she works, and her collection of treasured rare books. Nora declares the importance she gives to her experience of reading through Kathleen:

> She [Cecilia/Phoebe] was helping people become whoever it was they were going to turn out to be. Because when you read a book as a child it becomes part of your identity in a way that no other reading in your whole life does.

Nora remembered her mother not just through their shared love of literature. She was proud of her mother's work. Phoebe, like Cecilia, is well remembered because of her career. She was one of only a few successful women screenwriters working in Hollywood during the 1940s and 1950s.[65] She is documented as one of the significant women who worked in film.[66] In Nora's film Kathleen is to meet her email friend at a café, but instead Joe Fox turns up and forces a conversation with her. Towards the end of the conversation Kathleen says angrily to Joe that he will not be remembered and perhaps neither will she but "plenty of people remember my mother and they think she was fine." Kathleen's words are Nora's words. This is as much an acknowledgment of Phoebe as it is of Cecilia.

Nora also poses a question in *You've Got Mail*. Fox Books is opening for the first time. As the camera pans across the activity in the new book store it holds on the title of a display book, the title being *Are You Your Mother?*[67] An interesting question, given that Nora spent a lot of time talking, writing, and asserting that she was not, in fact, her mother. "I've always said you have to work very hard not to be your mother."[68] The book title is a somewhat ironic note from the woman who wrote the speech in which Kathleen praises her mother, but it is a note that functions to keep perspective. Although Nora has almost always been positive about Phoebe with regard to her professional success, as the child caught in the tension between Phoebe Ephron—successful playwright and screenwriter, and Phoebe Ephron—less-than-perfect mother, there was an unresolved conflict.

Nora referenced the less-than-perfect mother in *You've Got Mail* as well. Twice within the narrative Kathleen wishes her mother were there to advise her, and each time she is left unfulfilled. After the publicity campaign to try to save her shop from closure, Kathleen and Birdie meet. They discuss the lack of improvement of the shop's finances. Kathleen asks Birdie what she thinks Cecilia would have done. Birdie has a moment of play-acting—Cecilia's response, according to Birdie, is that she has no idea, but she thinks the window display is lovely. Earlier in the film, when Kathleen is writing to her email friend, she expresses the wish that her mother was there to make her cocoa and tell her that all the things that are going wrong in her life will eventually sort themselves out. On neither occasion does Cecilia help. Birdie, who knew Cecilia well, knew she would be of no assistance to her daughter. Kathleen is responsible for her own problems and for finding her own solutions. Cecilia was a practitioner of the Phoebe Ephron school of mothering: "Our mother called her brand of mothering 'letting them make their own mistakes.'"[69]

Although gentle, far gentler than Nora has been elsewhere with regard her mother's lack of maternal support,[70] there is still a noticeable lack of constructive support for Kathleen by her mother. Although Cecilia is dead there is nothing in Kathleen's memory of her mother's way of being that provides her with direction with regard her problems, except, perhaps, her acceptance of the circumstances of her life and her ability to make the best of a situation. The relationship between Cecilia and Kathleen bears a strong resemblance to the relationship between Phoebe and Nora, albeit a romanticized and fictionalized one.

Along with all the structural recipes and themes she clipped from other people's work, Nora added her own extra seasonings to the recipe for You've Got Mail. Her opinions flavor the film. It is Nora's opinion that the "happy ever after" ending is the fantasy of the romantic comedy genre. It is Nora's opinion as to what constitutes a "good man." And the film, particularly regarding the character of Cecilia, is an homage to her mother.

It is also Nora's view, her understanding of the Fourth Estate—garnered over her many years of working as a journalist—when she exposes the art of media manipulation. In the scene when Joe is at the gym on a treadmill and watching the televised reporting of the protests against the opening of his book store, he is shocked to find that an interview he has given has been dramatically cut and edited in such a way that all it shows is him declaring, "I sell cheap books—I do. So sue me." The reporter (Nina Zoie Lam) then says to the viewing public, "And that in a nutshell is Fox Books' philosophy." Joe looks dumbfounded, shocked beyond belief. Kevin, Joe's assistant, who is at the gym with him, looks at Joe and says, "That's what you *said*?" Joe, sarcastic in his anger responds, "Yeah, that's *not* what I said. I can't believe those bastards. I said we were great! I said you could read for hours and no one would bother you. I said we had 150,000 titles. I said we were a goddam piazza."

Media manipulation is a subject to which Nora regularly returns. It is one of her identifiable themes.[71] She knows "that people are constantly misquoted."[72] The inclusion of the scene, like so many other aspects of *You've Got Mail*, identifies and locates the film as belonging to Nora's body of work.

With *You've Got Mail* Nora has taken bits and pieces, recipes, from other peoples' work and made them her own. She has taken bits from Ernst Lubitsch (*The Shop Around the Corner*), Jane Austen (*Pride and Prejudice*), Henry and Phoebe Ephron (*Desk Set*) and used them to construct her unique work. In using Lubitsch and referencing Jane Austen, Nora has declared the romantic comedy construct of her piece and highlighted its historical antecedents. Through the use of music she has declared the romantic ideals played out in the course of the film to be a fantasy—a story which informs cultural expectations—one of "the romantic and sexual fantasies that are deeply ingrained, not just in society but in literature."[73] She has used other texts to frame her discourse on current cultural change (the home computer and email and the advent of the mega book store), and to express her opinion on those subjects. Nora has moved beyond the framework of other people's recipes in her exposure of how media manipulation works and with her ongoing examination of her relationship with her mother. She has made her work uniquely hers by writing aspects of herself into the character of Kathleen and through her manipulation of other people's recipes in order to create a work that is her own. *You've Got Mail* (1998) is a clear example of how the family credo, "Everything is copy," in its broadest application, operates in Nora's work.

4

Life Is a Story

There is only narrative.[1]
Life isn't just one thing or another. It's a combination of things.[2]

Storytelling was a powerful and pervasive part of the Ephron home. All four of Henry and Phoebe's daughters would become writers, storytellers, as a consequence of their childhood experience and their parent's expectations. For Nora writing became her life's work and her coping mechanism. Moreover and significantly, Nora's work reflects her belief in and is informed by her understanding that there is neither fiction nor nonfiction. The Ephron family's immersion in storytelling and blending nonfiction and fiction until all that existed was narrative informs both Nora's life and work.

Henry and Phoebe spent their entire working lives telling stories; it was their job, as it would become Nora's. The timbre of their existence was informed by their work. They lived in a world where the imagined and the living co-existed. In the most obvious and fundamental way, Nora was influenced by and followed in the footsteps of her parents. Like them she was a storyteller, a screenwriter and playwright; however her storytelling extended far beyond the scope of her parent's work, into journalism, directing, blogging, essays and a novel.

In the Ephron home the telling of stories was not confined to work but extended to their personal lives. Nora was caught in the world of the imagined before she was even aware of it, and the ramifications of growing up in the Ephron family can be seen across both her personal and professional life.

Nora writes that the end of her love affair with journalism marked the "beginning of my understanding that just about everything is a story."[3] She explains her understanding of "Everything is a story" by quoting

E.L. Doctorow: "I am led to the proposition that there is no fiction or nonfiction as we commonly understand the distinction: there is only narrative."[4] To her character John Cotter (Lucky Guy) she gave the profound statement: "You're born, you die. Everything in between is open to interpretation."[5]

It is likely that the years Nora spent working as a journalist was an attempt to escape from the world of narrative rather than a time of discovering the variable nature of truth. It is already documented in Chapter 1 that Nora saw her decision to become a journalist as an act of rebellion, as an attempt to escape the family business. Nora wanted to be a *real* writer—presumably reporting the truth rather than creating a fantasy, as her parent's had spent their lives doing. Her years as a journalist, however, rather than providing an escape simply reinforced that from which she was attempting to escape. Journalism confirmed for Nora that there is no such thing as fiction and nonfiction; there was only narrative. As she writes: "Journalists sometimes make things up.... Journalists sometimes get things wrong."[6] She added, "Now I know that there's no such thing as the truth."[7] Nora knew this to the extent that her screenplay for the film *Cookie* (1989) is founded on this premise. *Cookie*, written in collaboration with Alice Arlen, is a treatise on the nature of truth. It was one of many times Nora would return to this subject.

The film is an illustration of the belief that there is no distinction between fiction and nonfiction; there is only narrative, and it operates on many levels and is all pervasive. The first two-and-a-half minutes of *Cookie* sets up a situation that the rest of the film systematically deconstructs and, in doing so, exposes the questionable nature of truth. In the course of the film it is shown that newspapers lie, people lie, cultural beliefs and expectations are based on fantasies and governments, too, lie.

The film opens with a dog in a dark, empty back street. The scene is shot in black and white with just the slightest hint of blue. A large car turns onto the street, the horn sounds to move the dog. Italian opera is the musical backdrop to the scene. The car pulls up, a cigarette butt is dropped and stubbed out by a man's well-kept shoe. The man walks toward another large, parked car. The whole scene is immediately recognizable as having all the trademarks of a gangster film. The scene is set for the inevitable: the man gets into the parked car; there is a moment of stillness, then the car bursts into flame. At this point the title appears.

The next scene opens with the headlines from a newspaper, the

Daily News. The statement—"Dapper Dino Dead"—presumably announcing that which the viewer has just witnessed. A newspaper boy carries a bundle of the papers and moves among slowed peak-hour cars. The camera moves past a black funeral limousine. A woman's arm—draped in black-lace net—appears from the back seat of the car; money is given and a paper taken. The scene cuts to the graveside as a funeral is taking place. The gangster clan has gathered. Dressed in black, predominantly the crowd is made up of men. The tough-looking weeping widow, Bunny (Brenda Vaccaro), and the three women accompanying her are seated at the graveside. The name on the headstone is Dominick "Dino" Capisco. The camera pans across the crowd, now getting wet in the rain. Black umbrellas are raised. The camera holds on a young woman. She is in mourning, in black, wearing a very short skirt and a stylish hat with a veil covering her face. She is holding a red rose. The camera pulls in and the color changes to deep pink. The words "A few months earlier..." appear.

In the course of the film the newspaper headlines are shown to be inaccurate—journalists getting it wrong. Dino, whom the newspaper declares to be dead, isn't. The question, "Can you believe what you see or read?" is asked and answered. Just like a magician's trick we saw Dino die, but do we? Later the trick is explained and exposed. Ultimately, one person's truth is another person's fantasy. There are versions of the truth, each understood from the perspective of the individual.

Cookie does not just deal with the question of truth as it relates to the Fourth Estate. The film is an exploration of the far-reaching and all-encompassing role of storytelling in life. The complexity and layered construction of personal truth in determining who we are is a core theme of this early work. The central character, Cookie (Emily Lloyd), in the course of the film transitions from a teenage "Madonna" to the head of a mobster organization. As the backstory begins, Cookie is a rebellious young girl trying to be Madonna, the pop icon. She bases her physical appearance on Madonna as she appears in videos and performances—Madonna in her titular *Desperately Seeking Susan* (1989) incarnation, not as Madonna—Louise Veronica Ciccone—the person. Cookie identifies with and copies Madonna's creation, as do a number of Cookie's friends. With Cookie's emulation of her idol, the notion of truth is questioned at its most fundamental level. Who are we? How do we define ourselves? Particularly when we define ourselves in the image of something or someone else; more particularly, when that something or someone else is a construct and, in trying to be like that construct, having to imagine and recreate that which is already a creation. What is highlighted is the fantasy of who we think we are or desire to be. Further, the idea that Cookie should want to be like Madonna is in any way unusual is debunked. Madonna was who young girls of that time wanted to be. Cookie emulating her ideal is akin to Nora imagining herself as a modern-day Dorothy Parker as she might have imagined Dorothy Parker to be. We all play at being someone, defining ourselves in terms of a desirable image or achievement—an imagined other.

As Nora continues the already complex contemplation on the nature of personal identity she addresses how the expectation of others act as a determinant in how we present ourselves. Cookie is sent for by her father, Dino (Peter Falk). Dino is in jail, attempting to argue for early release. He has his minions pick Cookie up and take her to see him in prison where he demands that Cookie behave in a way which will reflect well on him. In other words, in a way other than her usual manner, which has led her to being charged with a misdemeanor. He wants her to be viewed in a much more acceptable and favorable light. Dino insists that Cookie live her life in line with the archetype of the dedicated young person and student. He wants her to attend school, come home, do homework and then watch a little television before an early bed in order to be prepared for the next day. Dino wants Cookie to live the parent-approved fantasy of the perfect teenager. Dino wants Cookie to be other than she is in order to advance his cause.

Cookie, in seeking a sense of who she might like to be, looks to popular culture for guidance on how to behave. She also has expectations forced upon her. The cultural expectation of the "good girl," a way of behaving as her father imagines a dutiful daughter should. In trying to create an image of herself in line with her own desires and the expectations of others, Cookie becomes an amalgam of the real and the fictional as she grapples with her sense of identity.

Cookie, as Nora's creation, can be seen as reflecting her own experience as a teenager when she was expected to go to college, be a writer and to have a "flashy career"[8] just like her mother. Like Nora, Cookie constructs a persona for herself based on the desirable but ultimately imagined (Madonna) and the forced expectation of a parent (the good daughter) which, in each case, is an expectation informed by fiction.

Family becomes another construct Nora puts under the microscope in *Cookie*. Having already touched on the notion of family, with Alice Arlen in the screenplay for *Silkwood*, where the housemates Karen Silkwood (Meryl Streep), her boyfriend Drew Stephens (Kurt Russell) and Dolly Pelliker (Cher) constitute a family, of sorts. This time, however, Nora uses irony to highlight the variable nature of the "truth of family." Cookie is the illegitimate daughter of Lenore (Dianne Wiest), the long-standing mistress to the married gangster Dominick Capisco. All Lenore wants is for Cookie, Dino and herself to be a family. For Lenore, her idea of family is not what she has: a married lover, an illegitimate child and a life spent as a single parent. For Lenore, family should be something like the image of family depicted on *The Brady Bunch*, which Cookie is seen watching on television.[9] Within the diegesis, Nora highlights the obvious. There is no possible connection between the "reality" of Lenore's family and the sitcom fantasy of what constitutes family. Lenore is the mistress of a married gangster. She will never have the white, middle-class dream family that is *The Brady Bunch*. Since its inception, television has been an arbiter of cultural norms and ideals. *The Brady Bunch* is one example of how cultural expectation is shaped by the stories told on television. Lenore does get her wedding and white picket fence marriage in Nora's world but only as a result of everyone—the government included—being involved in the deception, the denial of the real. Government-generated and sanctioned stories are not exempt from Nora's scrutiny. The resolution of the film's narrative sees Dino and Lenore marry under the pseudonyms of Vanessa and William. They have gone into the witness-protection program. They have been recreated with the assistance of a government agency and now they are "other" people. They pretend to be other people and pretend to live other lives. There is no truth to their existence. They live the ultimate fantasy.

When Nora creates her own fantasy, writes her own story, she never allows her audience to be deluded. She is never complicit in the deception. She ensures everyone understands her story of Cookie is just that—a story. In itself Nora's film is a fantasy, a narrative, and she lets her audience in on the joke. At the film's conclusion, in a return to the graveside scene of the film's opening, the young woman with the rose, now identified as Cookie, looks directly at the camera. She smiles a knowing smile at the viewer. It is a smile of acknowledgment. What Cookie is acknowledging is the privileged information she and the viewer share;

both are in on the deception. There is no truth, only a story. In that moment, in the transgression of the fourth wall, the illusion of any attempt at verisimilitude is shattered. Any illusion of a reality within the film's narrative is lost. Newspapers tell stories, cultural institutions such as television tell stories, governments tell stories. Nora tells stories. There is only narrative.

Cookie operates on many levels in its examination of the nature of truth. Nora deconstructs the nature of truth as presented in newspapers. She plays with the idea that governments have a vested interest in telling stories. People have a vested interest in believing the story and have expectations that are informed by believing the narrative. Lenore desires a family based on the unrealistic depictions of family life in television shows like *The Brady Bunch*. As Nora has written, television and film influence cultural norms and expectations. In *Cookie's* final moment, Nora reveals the illusion of the construct itself. When Cookie looks directly at the camera the illusion of the reality of the film's diegesis is broken, finally establishing that there is no distinction between fiction and nonfiction, there is only a narrative in which we all are invested and which we all, at some level, understand.

The blending of reality and fantasy to create the narrative of one's life is a characteristic Nora theme. *My Blue Heaven* (1990) and *Mixed Nuts* (1994) both continue to explore and play with the belief that there is only narrative. Taking up one of the themes begun in *Cookie*—the government-sanctioned world of pretend that is the witness protection program[10]—*My Blue Heaven*, for which Nora wrote the screenplay, saw her working from the same source material as her husband, Nicholas Pileggi.

Nora wrote the story of gangster Vinnie Antonelli (Steve Martin), while Pileggi wrote the story of gangster Henry Hill[11] (Ray Liotta). Vinnie and Henry are both characters based on real-life gangster, informant and witness-protection participant Henry Hill. Martin Scorsese's film *Goodfellas* (1990) was an outstanding critical and commercial success; *My Blue Heaven* was a disaster, both critically and at the box office.[12] Nora was unhappy with the film, but *My Blue Heaven* is not an inconsequential work. It explores the illusory nature of the life offered through the witness-protection program and it looks more closely at the mythology surrounding the FBI as an elite, secret government body. Writing of Nora's work with *My Blue Heaven*, Garry Wills posits that it is "typical of her unexpected blindside tackles of ideology: How many movies have you seen in which the FBI does the bidding of the Mafia?"[13]

As she did with *Cookie*, Nora clearly establishes that this is a story, a narrative, make-believe. Under the direction of Herbert Ross, whose background was in theater, dance and musical films, *My Blue Heaven* is a highly stylized film with vibrant color and, at times, almost surreal sets. The dance scenes are particularly theatrical, with the dancers not only dancing within the staged sets, but also transposing from a set to a "real" beach at one point.

Nora's script for the film is constructed in the form of a book, with intertitles operating as chapter headings. Within the diegesis the intertitles refer to the chapter headings of Vinnie's book, *How I Got Here*, which is launched at the film's conclusion. The film is the visual reading of the yet-to-be published book. Although the film is based on the life of the larger-than-life Henry Hill, Nora makes sure this film is not mistaken for the truth. Nora used a number of devices, including those described above, as well as a transgression of the fourth wall to expose the artifice of the construct. FBI agent Barney Coopersmith (Rick Moranis) looks directly at the camera mid-dance, raises his eyebrows to the audience as an acknowledgment of his ability on the floor, a look which says—"Can you believe I am doing this and how cool I am?"—then dances on. Having convinced everyone that this is only a story and that it not be mistaken for the truth, Nora uses the safety of the created space of the film script to explode the myth of an elite FBI. In her world, the FBI is populated with inept agents with very human foibles. Barney Coopersmith, for instance, is the FBI agent responsible for the relocation and care of Vinnie until he appears in court to testify against the other mobsters. But rather than the usual depiction of members of the FBI service—silent, intelligent and resourceful—Barney is hapless. He revels in the mythological status of the title "FBI agent," while the narrative reveals his secret service reality as spending most of his time at the bureau, doing paperwork. Of his glamorous life as an important FBI agent, the highlight, during his limited undercover work, was "once when I was undercover I got to drive a BMW."

Nora embraced the irony of the witness-protection program, in which a person who has committed a serious crime can live a make-believe life sanctioned, encouraged and financially aided by the government. Through the use of artifice, in this instance a highly stylized film construct, Nora can say whatever she likes. She can challenge an institution as untouchable as the FBI because the story the film is telling is not true. Nora took on an institution that is above scrutiny; that is so important that it should not be criticized.[14] But she was able to disclaim the challenge she mounted because of the highly artificial form of the construct. It is only a funny story she is telling, after all—not real in any way!

There are moments when one fiction confronts another in *My Blue Heaven*; when one protected witness discovers he is not the only person living a life of make-believe. With the discovery of multiple fictions, another level of narrative complexity evolves. Within the fictionalized account of Henry Hill, Vinnie, based on Henry Hill, pretending to be someone else, discovers colleagues from his former life; other people who have also taken on other personas and live other lives with the assistance of the government. The witness-protection program in the instance of Nora's story leads to one fiction bumping against another until it becomes obvious that *everything* is a fiction. With the discovery of other witness-protection participants, Vinnie concludes that within the pretend life they are all leading many have resumed a variation of their old life. They are living a life within a life within a life. Their lives are a combination of things.

Nora just keeps adding layer upon layer of complexity to the already complex exploration of the "narrative which composes life." Vinnie, having gone to a pet shop, discovers the owner of the shop is another gangster, also in the witness-protection scheme. Vinnie identifies himself, one gangster to another, by evoking the world of gangsters with a film reference. Vinnie sends a coded message via one of the most famous of all celluloid gangsters, the actor James Cagney. Cagney, of course, is an actor playing a role—not a gangster at all. Vinnie quotes Cagney's gangster personification when he says to the store owner, "You dirty rat." In having her character Vinnie quote Cagney's gangster character, Nora declares the core sentiment of her screenplay. The line, "You dirty rat," was never said by Cagney in a film. It is a legend built on a misquotation and is one of American cinema's most persistent myths. In *Blonde Crazy* (1931) Cagney's character Bert says, "Mmm, that dirty, double-crossin' rat!" and in *Taxi* (1932) his character, Matt Nolan, says, "You dirty yellow-bellied rat." At every level for Nora there is only a story.

Mixed Nuts, based on the French film *Le Pere Noel est une ordure*

(1982), has the feel of a French farce. It is the perfect context for Nora to continue to discuss her philosophical position that there is no single truth, only narrative. Set in and at times filmed on location at Venice Beach, California, this film, like *My Blue Heaven*, is very stylized. The film at no time attempts to appear to be real. Venice Beach is depicted in the film in much the same way as it is reputed as being: a fantasy, a staged setting. It doesn't look like the real world. It is a geographical location but it is one of those places, a Disneyland-like fantasy, where the imagined has taken almost full possession and in doing so the place—Venice Beach—has become a combination of nonfiction and fiction. Venice Beach has its own mythology. The location has become an amalgam of the real and the imagined and a home for the not quite "real" people who are drawn to it. The film opens on a bicycle rider riding past a blank wall on which is a sign indicating the space is available; a blank space waiting to be filled. The opening sequence is shot in shades of grey, with the credits appearing in orange. As the bike rider rounds the corner at the end of the wall, palm trees and a large decorated Christmas tree are revealed. The streetscape is now evident, and the rider is identified as Philip (Steve Martin). The background changes color from shades of grey to grey-infused, subtle color. As he rides on, Philip passes a row of seven child angels and an adult angel sitting at a bus stop. The bus stop sign is decorated in colors of red and white. The following shot opens on a 19th-century Christmas scene. A couple is riding through the snow-covered countryside in a horse-drawn sleigh. The camera pulls back to reveal the image to be a sidewalk artist's rendering of a Yuletide scene. It has the appearance of a painting from the Victorian Era, or a still from a film such as *Christmas in Connecticut* (1945). The illustration on the sidewalk is a Western culture imagining of Christmas. As Philip rides on, broad expanses of beach are visible. Roller-bladers ride on the boardwalk and palm trees stand tall in front of the Venice Beach shop fronts. There is a pianist playing a piano on wheels on the boardwalk. There are palm trees with their trunks wrapped in tinsel and a group of three pretend-Magi and two donkeys with whom you can have your picture taken for $2.00. There are carolers dressed in green robes and a snowman made of sand. A "snowman" on roller blades rides by and two roller-bladers with a Christmas tree pass Philip. The whole of the diegetic world is depicted as bizarre; an absurdist view of life. The credits conclude at this point.

It is clearly Christmas, Californian style, at Venice Beach. The absurdity of the expectations of Christmas revealed through the parallel visual and aural portrayals of Christmas. Against the visual backdrop of Venice Beach dressed up for Christmas in cold climate garb can be heard the Drifters' rendition of "White Christmas." This is a truly bizarre situation where the fantasy of Christmas, white and snowy, is juxtaposed against the world of palm trees and beaches and sunshine and sand snowmen and angels sitting at bus stops, at a place which is itself a fantasy—Venice Beach, home of "muscle beach bodies," 1970s counter-culture hippies and the cool, hip people. Venice Beach is known for its fantasy, it has a created persona, a dreamscape pretending to be real.

The people who congregate there are also outside the mainstream. Philip operates a help-line service for people in need, which has lost government funding and is destined to close. He has been issued with an eviction notice and his fiancée has broken up with him. Philip, like Barney, is another of Nora's hapless souls who ultimately hasn't a clue as to what he is doing. In frustration at his situation, he explodes at a phone client, "All I do all day is deal with nuts like you." Along with Philip, working at the help-line center is Catherine (Rita Wilson), a quiet, conservative woman in her mid-thirties who still lives at home with her mother and Mrs. Munchnik (Madeline Kahn), whom Philip describes as "a woman in a bad mood." Felix (Anthony LaPaglia) and Gracie (Juliette Lewis), who live nearby, are, respectively, a "wall artist" or "loser" (Felix), depending on who is asked, and the owner of a colorful second-hand shop (Gracie). Felix and Gracie are the bickering prospective parents of a soon-to-be-born baby. There is a transvestite named Chris (Leiv Schrieber) struggling for acceptance from his less than embracing family; a singing, downstairs tenant (Adam Sandler); and a vet, Dr. Kinsky (Rob Reiner), who says of his life: "I'm up to my eyeballs with people who think their animals have feelings." This is just before he says goodnight to all the dogs in his care, addressing each of them respectively by his or her name.

The plot is predictable: Philip and Catherine fall in love; Felix and Gracie have their baby, born under the Christmas tree; Mrs. Munchnik has sex with a man she has previously hated and is no longer in a bad mood; and, after Grace receives a windfall, she gives Philip the $5,000 he needs to keep his help-line operating. (Gracie comes by her money by accidentally killing the "Seaside Strangler," thereby receiving a reward for his capture.) All of the predictable plot outcomes are not significant in the film. The plot provides the vehicle for the exploration of the stories people tell themselves[15] and the location, Venice Beach, is a home for this collection of "mixed nuts."

Mixed Nuts, the story of a quirky collection of people is also, as the opening suggests, an exposition of the absurdity of the notion of The Christmas Story—the birth of Jesus—imagined by most Western cultures as being wrapped in the snow and glitter of a Northern climate but which, in fact, has a closer alliance with Southern California, where the climate is more in line with that of the Middle East. But more than a confusion of climatic conditions, Western culture's Christmas celebration is an amalgam of stories. The day is a celebration of the birth of Jesus but nobody knows exactly when he was born or if in fact he existed. In Western society the story of Jesus has melded with the story of the Greek Saint Nicholas, believed to be a benefactor to children, who lived sometime in the third century and whose image evolved and changed until the red-suited, fur-trimmed Santa universally recognized as Father Christmas or Santa Claus emerged as the result of the depiction of him by American artists such as Norman Rockwell and N.C. Wyeth. In 1931, the most instantly recognizable Santa appeared as the result of a long-standing advertising campaign mounted by the Coca Cola Company.

The Christmas story, fundamental to Western culture and the basis of Western religion, is exposed by Nora for what she believes it to be: an ever-evolving story, a narrative, an ever-shifting "combination of things" which, in its current incarnation, is the product of a very successful and long-standing advertising campaign.

The final irony of the story of Christmas in Nora's film world is that the event is being celebrated by a number of Jewish characters as well. Such are the stories people tell themselves and the beliefs and fantasies of their lives. There is no fiction or nonfiction in *Mixed Nuts*, only a jumble of narratives and a collection of "mixed nuts" who may or may not believe the stories they tell themselves in order to understand their lives. Nora, with her exploration of the Christmas story, challenges one of the fundamental events of the Christian calendar and a tenet of the Christian ideology which informs Western society.

The three films—*Cookie, My Blue Heaven* and *Mixed Nuts*—are overwhelmingly complex because Nora challenges so many of the concepts on which Western culture is premised. They are so full of ideas and have so many layers of understanding built into them that they are little understood. Although they had little commercial success, they are three of Nora's most interesting and revealing films. Her humor and affection for the quirky and absurd, and her understanding of the world, comes to the fore in these films. Through the use of comedy, humor, Nora exposed the basis of legal, cultural and religious belief systems for what they are—a collection of stories. Life is neither nonfiction nor fiction; just about everything is a story.

It is not surprising that "the narrative that comprises life" is a theme Nora often returns to in her work. Her whole existence is a narrative. Benjamin Markovits describes Nora as a "practised personality,"[16] an apt description given the circumstances of her life. Nora's "practised personality," so shrewdly observed by Markovits, is one that has been rewritten and refined each time it has been worked into a story or an amusing anecdote.

As is evident in works such as *Heartburn* and *This Is My Life*, Nora was profoundly affected by her parents' use of life as the raw material for their work; their conflating of the factual and the fiction of life into a story. Nora's belief, that there is only narrative, is far more complex for her than in the work of her parents or for her characters, with the exception of Erica Engels.[17] Erica is probably the most important of all Nora's characters because she is the character who is the voice of Nora, the child. Erica is the victim in her mother's propensity to conflate nonfiction and fiction. Nora and Erica think deeply, considering the ramifications of the telling of stories. They are intelligent and introspective.

Henry and Phoebe with their move, first into theatre and then into screenwriting, changed the fabric of their lives and, subsequently, the lives of their children. From the real they created the fictional and, in the transposing of life to fiction, there came a third tangled, intertwined being that that was neither fact nor fiction—a narrative emerged. The narrative included themselves and their daughter Nora. At this point their life became part fiction and their fiction became part fact. Neither would be purely one or the other again.

What is known about Nora as a baby comes largely from a fictionalized account of her life: Henry and Phoebe's play *Three's a Family.* Baby Susan was based on Nora, and her parents, Kitty and Gene, were based on Phoebe and Henry. The other source of information about Nora as a small child is Henry's memoir but Nora has challenged Henry's account, contending it is flawed. Nora has written of her father's book: "In it are several completely unbelievable episodes."[18] Nora is also quoted as saying, "Almost nothing about me in the book is true."[19] Therefore what is known of Nora as a child and of her childhood is a fictionalized or, at least, a questionable truth. From the beginning of Nora's life there is only a narrative. In a recent essay on growing up in the Ephron family, Hallie—the third daughter—comments on a photograph of her mother and Nora as a tiny baby, questioning the veracity of the scene.[20]

The ritual of the family dinner table, so central to Nora's happy recollections of her childhood, was fundamental in the development of her belief that there is only narrative. It was here Nora was taught to turn the events of her day into funny stories. Here she was taught not to tell the stories of her day as she understood them, not to tell what she perceived as really having happened, including her emotional response to the events of her day. Nora, through the continual practice of altering her perception of events, was taught to deny her own feelings and responses. It became an internalized process for survival and acceptance. She had to deny the reality of the events of her life as she understood them. Nora has said, "I'm very into denial."[21] She had been taught to deny anything negative from a very early age. She had to re-score her stories to a funny tune to bring to the dinner table.

Nora also learned as a child that any of her stories, the stories from her life, could be taken from her, from her ownership of them and from the life on which they were based. Nora's stories could at any time be incorporated into a screenplay by her parents. They could be removed from their circumstances and context. Nora's stories became her parents' stories. Such was her experience as a young adult when moments from her life at school, recorded in letters to her mother, as stated earlier, became the basis for her parents' play and Broadway hit *Take Her, She's Mine*.

In the stage production the character based on Nora was portrayed by Elizabeth Ashley. Ashley was an actress known for her intelligence, edginess and bite, not unlike Nora herself. However by the time the play became the more widely seen film, Nora and her experiences had altered substantially. There was nothing to identify the character based on Nora as Nora. By the time *Take Her, She's Mine* reached the screen Nora had ceased to exist; only she *did* exist because her words remained. In the film the character based on Nora, the character who spoke and wrote (in letters home to her parents) Nora's words (in some instances verbatim) in the play and film was now depicted as "a dish" rather than a brain and played by Sandra Dee. Nora, twice removed, had become a blond ingénue, more beauty than brain. Rather than the spikey, dark-haired, brain—from an intellectual, culturally Jewish family—Nora had transmogrified into Sandra Dee. In the film version of *Take Her, She's Mine* Nora's words do not fit Sandra Dee's characterization of Mollie, nor her screen persona. It is of no surprise that Nora has written that she and Los Angeles were not a good fit. Her words and sentiment and intellect did not fit the blond, dumbed-down image that is readily identifiable as Southern Californian.

Nora, the person, became lost many years ago, and her life became legend. For Nora, there was no one truth of her life, rather a number of variations of the truth—a narrative. The experience she took from life informed her work and, with her work, she continually reiterates the notion that there is no one truth, only a collection of stories. Linda Obst, with whom Nora had an ongoing professional relationship, describes Nora's character Annie (as played by Meg Ryan in *Sleepless in Seattle*) as "the girl-next-door version of Nora—sophisticated and urban without being New Yorky."[22] Coburn, the author of the article in which Obst is quoted, goes on to suggest that this may be a result of Nora, an intellectual Jewish woman from New York—as depicted in *Heartburn* and *This Is My Life*—not being palatable to the general public. If box-office results are any indication, then Coburn's suggestion is supported. Her life is not acceptable until it has been fictionalized. She is not acceptable until she has become a fictionalized version of herself.

In all of the blurring of life with art where does the real Nora fit in the depiction of her that is the public documentation of her life? Is she the baby that Gene threw and Kitty wanted to return to work to get away from? Is her type of young woman so unacceptable to the American public that she had to be transformed into a blonde ingénue? Is she the woman who as an adult was found to be unpalatable by the general viewing public; the films in which the lead female character most closely resembles her, *This Is My Life* and *Heartburn*, were box-office failures.[23] Is she the child who was never allowed to be who she was and feel what she knew she felt? Given the constant and re-enforced feedback that the person Nora Louise Ephron is only acceptable in a fictionalized form, it is not surprising that she did not believe that fact and fiction are separate, that she believed in narrative, a melding of the two. Her life has always been reconfigured into a fiction and her fictional self was more acceptable to both her parents and the general public.

Leslie Bennetts writes of Nora: "Ephron doesn't give anything away for free, and what she does share has long since been packaged as part of the ongoing mythology of her life."[24] Nora knew no other way of being. Her life from the start had been a narrative, a conflation of fiction and nonfiction; the narrative of her life her survival mechanism both personally and financially. Nora's world—including her work—is informed by her experience. The process of becoming an intermingled third being, a narrative, a combination of fact and fiction saved the woman who, because of the unique circumstances of her upbringing, could not find acceptance as herself.

The alteration of perspective through the repackaging of life events into funny stories is only one aspect of the complex and compounding influences which shaped Nora's understanding of the nature of truth. Nora believed that literature and movies have a role in autobiography. She once said:

> Movies are the literature of this generation, and all subsequent generations. It is exciting to know that if you make a movie that in some way works, you are going to reach people, to become part of their autobiography. Just as you went to the movies when you were a kid and got all your ideas about x or y from the movies you can be part of that for people, you can give that.[25]

It is Nora's contention that personal belief systems, those which inform who we are as individuals, are, in turn, informed by the books we read and the movies we watch. In relation to the books we read, she gives particular importance to those books we read as children. Again, this is not surprising given the importance reading held in her childhood. It was the one place she truly shared a love and a bond with her mother. It was a positive in an otherwise dysfunctional upbringing. It was also where Nora imagined how she wanted to be in the world and where she began to identify with the strong women characters which would shape her own character. This more intellectual consideration of the role of film and literature in the shaping of society was something Nora's parents had contemplated and debated. It was part of the intellectual atmosphere in which she grew up. *Always Together*, as already discussed, reflects upon the role and impact of film in the shaping and informing of cultural norms and expectations. The impact of storytelling in the shaping and informing of cultural norms was something Nora had always understood.

Nora's exploration of the role of storytelling in the shaping of cultural norms began years before she wrote the essay in which she quotes Doctorow or wrote the screenplay for *Cookie*. In 1972, Nora wrote another essay, "Fantasies,"[26] which provoked an outcry from some quarters, particularly by those in the Women's Movement who were outraged that Nora, a declared feminist, should write about rape fantasies. "Fantasies" provoked criticism because Nora not only confessed to having a sexual fantasy, a rape fantasy in which she is "dominated by faceless males who rip my clothes off,"[27] but it was a fantasy she thought of as "terrific."[28] It is a fantasy which, with only minor variation, remained the same from the age of eleven years. Sally has the same sexual fantasy in *When Harry Met Sally* (1989).

In an article by Tamara Straus, in what is ostensibly a comment on *Hanging Up* (2000), the author rages against Nora's entire body of work and what she sees as Nora's tenuous allegiance to the feminist movement. Straus objects to Nora's depiction of one-dimensional female characters and her achievement of "perfecting the art of emotional shallowness." Straus concludes her article by wishing for future female screenwriters the success of Nora Ephron; that they achieve her stature but "not by dishing out pseudo-feminist fluff" wherein modern American women "become a bad joke."

Straus, and others like her, those who took offense at "Fantasies" and continue to take offense at what they perceive to be Nora's lightweight work and women characters, missed the point. From a feminist perspective, if the writings of Kate Millett,[29] to whom is attributed the coining of the term "patriarchy" as it is applied to the contemporary social structure of the 1970s, and Susan Brownmiller, who argued "that rape, the act of forcing a woman to have sexual intercourse against her will, was the secret of patriarchy"[30] is the accepted ideology, it is understandable that offense was taken at what they understood Nora to be saying. It flies in the face of all they stood for. However, Straus mistook style for content. A closer examination of Nora's essay reveals something quite different and much more complex than that which Straus is proposing. Nora's alter-ego, Sally, says, "I have just as much of a dark side as the next person,"[31] only Nora had been taught to repackage her dark side for a laugh. Nora's style belies the seriousness of her content. She always understood comedy as a medium through which it is possible to examine and explore and process the difficult aspects of life. She always understood that "comedy has the power [to] make us think about things we never thought about before."[32] The issue for Nora in "Fantasies," the issue about which she was writing, is not rape fantasies and the nature of her personal fantasy; that is simply how she packaged it. As Nora had always done, she used her life as the prism to reflect the world around her. What she was *really* writing about, other than herself, was: "So many of the conscious and unconscious ways men and women treat each other have to do with romantic and sexual fantasies that are deeply ingrained, not just in society but in literature."[33]

For Nora the fantasies and stories which are so culturally embedded, so much a part of our psyche, subliminally inform our thinking and expectations. Nora, in "Fantasies," was not standing in the way of change. What she was arguing was that change is almost impossible until the stories, the fantasies, change, and that is a lot harder to do than dividing up housework. Through relaying her own experience, Nora was acknowledging the gap between the rational and the emotional, exploring the complexity of the internalized stories women told, and continue to tell, themselves.

Nora's understanding of the complexities of the human condition is found in her writing and in her films. "That's one of the subjects in all my romantic comedies—the role of other films (or, in the case of *You've Got Mail*, books) in that fantasy."[34] The influence of the internalized stories and literature in all its permutations and the ingrained fantasies of our culture inform *This Is My Life* and is the subject of *Sleepless in Seattle*,[35] *When Harry Met Sally*, and *You've Got Mail*.

Sleepless in Seattle is an exploration of the concept of romantic love as it is understood in Western culture. In the film, the intent is articulated and foregrounded when Becky (Rosie O'Donnell) says to Annie (Meg Ryan), "You don't want to be in love, you want to be in love in the movies." Nora's romantic comedy, on its way to having the two lovers meet, meanders through theoretical contemplations on the notion of love. Western culture has a number of stories to explain love. In *Sleepless in Seattle*, Nora touches on some of them, ranging from love as depicted in the movies to psychology's story of love where "his neuroses meshed perfectly with yours."[36] Nora once said of the intention behind *Sleepless in Seattle*: "Our dream was to make a movie about how movies screw up your brain about love, and then if we did a good job, we would become one of the movies that would screw up people's brains about love forever."[37] With *Sleepless in Seattle* Nora achieved her aim. Most of the viewing public missed the point of the film and it has become the television Valentine's Day staple.

When Harry Met Sally, made in 1989 under the direction of Rob Reiner and predating *Sleepless in Seattle*, is frequently written about, particularly as it contains one of the most quoted lines in the contemporary history of American film.[38] This film, along with *Sleepless in Seattle* (1993) and *You've Got Mail* (1998), make up the three most successful of Nora's romantic comedies. Harry and Sally discuss relationships and what women want from them by referencing *Casablanca* (1942). Sally says that women, including herself, do not want a life with Rick, the character played by Humphrey Bogart; they would rather have the stability of the other guy (in that case, Victor Laszlo, played by Paul Henreid). Harry cannot believe this, but both he and Sally alter their perspective over time, even when *Casablanca* remains the reference point to which they return in their ongoing conversation about relationships.

The audience expectation of what will happen to Harry and Sally is informed by our film experience. In the commentary accompanying the collector's edition of her film, Nora says of our expectation of the outcome for the protagonists: "And we have seen just enough movies to believe that because we don't like them we are destined to be with them forever,"[39] by which she means that the tradition of romantic comedies tells the viewer that the two people who are a couple at the conclusion of the story usually begin by not liking each other. Rob Reiner and Nora also comment on how the design of the film—the use of the split screen—evokes other films, including *Indiscreet* (1958) and *Pillow Talk* (1959), films which have been instrumental in informing the viewer's expectations of love.

As with *When Harry Met Sally*, film informs and defines the male and female positions on relationships in *Sleepless in Seattle*.[40] *Sleepless in Seattle* overtly references *An Affair to Remember* (1957) as the style of film which informs Western culture's views on love. It sets the benchmark for true love, and Cary Grant is identified by Sam (Tom Hanks)

119

and his friend Jay (Rob Reiner) as being the arbiter of all behaviors desirable in the courting male. The irony of Cary Grant being considered the benchmark for heterosexual male courting behaviors, not lost on Nora, is that for much of Grant's career (and still today) there was much speculation as to his sexual preference.

You've Got Mail, as discussed in the previous chapter, operates from the same premise, and, as with the two earlier films, the plot device is foregrounded in the film. This time the film referenced is *The Shop Around the Corner*. Nora has been quoted as saying that all romantic comedy comes from two sources: *The Taming of the Shrew*[41] and *Pride and Prejudice*. In particular for Nora, *Pride and Prejudice* is her reference point. It is literature which helps to form our culturally conditioned expectations of love. As Nora wrote in July 1972: "Even after the revolution (Women's Liberation), we will be left with the literature."[42]

Nora, by drawing attention to films or literature within the diegetic world of her characters, destroys the illusion of the reality within the text to illustrate the point she is making. She draws attention to the device and, in doing so, brings to the fore the artifice of the construct. In that way, Nora signifies that she is aware that films are part of the fantasy that inform and contribute to the cultural expectations of love. Nora is acknowledging that fantasy influences "reality," confirming her belief in the "proposition that there is no fiction or nonfiction as we commonly understand the distinction: there is only narrative."[43]

Nora's work is informed by her belief in the role of the unconscious: deeply embedded culturally determined fantasies and literature, in all its connotations, in determining, in part, our behaviors, expectations, hopes and dreams. Her work is further informed by her belief that literature, including movies, is part of our collective autobiography.

Because Nora lived in a world of stories, she not only learned to tell stories within a particular framework—from the perspective of telling a funny story—she also lived, from an early age, in a world where the fictional and nonfictional co-existed. Henry and Phoebe were readers and they "were movie buffs long before it was fashionable."[44] They were immersed in the fictional world of reading and film-going. They introduced and immersed their children in that world. Henry writes that he was expelled from college six weeks before he was due to graduate because he was caught stealing books from the campus book store; writers like Spengler, Dewey, Laski, T.S. Eliot, James Joyce and George

Bernard Shaw.[45] Phoebe loved Jane Austen. The first three weeks after Ernst Lubitsch had a heart attack which resulted in the Ephrons having nothing to do, they "lay around reading James Joyce (me) and Jane Austen (Phoebe)."[46] Later, Henry wrote of an incident where Phoebe spoke "in her best Jane Austen tone."[47] Of course, Jane Austen's tone can only be imagined. That Henry believed Phoebe spoke in a Jane Austen tone indicates that, for him, the imagined was as much a part of life as any other aspect of life. The imaginary was part of their biography.

Even the source of the information about Henry and Phoebe's life together, Henry's autobiography, is a narrative, a melding of fiction and nonfiction and selective recall. By its very nature, autobiography—the events of one's life as recorded by ones' self—implies subjectivity, "fact and fiction inextricably mingled."[48] However, given the nature of their existence, the immersion in a world of narrative and a life lived as an amalgam of nonfiction and fiction or fantasy, to dispute Henry's memories and to ask the question—are they less valid because they are subjective?—somehow seems redundant. Henry can write about the life he and Phoebe led, that they were movie buffs, that they were readers and, while all that might be true, a confirmation of their truth is revealed in their work. It is through elements of their work—the repeated identifiable Ephron traits—that their belief system comes into focus. For example, we know the Ephrons were movie buffs. We know Henry went to the movies most mornings ("The early bird matinees at the Edison Theater on Broadway. Two pictures for a dime. I went every morning except Saturday and Sunday")[49] because his alter ego, Sam Whitaker, went to the movies on most days as well. Irma says of Sam's daily movie ritual: [He's] "off to the movies to beat the two o'clock change in prices."[50] Henry and Phoebe used life as the raw material for their work. Sam goes to the movies every morning in their play, and Henry went to the movies in his life. Life for Henry and Phoebe was a narrative. They lived across fiction and nonfiction; they existed in both worlds.

When Henry and Phoebe began their screenwriting career, one of their first works dealt directly with the influence of films. Their early screenplay for *Always Together* sees their lead female character, Jane Barker, convinced that if the wife in a marriage has more money than the husband the marriage is doomed. This is what she has learned from the movies. By 1957 Henry and Phoebe had become less self-conscious about the place of movies in the lives of their characters. They were more open in their belief that life was a blending of fact and fiction. By the time they adapted *Desk Set* for the screen it was a given that movies were part of the public conscience, a part of individual autobiography. In *Desk Set* when Mike Cutler (Gig Young) returns from a business trip just before Christmas he enters the Reference Department carrying a large pink rabbit. Bunny's quick-witted response to the rabbit is "Aren't you going to introduce me to Harvey?" The reference to the invisible six-foot, three-and-a-half-inch rabbit Harvey from the 1950 film adaptation of Mary Chase's Pulitzer Prize–winning play of the same name operates on many levels,[51] the most obvious being the understanding by the characters within the diegesis and the viewer of who Harvey is. The invisible rabbit is part of the autobiography of Bunny Watson and Mike Cutler, Henry and Phoebe Ephron as well as the viewers of *Desk Set*. As Henry writes in *We Thought We Could Do Anything*, "Everyone knows about Harvey now."[52]

Not only did the Ephrons create characters who included the imaginary in their daily lives, Henry saw himself and Phoebe in terms of fictitious characters and imagined settings. In Booth Bay Harbor, Maine, for the filming of *Carousel*, Henry writes of the night the Clambake scene was shot: "That night Phoebe and I sat in the porch like two characters from *Our Town*."[53]

There was a comfortable blending of the everyday and the imaginary in the life and work of Phoebe and Henry, and when Nora began to make films almost all her characters, too, exist in a world where fiction and nonfiction co-exist. Where film informs life and where life is a "combination of things," a melding of fiction and nonfiction.

The assimilation of the imaginary and the real is evident in how Nora wrote and spoke about her life and how her characters live in their worlds. Even with screenplays as disparate as *Silkwood* (1983) and *Bewitched* (2005) there is a shared belief by the characters in something other than the physical. *Silkwood*, written in collaboration with Alice Arlen, a drama based on actual events and a film with a serious subject, is out of the ordinary for Nora but it still characteristic of and identifiable as having a Nora Ephron sensibility.

The establishing moments of *Silkwood* introduce the world of the character Karen Silkwood. A plutonium factory worker, Karen is an ordinary person working with ordinary people. As she arrives for work and takes up her position on the production line, one of her co-workers is telling a story of a faith healer he witnessed at a revival meeting. He describes the woman, dressed in white, looking like an angel, calling for the people to come forward. "This kid came up with an arm that was almost pitch-black from blood poisoning. But that woman held his arm and she prayed over it and it turned pink right in front of your eyes." As he tells his story it is obvious there are skeptics in the room. Wesley (David Strathairn) makes a joke of the story but it is obvious the man relating the incident truly believes what he saw. A little later in the scene another person tells the story of Jean Dixon's appearance on *The Tonight Show Starring Johnny Carson*.[54] Dixon was an astrologer and psychic who, during one appearance on the Carson show, told of how she had predicted an air crash and advised her niece, who was booked on the flight, not to go. The plane did crash, and as another of Karen's work colleagues says of Jean Dixon, "She's got the gift all right."

Within Nora's fictional world of ordinary people the characters hold a variety of beliefs. That people desire and have a willingness to believe in the possibility of something other than the tangible wraps around another story in *Silkwood*. This time the story is the misguided and misinformed belief that radiation is like a sunburn: "Radiation can't hurt you unless you are careless." This is what the manager of the plutonium plant tells new employees on an induction tour.

The accounts of the faith healer and Jean Dixon form part of the trilogy of "far-fetched stories" that includes the supposedly benign nature of radiation exposure. Each story can also stand alone as a comment on people's need and desire to believe in something other than the concrete; the desire to believe in the unexplainable. The Jean Dixon story has even more credibility in terms of reason to believe in the "other" because she was on *The Tonight Show*, and Johnny Carson was a trusted social commentator, and a hero to his loyal viewers. He was the boy from Nebraska.[55] If Jean Dixon appeared on his show and he didn't discredit her, as he had with illusionist Uri Geller, then she must be the genuine article. The faith healer similarly had credibility—the man telling the story was present at the time: "I was there Wesley; I was sitting right there."

The fact that there are characters who consider the possibility of something other than the quantifiable is well within the bounds of *Silkwood*, which is an examination of the untruths told by the government and corporations and an imagining of what can happen if "truths" are called into question. "*Silkwood* may be the most serious work Mr. [Mike] Nichols has yet done in films,"[56] wrote Vincent Canby of the *New York Times*.

A film based on actual events and a film different from the now expected Nora fare, *Silkwood* is an exploration of the concept of truth, a repeated subject in Nora's work. At a forum held in March 1992, Nora was on a panel discussing the "duty of art to history" and "fiction to fact." At the discussion she spoke of the nature of films like *Silkwood*, wherein the objective "is to create 'not the truth' but what it was like—sort of, maybe."[57] Nora was acknowledging that everything is a story, someone's version of events and, in the case of *Silkwood*, a proposition of what might have happened; the telling of a story in order to understand the unaccountable. In other words, Nora again returns to her theoretical position: there is only narrative.

Bewitched is a film so far removed from *Silkwood* that it is hard to imagine they are both the creation of the same mind. Where *Silkwood* was the "critics pick" when it was reviewed in the *New York Times*, *Bewitched* was belittled, as were Nora and Delia as the screenwriters.[58] *Silkwood* is serious, political and controversial. It takes a set of life events and speculates on the possibility that Karen Silkwood was murdered before she could expose the unsafe conditions of a plutonium factory. Conversely, *Bewitched* is seemingly fluff and inconsequential in theme. It is about a television show. However, *Bewitched* is not inconsequential. This film covers the same territory as *Silkwood*, even if the packaging is vastly different. *Bewitched* shares with *Silkwood* Nora's understanding that life is "a combination of things." In *Silkwood*, ordinary people are depicted as living a combination of nonfiction and fiction, while in *Bewitched*, Isabel Bigelow (Nicole Kidman), is a witch, an extraordinary being, who decides she wants to live the life of an ordinary person. With her bid to live a "normal life" what is revealed is that to which she aspires is a fiction. Nora said of *Bewitched*, "Our whole idea for this movie ... was the word 'normal' and not just normal but 'heightened normal,' a fantasy of normal because that's what she wants."[59]

There are multiple levels of reality in *Bewitched*, a tangle of realities. Isabel tries to live her life as she imagines an ordinary person might. Isabel attempts to shape a life by drawing on the representations by which she finds herself surrounded. But just as the lives of the people who work in the plutonium factory are comprised of a combination of things,

Isabel's life is also a combination of things. That is the ultimate understanding. There is no one truth or way of being, there is only a narrative.

Nora's wish for *Bewitched* was that, after viewing the film, people "may go off from this movie and have a little conversation about some of the levels of reality that are in it 'cause there are several."[60] There is no clear division of one level of reality from another—reality is a construct operating on every level in this work. Isabel, the witch, wants to be "normal" so she finds herself a normal house—pretty and cute and perfect—but hardly normal for most people. She also procures her house through the use of witchcraft. (Life isn't one thing or another!) Isabel then heads to Bed, Bath and More to buy linens. The store is of mammoth proportions, a universe unto itself. Shopping there is akin to believing your home will become the "Ikea" home; an alternate reality which seems a possibility when you are immersed in the experience of that store with its stylishly constructed rooms.

In a series of "hats on hats,"[61] the realities at work in *Bewitched* become a confusion of and a complex mingling of understandings about the narratives which underpin contemporary Western culture. Stories are told to create order out of confusion, the otherwise seemingly arbitrary nature of life. *Bewitched* is a film about the making of a television program—television being one of the most influential and significant vehicles for story-telling in contemporary culture. The show being made is a remake of the actual 1960s television series of the same name. *Bewitched* is a construct, a film, about the construction of a construct, the television series. During the process of reconstructing the construct, the actors lose themselves in the multiple realities of the television program. Isabel is a witch trying to live a human life, who, much to her surprise, is "discovered" and cast as the witch Samantha Stevens (who was played by Elizabeth Montgomery). Samantha is also a witch trying to live without resorting to magic. Isabel is unaware of Samantha or the television show when she moves to contemporary Los Angeles.

In *Bewitched* the film, veteran actress Iris Symthson (Shirley MacLaine),[62] cast in the role of Endora, (originally portrayed by Agnes Moorhead), Samantha's disapproving witch mother, reveals herself to be, like Isabel, a witch in "real life." Jack Wyatt (Will Ferrell), is the actor playing Samantha's mortal husband, Darrin, (essayed in the series by, consecutively, Dick York and Dick Sergeant). Two other memorable characters from the original series were featured: Uncle Arthur (Steve Carell, first played by Paul Lynde), and Aunt Clara (Carole Shelley, originally played by Marion Lorne). Characters from the fictional world of the 1960s television series live among the "real people" who are actors cast in the roles of the characters from the television series. This is an illustration of Nora's belief that "films and television become part of autobiography."

To further compound the levels of reality in operation in *Bewitched*, when the actor Jack Wyatt and the witch Isabel Bigelow fall in love they can only express themselves, not in their "real world," but in the constructed world of the television set. In a moment which recalls the scene from *Singin' in the Rain* (1952) in which Don Lockwood (Gene Kelly) declares his love for Cathy Selden (Debbie Reynolds) on the sound stage, Jack and Isabel declare their love on the *Bewitched* sound stage.

Singin' in the Rain, like *Bewitched*, examines the multiple levels of reality which operate in the illusion of the construct that is a Hollywood film. *Singin' in the Rain* operates within the conventions of the industry's own dismissiveness of film as "a complex aesthetic object."[63] Richard Maltby's statement in relation to *Singin' in the Rain*: "What appears on one level to be banal and conventional—the love story between two stars—is on another intricately complex"[64] is as applicable to *Bewitched*.

Bewitched has a depth and complexity only accessible when Nora's world view is understood. The film is a contemplation of the multiple narratives which inform daily life. It is also a contemplation of the role of film as informer and arbiter of cultural norms and an illustration of Nora's belief that there is no fiction or nonfiction, only narrative. Nora's many characters lead lives in which nonfiction and fiction, or the corporeal and the imagined, co-exist comfortably. Consider Dorothy Winters (Andie MacDowell) and Frank Quinlan (William Hurt), who are brought together by a big, untidy, cigarette-smoking, sugar-eating angel named Michael (John Travolta) in *Michael* (1995). Throughout the film, both Frank and Dorothy continue to be skeptical about the authenticity of Michael's claim that he is an angel, while their colleague, Huey Driscoll (Robert Pastorelli), accepts Michael as an angel without qualification, although he can't bring himself to tell his wife of his experience. After Michael has left, there is still an imprint of him on their lives. Dorothy and Frank don't know what to believe but still chase the possibility of Michael, which is what finally brings them together.

Nora's contemplation of the "narrative" and multiple levels of reality in life is not always so complex as it is in *Bewitched* and *Michael*. Sam Baldwin (the protagonist of *Sleepless in Seattle*) has conversations with his dead wife, Maggie (Carey Lowell), imagining her to be in the room, talking with him. Maggie does not appear ghost-like in the film; her presence is solid. She is sitting at the end of the lounge, talking to Sam. Implicit in the scene is the realness of the imagined. *You've Got Mail* and *Julie and Julia* both have moments when characters have conversations and relationships with those not physically present. In *You've Got Mail*, Kathleen and Birdie have conversations with Kathleen's mother, Cecilia, who had died years before; Julie Powell (Amy Adams) has conversations with and imagines a relationship with Julia Child (Meryl Streep), the renowned chef she admires but has never met. In both instances, the relationships are imagined but are no less diminished than any other relationships the characters in the respective films might have.

A fictionalized depiction of Nora's own life can be accessed through her novel *Heartburn* and her character, Rachel Samstat. In the film version, many of Rachel's traits and behaviors are ascribed to other characters but, essentially, the film illustrates the nature of Rachel/Nora's life.

In *Heartburn*, films are part of the biography of Nora's characters just as fictional characters are part of her autobiography. The scene in which Rachel goes into labor with her first child opens as Arthur (Richard Masur) and Mark (Jack Nicholson) are listing female actors they find attractive: Veronica Lake, Janet Leigh, Rita Hayworth, Ava Gardner and Ann Blyth. When Arthur names Ann Blyth the reaction from the others prompts him to respond, "What can I tell you? I have always had a thing for Ann Blyth." So readily a part of the lives of these men are these women—women who are constructs; nothing more than "point-in-time" images from films or magazines, in reality either dead or much older than the men discussing them. The image the men hold of these women is not based in reality but that of the movie star, the fantasy, the construct. Arthur and Mark bring the dream of these women into their respective lives.

Rachel herself has a rich fantasy life. In Nora's book, Rachel imagines herself as being somewhat between an "Imogene Coca or an Elaine May."[65] She entertained fantasies about strangers on trains.[66] She imagines the funeral of her first husband once she hated him; what she might wear, whom she might flirt with.[67] She fantasizes about life with the detective who interviewed her after her therapy group was robbed.[68] Rachel's perception of how the police might behave when they come to your home is based on many years of watching *Dragnet* on television.[69] Rachel also looks for "signs." When her engagement ring was returned to her after it had been stolen, the stone was loose. Rachel saw it as a "sign" that something was wrong. When she told Mark of the robbery he glared at her—another sign.[70] Rachel, searching for evidence of Mark's infidelity, identified herself as a character from a trashy novel.[71] Rachel's life, just like Nora's, is an amalgam of fiction and nonfiction, a narrative.

While the detail of Rachel/Nora's life did not survive the transition from book to film, the essence of who Rachel is and where she comes from remains. The night prior to her father's return to his New York apartment, the apartment Rachel is staying in during her separation from Mark, she finds herself on television, incorporated into the "Arm-chair Theatre"–type television show she is watching. As Rachel eats her comfort food, mashed potatoes, the television show begins. As Rachel watches, the moderator (John Wood) provides a catch up on Rachel's situation to this point, concluding with: "Rachel closes her weary eyes and sobs herself to sleep." This is where the television show concludes and the camera reveals Rachel, who has indeed cried herself to sleep. There is no joke, no "What's going on?" look on Rachel's face. Nor is there any indication that the scene was a dream. It was the exterior and interior life of Rachel in operation, co-existing, comfortable; a rich and fully formed biography.

Later, when Rachel has returned to her life with Mark in Washington, the British moderator visits her again on television to provide an update of her situation. From his television armchair, he begins: "Alone in the still unfinished house in Washington, Rachel has turned on the television set. And as she switches channels everything she sees seems to be an echo of her own dilemma."

The penultimate scene, when Rachel puts a Key lime pie in Mark's face, is the moment where the dream and the reality of her relationship meet. Even though the reality of the situation does nor meld with the dream, the dream is not vanquished. Rachel comes to realize the dream of her marriage to Mark did not match the reality, so, rather than stay in a reality which is unbearable, she chooses to leave and dream another dream.

Rachel's world is one where the living and the imaginary simply co-exist. Her exterior and her interior lives together comprise her biography. Rachel is a fictionalized Nora, and Nora is the creator of Rachel and all her other characters; characters whose lives are "a combination of things," a narrative. When Sally tells Harry, "I have just as much a dark side as the next person,"[72] Harry scoffs. In his mind, *he* is the deep one; Sally is bright and perky—not capable of deep emotion. Nora Ephron is also thought of as bright, perky, funny, a maker of romantic comedies, not capable of deep thought. But Nora Ephron's style should not be confused with its content. To hold a view of the world where "there is only narrative" is a deeply considered view of life, a view which reflects her childhood. A childhood controlled by the story; a childhood so immersed in the telling of stories, whatever their purpose, that as an adult Nora's view of the world as reflected in her work verges on the absurdist—particularly demonstrated in *Cookie, Mixed Nuts, My Blue Heaven* and *Bewitched*, but present in even the most ordinary of lives.

5

Julie and Julia

*Fans are going to see this as the essential
Nora Ephron movie.*—Amy Pascal[1]
The cookbooks I write do well.—Rachel Samstat[2]

Julie and Julia is the quintessential Nora Ephron film. It is a Hollywood film with mainstream appeal and it was a financial, commercial and critical success.[3] The film is also personal and idiosyncratic. Nora's work has been identified as being informed by the life and work of her parents—informed by the experience of being their child and growing up in their home. Her work has been identified as being about her: her life and interests. It has been demonstrated how Nora's work operates as a vehicle to process the experiences of her life. It has further been identified that Nora uses the work of others to construct a framework for the discussion of themes and subjects which are of interest to her: relationships, technology, communication, food, the role of literature in determining cultural norms as well as to chronicle the culture to which she belonged. Nora's world view—there is only narrative—is consistent across her work, which is informed by her philosophical position. The focus of this final chapter—a case study—is to demonstrate that this mainstream success, Nora's final film, contains all the characteristic traits of Nora's work identified in the previous chapters. The overarching credo of Nora's work, consistent throughout is that "everything is copy." *Julie and Julia* is an illustration of that assertion.

    Julie and Julia is ostensibly a biopic about the famous mid–20th-century American cook Julia Child and the contemporary blogger and recreational cook Julie Powell. Powell, a New Yorker, became known for her project to cook her way through the entire Julia Child recipe book *Mastering the Art of French Cooking* (Beck, Bertholle, and Child) over a twelve-month period, while at the same time writing a blog about her experiences as she attempted the task. Powell later wrote a book about her year.

Julie and Julia is, however, much more than a biopic. Nora's work is characterized by her ability to manipulate the filmic form to produce a commercially viable project which, at the same time, is both unique and personal. *Julie and Julia* is one such film.[4] Of *Julie and Julia*, Nora said: "There is nothing autobiographical here. I could practically footnote every scene." However, in the same statement, Nora, when speaking about filmmaking in general, said, "You hope that you make movies that feel personal to you." This is a very personal film.

Responding to her claim that there is nothing autobiographical in *Julie and Julia*, Mike Nichols, who directed *Heartburn* and counted Nora as a close friend, didn't accept her statement. "Nora is stronger, funnier, sexier than ever," he said. "You do feel like this movie is plugged into the life she's living."[5] When he was responding to her claim, Mike Nichols, along with many of Nora's friends and associates, did not know that at the time she was making *Julie and Julia* Nora knew she was terminally ill, and being "plugged into the life she was living" was, in fact, part of the story, the pretending, the denial of that which was happening elsewhere in her life, to her life. In retrospect, Nora's last film can be read as her swan song; an ode to the things important to her and that defined her life. *Julie and Julia* is the Nora Ephron film about Nora Ephron.

Nora's belief that biography is composed of both the events of living and the imagined; that life is a combination of things, is at the heart of this film. *Julie and Julia* is the story of an imagined relationship. It was not the first time Nora had broached the subject of imaginary relationships. As previously discussed, there had been references to the idea of the role of the imaginary in life in much of her work, including her play *Imaginary Friends*, which speculates on an imagined relationship between Mary McCarthy and Lillian Hellman; however, Nora had not successfully foregrounded the idea until *Julie and Julia*.

Most pertinent to understanding the film is the understanding that the relationship between Julia and Nora was entirely imagined. Nora and her characters, Rachel Samstat and Julie Powell, all have a relationship with Julia Child. The relationship Nora had was not just one of subject (Julia Child) and writer (Nora Ephron) or of cookbook writer

(Julia Child) and cook (Nora). The defining characteristic of Nora and Julia Child's relationship was that it was personal and entirely make-believe just as the relationship Julie Powell has with Julia Child is personal and imagined. That the relationship is imagined does not diminish its importance at all; it is indeed its most important characteristic. Julia Child becomes part of Julie Powell's biography in *Julie and Julia* as she has in the life of the person Julie Powell.[6] Nora said, "I do think you have an amazing imaginary relationship with people whose books you cook from if you're a cook like me."[7] Julie (the character), in voice-over says, "And as I cook it, I almost feel as if Julia and I are communicating over space and time on a deep, spiritual, mystical level."[8] Nora wrote of her imaginary conversations with Julia Child, "Julia was nicer and more forgiving—she was by then on television and famous for dropping food, picking it up and throwing it right back into the pan."[9]

The central significant relationship of the film, that which exists between the two cooks, is not the only level of imagining in *Julie and Julia*. The story is Nora's imagining of the relationship between Julia Child and Julie Powell, and Nora's interpretation of both Child and Powell's lives as well as how Powell might have imagined Child's life to be. Consequently, the film is a combination of imaginings, the telling of a story built upon a story upon a story.

Julie and Julia is the embodiment of Nora's statement, "You hope that you make movies that feel personal to you," and refutes her claim that there is no autobiographical material in this film. The film is personal and idiosyncratic, recalling and continuing the processing of her life. It is identifiable as the work of Nora Ephron because it has the Ephron sensibility. The film "is plugged into the life she's living," and life, by her own definition, is a combination of things and that combination of things is informed by the experience of growing up in the Ephron family.

The subjects of the film are, like Nora, unusual women—women at odds with conventional expectations. As was her final collection of essays *I Remember Nothing*, *Julie and Julia* is a précis of her life. The other subjects of the film—writing, food, relationships, communication (both in terms of technological advance and source of information)—are Nora's motif subjects. Nora's continued examination of her relationship with and understanding of her mother, Phoebe, which is beautifully and carefully embedded in her story of the two cooks, is a prominent theme of her work as is her ongoing chronicle of the world around her. The essence of *Julie and Julia* is Nora Ephron and consequently only Nora, with her distinct personality, world view and the unique circumstances of her life, could have written and directed *Julie and Julia*.

Nora's ability to manipulate the filmic form in order to create a commercially viable product which is also personal to her is directly related to her experience as a child of the old Hollywood and her exposure to the industry, her experience of the industry and her understanding of the industry. Ultimately, it is the result of Nora's experience of growing up in the Ephron family. That Nora made mainstream films is a defining characteristic of her work, but making mainstream Hollywood films was not really a matter of choice for Nora; rather, it is the result of the expectation of someone who spent her childhood immersed in Hollywood filmmaking. As stated in Chapter 1, Nora went into the family business because it is what she knew.

Nora, working in the contemporary film industry, created works with universal appeal which, at their core, are about her life and experiences. That is the poetic conceit of her work. She, at some level, is the subject of all of her work, never more so than with *Heartburn, This Is My Life* and this, her last film. The point of difference between the two previous films and this one being that the two earlier films were overtly about her life but *Julie and Julia* is extremely personal in a covert way. It is expected that, as the author of her written work, Nora's life experiences and opinions are the subject of the piece, but there is not the same expectation of her film work. Generally, Nora Ephron, credited as director or screenwriter, denotes an expectation of romantic comedy or other lightweight fare. There is little recognition that her films will reflect her life experience and her world view in the way they do.

Nora made a career for herself because of her ability to share her stories and experiences with others in a voice that resonates with her audience. In part, her success was dependent on her historical time— New Journalism, the Women's Movement and the emergence of auteur theory[10]—but, ultimately, it is her skill as a storyteller that brought her success.

Julie and Julia is a work in line with the Ephron family oeuvre. It is an "intellectual, word driven, film with strong female characters"[11] in the style of Nora's other works. Works which are, in turn, influenced by the work of her parents and, before that, the style of New York theatre of the 1930s and '40s, where Phoebe and Henry learned their craft. *Julie and Julia*, in line with the expectation of the Ephron oeuvre, is also humorous. Humor is intertwined with Nora's world view and, as such, serves a dual purpose in her work as it did in Henry and Phoebe's work. Comedy makes a story entertaining, and therefore, palatable,[12] and comedy creates the space for contemplation of the serious without it being overwhelming.[13] This is very much in keeping with the Ephron family tradition. Turning a sad story into humor was a requirement of living in the Ephron family and a nightly ritual at the family dining table.

From early in her career as a journalist and essayist, Nora has written about herself and her interests. Nora writes in the introduction to her collection of essays *Wallflower at the Orgy* that she writes about "what I like to think of as frivolous things. Fashion, trashy books, show business, food."[14] She calls these subjects "Popular Culture" and says she likes writing about them so much "that I hate to think they have to be justified in this way—or at least I'm sorry if they do."[15] Nora also provides a context for her interest in these subjects. She writes of an incident when, as she was being interviewed on radio about an essay she had written on Helen Gurley Brown, the other guest on the program, a folk singer, interrupted her to protest the frivolity of the subject when the Vietnam War was being waged. Nora responded by saying that she cares and protests against the war in Vietnam, but "much of my life goes irrelevantly on, in spite of larger events. I suppose that has something to do with my hopelessly midcult nature, and something to do with my Hollywood childhood."[16] For Nora, nothing changed between 1970, when she wrote the introduction to *Wallflower at the Orgy*, and 2009 when *Julie and Julia* was released. Frivolous things, aspects of Popular Culture, are played out against a background of larger events in her last film.

The larger events, the background against which the story of *Julie and Julia* is told, is one of unimaginable devastation and rebuilding. The background provides a chronicle of the times in which the film is set: post–9/11 New York and post–Second World War France. *Julie and Julia* begins with the arrival of Julia (Meryl Streep) and Paul Child (Stanley Tucci) in France, in 1948. Nora, in making the film, was diligent to ensure the larger events against which her story is told are accurately depicted and clearly in evidence. One example involves the visual recreation of postwar conditions in France. The external shots of the building used as the façade of a restaurant in Rouen needed to be just dirty enough to be authentically postwar. Watching the film, the viewer is likely to be unaware of this small production detail but Nora, insisting that it be just right, repeatedly digitally altered the degree of griminess of the external walls until she was satisfied because "it bothered me."[17] Nora was determined to ensure the larger events were evident and authentically reproduced as the backdrop against which her story is played out—even if no one noticed. She wanted to make sure her chronicle of the time was authentic in her documentation of it.

Nora's attention to the detail of her social and historical chronicle is again highlighted in the scene where Paul and Julia are sitting, working, in their Paris apartment. Both are wearing Chinese jackets. The jackets—out of character for two Americans living in France—allude to the Childs' association with China and also suggest the austere nature of postwar living conditions in France. The jackets were worn by Paul and Julia not for purposes of fashion, but to keep themselves warm in their frequently unheated apartment—a common condition of postwar Paris. The Chinese connection is picked up by Nora later in the film and brought back into focus. In 1955, just after the height of the McCarthy years, Paul Child was investigated by the United States Information Agency, Office of Security.[18] There is some suggestion that Paul and Julia Child were spies because of their time in China and their opposition to Senator Joseph McCarthy. Paul Child was considered to be a possible security risk and, consequently, investigated and interrogated. Nora acknowledges the suggestion that the Childs had been spies when, at a Valentine's Day dinner party, she has a dinner guest ask, "Were you spies?" to which Paul responds, "*Us*? No." But the question of their being spies is left to linger in the mind of the viewer when a second dinner guest queries Paul's response with, "You were in the Office of Strategic Services and you *weren't* spies?" Julia responds, on her own behalf, "I was only a file clerk,"[19] leaving open the question: what was Paul doing? The McCarthy era and the suggestion that the Childs may have been involved in espionage during their time in China inform not only the historical background against which the story of Julia Child is told but also the shaping of postwar life.

The larger event against which the parallel story of Julie Powell is told is one that affects both Julie Powell and Nora deeply. In her essay "Where I Live," Nora writes:

I live in New York City. I could never live anywhere else. The events of September 11 forced me to confront the fact that no matter what, I live here and always will.[20]

New York, in the aftermath of September 11, 2001, is the larger event, the catastrophic event against which the story of Julie Powell plays out. New York—more specifically, Queens where Julie Powell lives, and Manhattan where she works—is not depicted as the center of major technological change as it was in Henry and Phoebe's *Desk Set*, nor is it the beautiful and twinklingly lit wonder of the New York of *You've Got Mail*. In contrast, Nora's New York of *Julie and Julia* is a bleak and sad place, recovering from a devastating and traumatic assault.

Nora describes the location of the Powell's new home into which they are moving at the start of the film, as "a bleak area in Queens near the Triborough Bridge." The building where they are to live is "a rundown, two-story building," and their home "a decrepit loft."[21] To get to their new home, the Powells drive through a cityscape of abandoned, derelict buildings—scenes reminiscent of the abandoned and destroyed cityscapes of the "Pruitt Igoe" sequence of *Koyaanisqatsi* (1983).[22] In none other of her films does Nora depict New York is such a way. The world of New York in 2002, in *Julie and Julia*, was one of "life out of balance." *Koyaanisqatsi,* the title of Godfrey Reggio's film, is a Hopi Indian word which translates as "life out of balance." The film has been described as an apocalyptic vision of the collision of two different worlds.[23] *Julie and Julia* was set against a backdrop of the collision of two worlds; the first being Europe in the aftermath of the Second World War, and the second, a collision by which Nora was deeply affected, the assault on her home city by terrorists.

Not only does Julie Powell (Amy Adams) live in an area that is rundown and desolate, she is shown walking through a barren, littered, deserted streetscape on a hot summer's morning to the train station crowded with people who, like her, are hot and miserable—she works in a desolate and desperate place as well. After traveling in a crowded train, Julie walks to the Lower Manhattan Development Corporation[24] building, located at Ground Zero. She works there, taking calls from people affected by 9/11. To get to her small cubicle in her crowded office she must walk past "yellow trucks, excavators, firemen, trucks taking debris away."[25] After walking past the walls of tributes, smaller than they were just after the bombing but still visible, she spends her day listening to the overwhelming stories of people affected by the bombing of the twin towers. So immense is the catastrophe that Nora depicts Julie as being unable to have any control over her world. Julie is incapable of providing the help her callers are seeking: "Do you have any power?" asks a man on the phone.

Julie replies, "No."

This vision of New York, this vision of a city struggling in the aftermath of a devastating assault, is one which can get lost in the narrative of *Julie and Julia*. Nora does not dwell on the overwhelming in life. The scenes of New York, broken and decaying, fall away in order to tell the personal story of the woman who cooks her way through the Julia Child cookbook. But in the same way the statue of Prometheus defines the world of *Desk Set*, and leafy streets, lovely brownstone buildings and the quaint and quirky shops of the Upper West Side defines the world of *You've Got Mail*, the hot miserable drudgery of people living in the shadow of September 11 defines the world of *Julie and Julia*.

Julie Powell is funny and sad and compassionate and, ultimately, rendered helpless by her life as a would-be writer and as a New Yorker after September 11. But, as Nora wrote in 1970, life goes irrelevantly on despite the larger events. Julie Powell had to find a way to survive and she did so with her cooking project. Nora also had to find a way to personally survive the devastation of September 11, and she did what she has always done. She processed the events of her life in her work. It is her chronicle of the events of her time and society and it is her homage to a city she loves, her home, as it responds to the devastation of attack. In *Julie and Julia*, New York responds to the assault in the same way Nora has always responded to adversity—find a way through it, get on with it and live a life largely irrelevant to the larger events that are taking place around you. Everyone is living with the hole that is Ground Zero, rebuilding their lives and voicing their opinion about what is happening, including a man on the phone who complains to Julie, "I don't like the plan for the memorial that was in this morning's *Times*," to which Julie replies, "I don't like the plan either."[26]

Set against a background of devastation and rebuilding, each of the two women at the center of Nora's story is trying to find something that defines who she is, something that provides meaning to her life. The thing they both find is cooking and writing. Food is one of the frivolous subjects about which Nora liked to write, and Nora is another woman known for her ability as a cook and a writer. She was also someone for whom cooking provided an emotional anchor. As a cook, Nora said of herself, "I'm not a serious cook—I'm a feeder."[27] And she wrote of herself when she writes of her alter ego, Rachel Samstat, in *Heartburn*: "Rachel Samstat, she's bright, she's funny *and she can cook*."[28] When asked what she considered her greatest achievement, Nora responded, "My ability to cook dinner for a large number of people in a short time."[29] As a director, Nora claimed "that filet of sole is my proudest achievement."[30] That filet of sole is the shot of the fish being presented to Julia Child in the restaurant in Rouen, where she was transported for the first time by the experience of eating French food. Of the regrets in her life, Nora cites as significant not having done the catering herself for her wedding to Nick Pileggi.[31] There is no question that food and writing are the subjects connecting Julie Powell, Julia Child and Nora Ephron and, in doing so, define *Julie and Julia* as a film by and about Nora Ephron.

Food is more than just a subject Nora liked to write about, and it is more than one of her defining personal traits. Most significantly, it is food which is the link to her childhood, her mother, her world view and her work. Much of Nora's work has, in one way or another, involved food. Nora wrote about particular foods,[32] recipes,[33] the food establishment,[34] food magazines,[35] food as biography,[36] food conventions,[37] food named after her[38] and, ultimately, she used her work to give herself another life as a food writer. As Rachel Samstat, Nora can say of herself, "I had a career as a food person."[39]

In her films food operated as an identifier of Nora's characters and is a recurring motif in her work. It links her life to her work and her characters and identifies the work as that of Nora Ephron, regardless of the form of the piece. Sally (*When Harry Met Sally*) is defined by the way she orders food. Nora was equally pedantic about what food she would order and how it should be served. In the film *Michael* there is an ode to pies. Dorothy (Andie MacDowell) sings her song about pie to the others at her table as they all eat pie. Nora notes in her essay "What I Will Miss,"—her list of things she will miss when she is dead—that she will miss pie.[40]

Nora's love of food stems from her childhood. As previously discussed, the incorporation of food references or the use of food as plot devices is a defining characteristic of Phoebe and Henry's work. Nora slyly references her parents' screenplay for *Desk Set* when she devotes a moment in *Julie and Julia* to Julia Child's dessert Floating Island.[41]

Food was integral to Nora's emotional well-being as much as it is for the two women at the center of *Julie and Julia*. It was not just the larger events that were beyond the control of the two women which were difficult, so too were their respective personal lives at the time that they both discovered food. Julia asks her husband, Paul, as they enjoy a meal together, "But shouldn't I find something to do? None of the wives here do anything, but that's not for me, it's just not me."[42] When Paul asks Julia what it is she likes to do, she responds without hesitation, "Eat. I like to eat."[43] As Julia searches for "something to do," the idea of learning to cook becomes more and more appealing until she finally enrolls in the Cordon Bleu school and, consequently, becomes an expert in French cooking. Cooking defined Julia Child's life and gave it meaning. Through the pursuit of her passion she "discovered I was fearless."[44]

In the same way that Julia Child found herself through her cooking, Nora's character Julie Powell also believes food saved her. At her thirtieth birthday celebration, Julie tells her husband, Eric (Chris Messina), and her birthday guests, "I thought it was going to be terrible. But ... thanks to Julia, it feels like I'm going to get through."[45] And, later, she says of herself and Julia Child: "Both of us were lost, and both of us were saved by food in some way or other."[46]

Nora and Julie Powell are at one in their experience of food as the provider of emotional security. As opposed to the obsession and passion Julia Child had for her work and not denying the emotional stability her work gave her, Nora and Julie share a different perspective on the role food and cooking play in their respective lives. In fact, in this respect Nora's character Julie Powell is no longer Nora's fictional representation of the person Julie Powell but rather her own voice when she has Julie say of cooking:

> You know what I love about cooking? I love that after a day where nothing is sure ... you can come home and absolutely know that if you add egg yolks to chocolate and sugar and milk, it will get thick. It is such a comfort.[47]

Rachel Samstat, Nora's alter ego, says of cooking, "It is totally mindless," and more pertinently:

> What I love about cooking is that, after a hard day, there is something comforting about the fact that if you melt butter and add flour then hot stock,

it will get thick! It is a sure thing! It's a sure thing in a world where nothing is sure.[48]

And Nora wrote in her 1973 essay, "Baking Off":

I don't happen to think that cooking is very creative—what interests me about it is, on the contrary, its utter mindlessness and mathematical certainty. "Cooking is very relaxing"—it's my bromide.[49]

Cooking was important in Nora's life, but not the all-consuming passion it was for Julia Child. As Nora said, "As much as I love food, food is not all I do."[50] Cooking was an escape from the uncertainty of life for Nora and her fictional women. It was relaxing, emotionally fortifying and certain when most other aspects of life weren't. It is a belief that Nora long held.

Food and the emotional security Nora found in cooking stems from her association of food with love and her life as a child growing up in the Ephron family. There is much in her work which would suggest that, for Nora, food operated as a way to define relationships and express love. Given that Phoebe could be very difficult, demanding and withholding emotionally with her daughters, food, along with books, was a positive in Nora's early relationship with her mother. Phoebe ensured her children had good food, even if she didn't cook it herself, and she gave Nora her first cookbook. The experience of the family dinner table: "The plates were heated and there were butterballs made with wooden paddles. There was an appetizer, a main course and dessert,"[51] and the telling of funny stories and stimulating discussion was an aspect of Nora's childhood she loved, remembered with unwavering fondness.

However, as with everything to do with her mother, Nora also reflected that food played another less positive role in her mother's life. Food, or, more precisely, the presentation of food, was an indicator of status, was one of the ways in which Nora's mother showed herself to be superior to other women: "a cut above the other mothers," even "a cut above other career women."[52] Not only did Phoebe have a career when most other women didn't, she had a husband and children, she dressed beautifully and "she served delicious food" which, as Nora writes, was "another way she liked to rub it in."[53]

That love and food should be connected in Nora's mind is only to be expected when she had internalized the connection between food and the love of her mother and the experience of food and good times from when she was a child. As an adult, Nora used food to recreate the emotional memory of her childhood. She "like[d] to cook so that people will sit at a table and you bring out all these things and everybody can talk."[54]

Julie and Julia is part of Nora's continued and extended contemplation of the connection between food and love. Earlier, by the time Nora had written *Heartburn*, she could say, as Rachel could say, "I've written about food and marriage dozens of times."[55] After Rachel and Mark (*Heartburn*) have sex for the first time, "Rachel brings him spaghetti carbonara in bed at 4 a.m.,"[56] and, later, food marks the end of Rachel and Mark's marriage. Rachel puts a Key lime pie in Mark's face— without the expected humor—just prior to her leaving him and their marriage. In *Sleepless in Seattle* the sharing of food is an integral part of the ritual of modern culture and the rituals associated with the declaration of love. Sam and his sister Suzy (Rita Wilson) and her husband, Greg (Victor Garber), have a funny and animated discussion about film over a meal; Annie and Walter (Bill Pullman) announce their engagement at Christmas Dinner; and Annie's father, Cliff (Kevin O'Morrison), outlines the menu for their wedding—salmon and strawberries. In *This Is My Life*, Dottie cooks flapjacks in the shape of the letters *E* and *O* for her daughters, Erica and Opal; an act of love. Nora wrote in *Heartburn*: "I'm very smart about how complicated things get when food and love become hopelessly tangled," and many years later defined the stresses on the marriage of Julie and Eric Powell (*Julie and Julia*) in terms of food—"too much food, not enough sex."[57] In the course of the film, Eric and Julie separate. To console herself, Julie begins to cook and, later, Eric, having decided he wants to come back to the marriage, indicates his decision to Julie when he asks her, "What's for dinner?"[58]

Nora's film work has always involved the contemplation of the romantic relationship, and not just in terms of food. It is another part of her inheritance and another marker that this is an Ephron film. Love, marriage and divorce are subjects which were of interest to her parents. They, like Nora, wrote screenplays for romantic comedies, and Henry writes that he and Phoebe would often "talk about love and marriage, and divorce among our friends."[59] Not detracting from the central relationship of *Julie and Julia*, that between Julie Powell and her imagined friend Julia Child and their connection through cooking, Nora also explores the principal relationships in the lives of these two women.

While still very much in the vein of her previous works, with its association of food and love, *Julie and Julia* marks a significant shift in Nora's portrayal of romantic relationships. A change that is not only appropriate to the narrative—Paul and Julia Child were, by all accounts, happy in their marriage—but also reflective of Nora's personal situation.

Nora had two failed marriages prior to her marriage to journalist Nick Pileggi. Both her previous husbands, Dan Greenburg and Carl Bernstein, were unfaithful. Nora's experience of marriage even before her own was one of unfaithful men. Nora's grandfather and father were both unfaithful to their respective wives. In her work, Nora's women did not have successful relationships. In *Michael* (1996) Dorothy (Andie MacDowell) and Frank (William Hurt), the ersatz work colleagues and potential romantic comedy couple, are both very wary of falling in love. Frank is a broken man, shattered by the death of his wife, and Dorothy, having had a succession of bad relationships, has written a song about her failed romances. Even in Nora's most famous romantic comedies, *When Harry Met Sally, Sleepless in Seattle* and *You've Got Mail,* each woman walks away from a ho-hum relationship with the potential for a new, lasting union. It is only in Rob Reiner's conclusion to *When Harry Met Sally* that the couple make a commitment to each other and, then, it is Harry declaring his love for Sally. Sally discusses the wedding and the wedding cake.

But in *Julie and Julia,* love is different. Julia and Paul Child's relationship is solid, companionable and supportive, and Julie and Eric Powell's relationship, although at times rocky, is again drawn as solid and settled. Ariel Levy attributes the change in Nora's depiction of marriage to her having "a different point of reference now."[60] Levy points out that, in the past, Nora "used to make a lot of jokes about [men] not being able to keep it in their pants. She cites *Heartburn* and *Mixed Nuts* as two examples containing such jokes. In *Heartburn* Rachel Samstat writes of her husband Mark Feldman "that he was capable of having sex with a venetian blind"; in *Mixed Nuts*, Mrs. Munchnik (Madeline Kahn) says, "Men are capable of having sex with a tree."[61] *Julie and Julia* is quite different. Both women are happily married, even though there are moments of conflict and issues to be dealt with in each relationship. Julie and Eric separate briefly, and Julia and Paul are unable to have children (an aspect of their marriage that distresses Julia particularly), but, in the film's narrative, both couples remain secure in their marriages. Julie sees similarities between her relationship with Eric and Julia's with Paul when she says, "A really nice guy married her; a really nice guy married me."[62] This similarity is not confined to the relationships of the film's narrative. Since 1987 when they married, and for the years before when they lived together, Nora was also with a "famously nice guy."[63] Levy noted (in 2009) that Nora and Nick Pileggi had been together for twenty-six years and quotes Nora's son Jacob Bernstein as saying, "I have never seen them have a fight."[64] Levy was not the only one to comment on the very different circumstances of Nora's third marriage. Leslie Bennetts also comments on the stability, security and happiness Nora found in her last marriage.[65] The articles, written 17 years apart, confirm the different experience of marriage Nora found with Nick Pileggi. This is reflected in *Julie and Julia.*

As stated earlier, Julia Child was part of Nora's life, her biography, long before *Julie and Julia.* Julia Child was one of Nora's imaginary friends. She was as much an integral part of Nora's life as she is of Nora's character Julie Powell. She played a pivotal role in providing the emotional security both Julie Powell and Nora were seeking through their cooking at particular times in their respective lives.

With *Julie and Julia,* Nora demonstrates how the imagined in life is as important as the corporal in informing and shaping biography. By allowing her character Julie to have an imagined relationship Nora is highlighting how much a part of the everyday the imagined is.

Nora's own long and imagined relationship with Julia Child is well documented. When Nora made a film about the celebrity cook Julia Child she was making a film about an aspect of her own life, a film about herself. Nora, in her essay "Serial Monogamy: A Memoir," charts the course of her adult life in terms of cooks, cookbooks and recipes. The title of the essay is suggestive of the connection between food and love, or a sexual liaison. Of the time of her move to New York to become a journalist in 1962, Nora writes: "Just before I'd moved to New York, two historic events had occurred: The birth control pill had been invented and the first Julia Child cookbook was published."[66] Such was the connection between sex and cooking for Nora: the pill gave women sexual freedom, and Julia Child's cookbook liberated the contemporary American cook from the strictures of cooking tradition.

As Nora writes of the time and the coincidence of the contraceptive

143

pill and Julia Child's cookbook: "As a result, everyone was having sex, and when the sex was over, you cooked something."[67] "Serial Monogamy" was written around the time Nora was working on *Julie and Julia*. Nora references her essay indirectly in the director's commentary on the DVD version of *Julie and Julia*.[68] Like so much of Nora's work, rather than the essay and the film being part of the same marketing package, it is more likely that "Serial Monogamy" and *Julie and Julia* are part of the ongoing process of Nora documenting her life and writing and making films about things that interest her. Between Child's cookbook and the contraceptive pill becoming part of American women's lives in the early 1960s, and the making of *Julie and Julia* in 2002, Rachel had sex with Mark and then made spaghetti!

Julia Child became part of Nora's life and work. Of living alone in New York in the mid–1960s, Nora wrote that she would cook an entire meal for herself from one of her cookbooks and, as she ate her meal for four, it made her feel "brave and plucky."[69] It made her feel that she "wasn't one of those lonely women who sat home with a pathetic container of yoghurt."[70] At times it was Julia Child who kept Nora company. "I cooked ... at least half the recipes in the first Julia [cookbook] and as I cooked, I had imaginary conversations with them both [Child and cookbook author Michael Field]."[71] Nora's alter ego, Rachel Samstat, has more than a passing interest in Julia Child. She imagines herself as the host of a public television cooking show as being somewhere between "a middle brow Julia Child crossed with a high brow Dinah Shore."[72] And Rachel, like Nora and Julie, would "pick a recipe from Michael Field or Julia Child and shop on the way home and spend the first part of the evening painstakingly mastering whatever dish I had chosen."[73] Julia Child was as much part of Rachel's personal life as she was her professional life. Julia was there when Rachel and Mark (Nora and Carl) broke up before they were married: "and then we had another big fight over whether it was his Julia Child or mine,"[74] and before that, in 1968, Nora wrote about Julia being one of the big four of the Food Establishment: traditionalists whose primary concern was French food and *haute cuisine*.[75] "Serial Monogamy" and *Julie and Julia* are recent references to the woman who had been part of Nora's biography since the early 1960s.

Although the relationship they each have with Julia Child is a defining characteristic of their lives, neither Nora nor Julie Powell is deluded. They are both well aware of the fabricated nature of their relationship with Julia Child. Julie Powell, the blogger and author, not Nora's character, in an interview with Amanda Hesser said of her relationship with Julia Child, "I do kind of like that she's sort of a construct. She's *my* Julia. I like interpreting what she says and thinks."[76] Eric says of Julie's imagined Julia: "The one in your head is the one that matters."[77] Eric's words are Nora's words, and, with those words, Julie and Nora acknowledge that the imagined is just that, imagined, but both believe the imagined relationship and the imagined person is important to them. Eric's acknowledgment of the importance of the Julia Child in Julie's head reflects Nora's belief in the significance of "the other" in her life.

The imagined was powerful and influential throughout Nora's life. From the time of her childhood there were imagined relationships and fantasies. Nora's relationship with Julia Child was just one of many. As a young woman Nora wanted to be Dorothy Parker, not the *person* Dorothy Parker but the *legend* who was Dorothy Parker.[78] Nora also had a relationship with Elizabeth Bennet, the heroine of Jane Austen's *Pride and Prejudice*. Of that relationship she has written: "I have spent twenty years knowing exactly what Elizabeth Bennet looks like.... She looks like me."[79] That Bennett is a fictional character—someone whose traits are, incidentally, quite different than her own—did not deter Nora from her fantasy. Nora knew she had more in common with another of Austen's characters: "Emma Woodhouse of *Emma*.... She's manipulative, bossy and controlling."[80]

Nora's understanding that biography is comprised of a combination of things is fully developed and realized in *Julie and Julia*: the imagined is the structure on which the narrative is built. The parallel narratives, the imagined story of Julia Child in France and the imagined story of Julie Powell in New York, unite as the film draws to its conclusion. Julie reconciles herself to the nature of her connection with Julia Child, an imagined relationship where she and Julia get along well, a stark contrast to the fact that Julia Child indicated she did not care at all for what Julie Powell was doing regarding her online experiment. Judith Jones (played by Erin Dilly in the film), Child's editor and friend, said in an interview that she and Julia Child heard of Julie Powell's blog, but after they had looked at it, "We both decided that it wasn't anything Julie should have anything to do with. Principally because I think, Julia felt you can't be serious talking about food when you have a vocabulary of four-letter words to describe things. And that was about what it was. Let her have her blog, that's when I called up and cancelled the dinner party. Or didn't come to the dinner party."[81]

Julie (in the film), having chosen the imagined relationship, her version of the relationship with Julia Child, confronts her last task—boning a duck. In the production notes, Nora writes of the scene, "We cut back and forth between Julia (on television) and Julie boning the duck …. it's as if they're one person."[82] Julia Child had become part of Julie Powell, part of her biography.

While Nora is convinced of her belief in the importance of the imagined in life she does not let that belief in the imagined sit comfortably or unchallenged. Julie says of her conversations with Julia: "although mostly I am just talking to myself."[83] Nora knows the imagined is just that—imagined—but being imagined in no way reduces its significance in life.

Communication, another of Nora's long-term interests, forms part of the narrative structure of *Julie and Julia*. Nora not only chronicles the changing nature of communication, the many technological and practice changes that have taken place in the area of communication over the period of time the film spans—Julie Powell is a blogger—she also uses information drawn from more traditional forms of communication. By doing so, Nora is characteristically using other people's stories as a framework for telling her own. It is through this aspect of Nora's world view—her belief that there is neither fiction nor nonfiction only narrative—is understood. *Julie and Julia* is based on two biographies: Julia Child's *My Life in France*, and Julie Powell's *Julie and Julia*. Nora's screenplay involves multiple levels of storytelling. The story of Julia Child's time in France (as told by Julia in the years just before her death and recounted with the help of Alex Prud'homme) is colored by the passing of years and the subjective nature of memory; Powell's book is a subjective rendition of her endeavor as well.

Nora is linked to her two woman protagonists through the art of writing. Nora recorded her life, wrote her memoir, as did Child and Powell. Unconventional, certainly, but Nora's work is no less a subjective documentation of her life as the writings of the women on whom she based her characters and through whose story she tells another installment of her own.

Communication in the form of letter-writing is another of the links which connects *Julie and Julia* to Nora and the Ephron oeuvre. Nora's reputation as a letter-writer of great skill, the Ephron tradition of letter-writing and using personal letters as the basis for works of art, her use of the Child's personal letters and Julie Powell's blogging as sources of material for *Julie and Julia* binds this final film to Nora's body of work and again foregrounds the subjectivity of personal history and documentation.

Julie and Julia as a documentation of technological change and the evolving nature of communication is a continuation of the Ephron family's long standing chronicle of the changes in technology, which began with *Desk Set*. As such, the introduction of blogging and the immediacy of this mode of communication is another subject of this film. Communication, in its various forms, is integral to the story of Julia Child and Julie Powell, as told by Nora. The story of the two cooks could have been told without the inclusion of the voice-over technique; it could have excluded Julie Powell sitting at her computer, blogging, and it could have omitted Julie Child explaining to her collaborator and friend Louisette Bertholle the nature of her relationship with Avis De Voto—they were pen pals— but, then, *Julie and Julia* would not have been a Nora Ephron film.

Writing and communication is not only a subject of the film but also forms the structure of *Julie and Julia*. The subjectivity of recollection and the questionability of "fact" is highlighted when the film's narrative is based on personal, subjective sources and selective recall. The truth of the "Two True Stories," on which Nora claims to have based her film, is that they, as with the other source material used as the basis for the screenplay, are neither fiction nor nonfiction but an amalgam of both— a narrative. They are both personal accounts of the events of each woman's life. Julia Child is writing a cookbook; Julie Powell is writing a blog; Nora Ephron has written a film, both literally and visually about Julie and Julia's writings and, in doing so, has written a subjective interpretation of the information which, in turn, has revealed information about the author. *Julie and Julia* forms part of Nora's memoir.

Nora used very subjective sources of material for her screenplay when she incorporated extracts from the letters written by Julia Child to her sister Dorothy and her friend Avis De Voto, and Paul Child's letters to his brother Charlie into the film. Julie Powell's blogs are, again, very subjective; they are how she communicates her thoughts, feelings and the events of her day. It is the use of the letters and blogs which provide much of the detail; the more intimate and personal information of the film. Nora has always used her work, in this instance her film, to communicate her thoughts. Extracts from Powell's blog, Child's letters and Nora's thoughts appear in voice-over. This narrative technique creates a sense of having access to the private and personal, the internal lives of the characters.[84] The intimacy and subjectivity of letter-writing and blogging sets the tone of the film. As Rachel says of her books: "They're very personal and chatty,"[85] and as Nora writes of her style, it is "chatty and informal."[86] *Julie and Julia* reflects this approach.

The story of Julie and Julia is imbued with Nora's own story and her reinterpretation of the already subjective stories told and retold by Julie Powell and Julia Child. Nora's story, the third story, the one woven throughout the screenplay, is the one which brings a depth of understanding to the film that is neither evident nor necessary in watching the film. That is, it is not necessary to the success of the film but, without Nora's story, the film is not complete and would be different in its telling. Nora manipulated the filmic form in order to make the film personal. The parallel narrative structure of *Julie and Julia* allowed Nora the space to process her reaction to the September 11 assault on her hometown, New York. It allowed Nora the opportunity to pursue her interest in food and to continue the discussion of how food functioned in her life. The film also allowed her to continue the documentation of the changing nature of communication, with the advent of blogging. For Nora, where there was no separation of fiction and nonfiction, this work illustrates how life is a combination of things, not only for herself but for others as well. The parallel narrative trajectories of *Julie and Julia* was not Nora's idea,[87] but it defines the film and it provides a structure for Nora's world view to be given full articulation.

Nora's ability to manipulate the filmic form is important and is evident in her use of her motif subjects, food and cooking—the subjects of *Julie and Julia*—to continue to inhabit her relationship with her mother, Phoebe. The created, imagined, world of her work always allowed Nora the freedom and safety to examine her life, most particularly those aspects that were too painful to address anywhere else. Phoebe is a presence throughout Nora's work. Phoebe's death, which occurred when Nora was thirty, was protracted, the result of years of alcohol abuse.[88] Nora writes: "Long before she died, I'd given up on her."[89] Even though Nora goes on to write in "The Legend" that she got back the mother she adored in 1978, her work suggests otherwise.

Heartburn was published in 1983, *This Is My Life* was released in 1992, and *You've Got Mail* in 1998. The still-conflicted nature of the relationship is evident in *You've Got Mail*. But by the time Nora wrote *Julie and Julia* there are indications that she had had shifted in her feelings about her mother. The mother Nora describes in *Heartburn* is the one "who was a washout at hard-core mothering."[90] In *This Is My Life* Nora depicts the mother figure, Dottie, as variously loving and self-absorbed, not unlike Phoebe. The situation in which the daughters, Erica and Opal, find themselves in with their mother is largely unresolvable. Later, in *You've Got Mail*, Nora was able to honor the way in which her mother was able to show love. Through the giving and sharing of books, and the strong female role models found in those books, Cecilia was able to show love to her daughter Kathleen, as Phoebe was able to show love for her daughters. However neither mother, Cecilia nor Phoebe, could be there for her daughter in other aspects of her life. With *Julie and Julia* there is a sense that Nora had reached a more comfortable place, a place of resolution in her relationship with Phoebe; a place where Nora reconciled the nature of her relationship with her mother.

Keeping within the narrative integrity of the film, butter operates as the point of reference to Phoebe and the point of connection between Nora and her mother. Julia Child is famous for her use of butter. There is no question that the significance of butter in *Julie and Julia* is appropriate to the narrative.[91] But butter is also strongly associated with Phoebe. In *Julie and Julia*, butter operates as the link between Nora and Phoebe. Butter and Phoebe are linked in Nora's recollection of her childhood. In *Julie and Julia*, Nora pays homage to Phoebe. The butterballs made with wooden paddles at the family dining table as a child; the mother who "had enormous flair when she was paying attention, and when she didn't feel like paying attention she threw in a lot of butter"[92]; the mother who instead of nurturing her daughter would go to the kitchen to toast almonds in butter,[93] and simply the mother who, when sautéing onions, stopped them from burning by "throwing more and more butter into the pan."[94] Butter and Phoebe were forever intertwined for Nora. One cannot be thought of in isolation. When Nora wrote "the butter scene" for *Julie and Julia* it was for her mother as much as it was relevant to the narrative. The film's imagery is unmistakable: butter melted in the saucepan, whipped butter, the words being typed as Julie writes about butter on her blog, Julie and Eric eating artichokes with hollandaise sauce and, to close the scene, a number of packets of butter in the fridge. At one point, Julie asks, "Is there anything better than butter? ... Here's my final word on the subject: you can never have enough butter." On the director's commentary, as this scene is playing, Nora says:

> All this stuff about butter is probably as close as I ever get to religion. I just believe in butter and I can never resist a moment to say so ... this movie was meant for that. My mother always said you can never have too much butter. She believed that. It was her credo and it is my credo.[95]

Nora, in this one scene in *Julie and Julia,* declared the depth of her feeling for her mother. The way she felt for Phoebe was as close to the sacred as she would ever get.

Julie and Julia is part of Nora's biography, not just because Phoebe informs *Julie and Julia,* not just because of Nora's homage to her mother and not just because the subjects of the film are Nora's motif subjects. *Julie and Julia* is part of Nora's biography because it is imbued with an Ephron sensibility. Part of that sensibility stems from Nora's attraction to strong, complex and unusual women. Phoebe was, of course, the first of the unusual women who interested Nora. Julia Child is also an unusual woman, which makes her interesting, too. As a woman writing a cookbook, Julia Child seems to be well within the parameters of conventional, but she was not.[96] Julia Child is part of a group of women who, like Phoebe and Nora, do not fit. They are women who defied social expectation and became very successful in their chosen fields, on their own terms. Nora belonged to a family of women who did not fit. Phoebe worked and had a family when most other middle-class women did not. Phoebe did not fit the conventional expectation, nor did Nora's great-aunt Minnie, who was a dentist and financial provider for her family while her husband looked after the domestic arrangements. Julia Child may not be an Ephron relative, but she is certainly part of the clan. When Julia says to her husband, Paul, that she wants to find something to do, that she doesn't want to be like the other wives who do nothing "that's not me, it's just not me,"[97] she is declaring herself to be different. Different in the same way Aunt Minnie and Phoebe were different. Different in the way Nora was different.

But it is not just the decision to work, to have a career and to be financially responsible for themselves which connects Nora and Julia. They are connected by physicality. Again, they both were different, unconventional. Nora spent the majority of her youth believing she did not fit in because of her physical difference and her intellect. Nora and Julia share a lack of conventional beauty, which marked them as different and united them in an understanding of what it means to outside accepted standards of womanliness. Growing up in Hollywood, Nora was smart, athletic and did not fit the expectations of southern Californian female beauty, particularly Hollywood-defined beauty. For Nora, her physical appearance and her intellect always separated her from others. Like Nora, Julia Child was distinctive because of her physicality. When Dorothy (Jane Lynch), Julia's sister, says to her: "Too tall. Let's face it. It's true. From the beginning, you just don't fit in, literally, so then you don't,"[98] she is speaking as much for Nora as she is about herself and Julia.

A woman six-foot-two-inches tall and solidly built, Child was not the average American woman, which set her apart: her appearance became part of her public persona. Nora's droopy eye, being a dark-haired "spiky Jewish girl,"[99] and her perceived lack of breasts ("If I had had them, I would have been a completely different person")[100] marked her as different. Nora's depiction of Julia Child is informed by her own experience of growing up different. As one of her high-school associates was once quoted: "I think Nora always projected herself as the ugly duckling. Her wit made up for not having the beauty."[101] In *Heartburn*, Nora is describing herself, when her alter ego, Rachel, describes herself as having "odd and interesting features."[102] Bennetts's comment that "Ephron claims she's long since gotten over any early insecurities about her looks, but her behaviour sometimes suggests there are enduring scars"[103] would indicate that while Nora's concern with her appearance may not have led to the overwhelming insecurity it once did, the feelings continued to linger. Nora continued to write about her looks in the essays "I Feel Bad About My Neck" and "On Maintenance,"[104] and Jacob Bernstein wrote of his mother in his exquisite essay on her final days "All sorts of men had rejected her when she was younger as cute but not beautiful. She wrote about it, turned it into a comic riff—everything is copy—but privately, it was heartbreaking for her."[105] It is not surprising that the subject of *Julie and Julia*, Julia Child, is another woman who was distinctive because she was not a beautiful woman, nor did Nora dishonor her by depicting her as one. Not being beautiful was very personal for Nora.

Meryl Streep won acclaim for her portrayal of Julia Child in the film. Streep's depiction of Child in no way enhanced her physical beauty. Julie Powell, in Nora's script, describes Julia Child thusly: "She's tall, she's awkward, she's gawky, she's goofy"[106]; Nora describes her on page 18 of her script in the following terms: "Julia is taller than everyone else and her feet are larger than everyone else's. She's like a big tree." There is a moment in *Julie and Julia* when Julia and her sister Dorothy stand looking at themselves in a full-length mirror as they prepare for a party. "They look as good as they can possibly look. But neither of them is any way stylish and they know it." Julia, looking at their reflection says, "Pretty good. But not great."[107] This moment is an echo of the scene in *This Is My Life* where Dottie Ingels tells her daughter how on one summer camp she looked in the mirror and recognized that what she saw was what she was and she knew she needed to make the most of it. Nora wrote in 1972: "I am obsessed with not being beautiful."[108] Julia Child was not beautiful but, like Nora and Nora's women Rachel and Dottie, and Nora's literary heroes Elizabeth Bennet, Dorothy Parker, and the amazing Marian Halcombe, the unconventional woman at the center of one of Nora's favorite books, Wilkie Collins's *The Woman in White*, she was strong, resourceful and successful. Julia writes to her friend Avis of her experience of being the only woman in her cooking class "and all of them very unfriendly until they discovered I was fearless, something I realized at about the same time they did."[109] Nora and her women are all fearless: Karen Silkwood, Rachel Samstat, Cookie, Sally, Dottie, Kathleen—even Isabel Bigalow—all dared to be different—as did Julie Powell, Julia Child and Phoebe Ephron.

Nora made a career for herself based on her ability to share her stories with others. She was able to make a career based on her life because she was unique; a product of her circumstances—"not everyone grew up in my family"—and because there is universality to her individual experience, which gives her work broad appeal. When Nora was asked, "Don't you feel odd that, because your work is autobiographical, your readers know that much about you?" she confidently responded, "Almost never … what you want is for them to say, 'Oh, you feel that way too, huh?' I've been incredibly lucky in terms of being so ordinary."

Nora might have promoted herself as ordinary but she was not considered by others to be so. Tom Brokaw described Nora as the "gold standard of smart thinking."[110] Benjamin Markovits, describing a book reading by Nora where she didn't turn up but was instead projected "larger than life" on screens "about eight feet high," saw this as an indication of the stature of Nora, who, in promoting *I Feel Bad About My Neck*, was also promoting herself and her life as "everyday." Nora's claim that she was ordinary prompted Markovits to respond: "The life almost ordinary [...] wouldn't interest us if it really were."[111] Ariel Levy observes: "Ephron isn't cold, but she is queenly: a Jewish dame."[112] Levy concludes her article on Nora with a critique of *Julie and Julia*, in which she attributes the contrast between the parts of the film dedicated to Julia Child and those dedicated to Julie Powell—the first "irresistibly vivid," and the latter "flat"—as being the consequence of Nora no longer being able "to understand half as well what it's like to be ordinary as she understands the remarkable."[113]

While Brokaw, Markovits and Levy might see Nora as extraordinary, Nora's work illustrates that she values and understands the ordinary. The story of Julie and Julia and Nora is not about the famous women they became but rather the time leading up to the fame—the time when they were ordinary. Eric insightfully tells the hero-worshipping Julie: "Julia Child wasn't always Julia Child."[114] For that matter, Nora Ephron wasn't always Nora Ephron. She was once just a child growing up in a family, but a family unlike any other. Nora, Julie and Julia are ordinary women who have done extraordinary things.

Nora liked to write and make films about aspects of popular culture, but as has always been her wont, she does so through the "prism of her own experience." As Tom Brokaw wrote of Nora's writing:

> She was able to pull off the journalistic hat trick of reporting the big picture, commenting on the telling details, and leaving just enough of herself in the piece so that the reader knew the writer had a personal stake in the story.

With *Julie and Julia*, Nora has done exactly that which Brokaw attributes to her writing. She has reported "the big picture"—the story of how Julia Child came to write *Mastering the Art of French Cooking*, and how Julie Powell came to cook the entire recipe collection contained in Child's book over a twelve-month period. Nora includes "the details" of the two women who embarked on their respective tasks and, finally, Nora leaves enough of herself in the film to let the viewer know that she has "a personal stake in the story."

Julie and Julia is the quintessential Nora Ephron film. She described it as "a little bio of myself in terms of food."[115] It has broad appeal, was financially successful and won critical acclaim. The subjects of the piece are those Nora had long contemplated in her work: food, love, communication, technology, and women who live normal lives and do extraordinary things. *Julie and Julia* is personal—Nora used her life as the raw material for her film and her life and her world view informs it. *Julie and Julia* was part of Nora's ongoing revision and processing of her life. It allowed her the opportunity to reflect on her relationship with her mother, to contemplate her life as a resident of New York after the events of September 11, and to illustrate the changed nature of her adult relationships. *Julie and Julia* is the work of Nora Ephron; a woman whose life was informed by her experience of growing up as a member of the Ephron family, where everything was copy. An experience she understood as unique: as she said, "Not everyone grew up in my family."[116]

Conclusion: The Ephron Modus Operandi

"What do you owe your parents?"
"My sense of humor; my ability to get over it,
whatever it is; and my love of food."[1]

All the Ephron daughters grew up to be writers—just as their parents expected of them. Nora, Delia, Amy and Hallie, all independent women, did what was right for them, but, ultimately, each decided to become that which was expected of her. Hallie writes suspense novels and magazine articles; Amy, a reporter, writes screenplays and period novels, as well as a food blog; Delia writes novels, essays, articles, screenplays (she was Nora's screenplay and play-writing partner).

No doubt it must, at times, be irksome to be one of Nora's sisters. To know that, despite their own talent and skill and successes, Nora will always be the most famous. Hallie recently wrote of her reaction to being asked about Nora—how at times she feels like responding that there are three other sisters![2] Delia wrote of her reaction, at her sister's memorial service, to Nora being credited with lines she actually wrote—she claimed her lines, if only to her husband beside her. There is rivalry, yes, but there is love, too. There is also the sense of understanding the life they shared as children and still not knowing very much about one another. Delia writes of her relationship with Nora: "Our lives were in some ways entirely separate and unknown to each other."[3] Hallie echoes that sentiment when she writes, "I knew her well enough to know I didn't know her that well at all."[4]

The daughters say much the same about their mother. Nora's death has allowed a space for her sisters to write about the subjects which had been almost exclusively her domain, most particularly their mother,

155

Phoebe. Delia recently has written about her mother, as has Hallie. The alcoholic mother of *There Was An Old Woman* allows Hallie a re-imagining of her mother's death; Delia wrote about her mother in her ironically titled essay "Why I Can't Write About My Mother."[5] Both of these works were published after Nora's death. This is not to say that the sisters had not written of their mother before, but now their consideration of their mother is foregrounded in a way it had not been previously. What is evident in Delia's and Hallie's prose is their struggle to come to terms with who Phoebe was. It is a struggle all the sisters shared; a point of the reference for all of them. Delia asks the question of her mother, "Did she just not really like me?"[6] Hallie wonders "how she felt about us. About me."[7] These are heartbreaking questions for someone to ask about their mother, but there remain issues so unresolved for Phoebe's daughters that they are still exploring them as mature women. They continue to struggle to come to terms with the complicated woman who was their mother.

Hallie, in her essay on growing up as an Ephron, not only questions how her mother felt about her, she questions the implied bond between Phoebe and Nora. Looking at a photograph of her mother holding her firstborn, Hallie writes, "The portrait is lovely, and yet the longer I look at it, the more it seems suspect, this semblance of domesticity."[8] Her feelings are understandable when one takes into account that the Ephron sisters grew up in a home where the brand of mothering they experienced was one of "Don't involve me, I have my own life," and then of living with an alcoholic. The image of the mother looking at her child, a personal and private bond of love, does not align with the experience of any of the daughters nor does it align with the image of the mother as she is drawn in any of the Ephron work. The work of the Henry and Phoebe writing team and the work of all the daughters, especially Nora, describe a very different woman and mother.

Hallie's writing about her life as an Ephron child is clear and direct. She astutely observes that, although the four sisters were ascribed different roles within the family, roles which reflect their attributes—Nora intelligent, Delia funny, Hallie obedient, and Amy a mischief-maker—they are very similar. All are bossy, opinionated, smart and witty. They are Phoebe's daughters and "to understand any of us, including Nora, you'd have to start with our mother—a woman well ahead of her time. Of all the Ephron women, she was surely the most exceptional, for better or worse."[9]

It is not just the similarities of personality that the sisters share; it is the similarities of personality they share with their mother which unites all the Ephron women. But Nora, Delia and Hallie have written at one time or another of their shared desire *not* to be like their mother. There are also similarities in their work—despite the differences of style, form and genre—that also unites them. All the Ephron daughters have written about growing up in the Ephron family and the inherent consequences. They all celebrate and honor Phoebe as a trail-blazing career woman in Hollywood, but they have continually sought ways to resolve who she was and to understand how she was with them, Nora famously so.

Nora struggled all her life to be comfortable with her relationship with Phoebe. The feelings she had towards her mother were conflicted, unresolved, always up for review. She vacillated between wanting, needing, to be nothing like her mother, to finding a way to accept that she was very like her mother. The photograph of Phoebe, in profile, and baby Nora reveals just how much Nora looked like her mother. Nora needed to know she was loved by her mother. Her work reveals the search she conducted all her life to find proof of Phoebe's love. Phoebe was instrumental in shaping the lives of her daughters, and she was instrumental in shaping their work. She was and is an ever-present influence. Phoebe is not the only subject of Nora's work, but she has been a consistent one to which the artist continually returned. Nora's writing is easier to access, more open than her films, which are far from simple, built as they are on layer upon layer of personal connections.

By the time of her death in 2012, Nora was adept at building multiple levels of meaning into her work. It is the idiosyncrasy of the Ephron modus operandi, and she had become its master. With the unmanageable knowledge of her terminal illness Nora did what she had always done, what she had been taught to do by her family: she addressed the issues of her life through her work. As already noted, Nora was a firm believer in denial and, in the face of her own mortality, she did what her mother had taught her to do. Nora did more; she copied her mother. As a severe alcoholic, Phoebe had a disease not even her closest friends knew about, but she revealed her concerns for her health in a play. Similarly, Nora's closest friends (with the exception of a select few) did not know she was dying. Nora, to the end, utilized the family coping mechanism. She used her work to process the things that were impacting her life. Tell a story and make it funny. Don't be the victim, be the hero. So Nora wrote about what she will miss when she died. She was the subject and heroine of her story. She got to tell her story *her* way. She heralded her death in her work.

In addressing her death, Nora had to tie up the loose ends of her life. Her work was where she did her final tidying. She discussed how she would leave her final instructions when she wrote of her friend Henry in "Considering the Alternative,"[10] even though she was not yet ill, she was deeply affected by the passing of some of her friends. She returned to the issue of her mother. In her 3,500 word précis of her life, she wrote her controversial, funny version of Phoebe's death; it suggests Henry killed Phoebe with an overdose of sleeping tablets. Nora makes a joke about her own naiveté; her sister Amy is so much more astute.[11] *Julie and Julia* is Nora's last film and, fittingly, it is the film, as noted in Chapter 5, in which she pays her final homage to her mother. As with *You've Got Mail*, her homage to Phoebe is deeply imbedded in the story. *Julie and Julia* operates at one level as a final reconciliation with the woman who had so great an influence on her life. The film also honors those other things she got from her parents. It honors the "ability to get on with things and get over things," and it honors food. *Julie and Julia* is a fitting tribute to the most fundamental influences in her life— her family heritage.

Nora's final produced work, the play *Lucky Guy*, opened on Broadway on April 1, 2013. Although the play was begun much earlier, in the 1990s, this final version was completed when Nora was very ill. It is a fitting tribute to her life. With *Lucky Guy*, Nora moved beyond the concerns of her family and wrote about how she had chosen to live her life. Not overtly, of course, but wrapped in a story about a subject close to her. The play centers on one Mike McArlary, and it is, in many ways, an oral history of Nora's beloved city, New York, and the profession she loved, journalism, as they were in the 1980s and early 1990s. On first reading it seems totally unconnected to Nora's personal life. However, on closer examination, it becomes obvious that Nora and McAlary shared more than a career in journalism. Mike McAlary worked up until the time of his death from cancer, won the Pulitzer Prize in the process and, in doing so, made life the main game and death a side issue, an approach to living and dying to which Nora ascribed. Jacob Bernstein wrote of his mother, who saw McAlary as a "role model not so much in life, but in death, in the way that he used writing to maintain his sense of purpose and find release from his illness."[12] In the same way Nora borrowed from her friend Henry in order to set out the template for what should follow her death, she drew strength from the story of Mike McAlary. McAlary, from what is written of him, was not a particularly likeable person, nor was he in the play; it was how he lived his final days that gelled with Nora.

Two things are frequently written about *Lucky Guy*. The first is that it is a play about the world of old-school journalists: hard-drinking, foul-mouthed men, working on the tabloid papers in New York, where Nora worked when she first moved to the city in the 1960s. The second is the asking of the question: who *is* the foul-mouthed fictional female journalist Louise Imerman? Lucy Komisar, in her article "The Imaginary Cursing Woman in Nora Ephron's 'Lucky Guy'" posits: "How could Ephron get this part of her story so wrong?"[13]

But Nora rarely got anything wrong. Toward the end of her life she wrote two books of significant essays and wrote and directed one significant film. *Julie and Julia* was the film—so perfectly a Nora Ephron film—with its homage to her mother, its celebration of a famous and unique woman, much like herself, the getting on with life after a devastating event and the story of getting a book published. The two significant books of essays were best-sellers and, within the covers, were stories of Nora's life at that point—just prior to and in the years after her diagnosis. There are two love letters in Nora's final book. "The Legend" is about Phoebe, and the other, "Journalism: A Love Story," is, its title suggests, about working as a journalist. It is obvious that Nora loved being a journalist, but that did not blind her to the shortcomings of the business. She wrote how she could now see that, at *Newsweek* at the time she worked there, just "how brilliantly institutionalized the sexism was…. For every male writer [there was] a female drone."[14]

Louise Imerman, it has been suggested, is more than likely a composite—even if no one recognizes on whom she is based. But she could also be Nora, imagining, observing from the sidelines the world of Mike McAlary, the boys club, the world of journalism she knew, loved and understood, even when women were excluded from that club. Louise could be Nora observing how the women were treated and making a comment on what she sees. Commenting not just for herself but for all the women who were treated with such disregard, all the women who would go on to break down the boys club. Nora has been described as frank and forthright; swearing is not something Nora would avoid in her work, but she would not use gratuitously, either—this woman, Louise, could easily be Nora Louise Ephron, a young female journalist who would go on to be far more famous than any of the men who were the stars of the day, the ones who treated their female colleagues so badly it became part of the legend of old school journalism. Nora devoted two paragraphs to journalism in her earlier essay "The Story of My Life in 3,500 Words or Less." The first paragraph describes the joyous moment Nora decided she would be a journalist forever, and the second: "I may not be a journalist forever" describes an incident in which Nora was set up by a male colleague—a managing editor—which resulted in her being drenched with water, an incident thought to be hilarious by the perpetrator and the male onlooker. This was significant enough for Nora to write about and significant enough to cause her to rethink her career. Nora would have been furious and humiliated. She could well have had something to say about being a woman in journalism.

Lucky Guy is Nora's final contemplation of one of her important motif subjects: her philosophical point of view. *Lucky Guy*, like *Heartburn*, is a declaration of who Nora Ephron is. The play goes to the heart of her being: how she had chosen to live until she died. It is her final reiteration of her position on the nature of truth. She gives to her characters John Cotter and Mike McAlary the discussion on the nature of truth—that there is no truth—there are indeed very few facts. It is Cotter who articulates Nora's belief: "Except for a few hard-core things, which for want of a better word we will call facts ... everything is a story."[15]

The question—of what relevance or importance is an understanding of the influences on the film work of Nora Ephron?—should be asked. Addressing this allows for the exploration of what is really meant when it is said of her work that it is biographical. The question draws attention to the work of an artist who has not, for the most part, been taken seriously. Nora Ephron, as stated at the outset, was the writer and director of mainstream films which are generally dismissed as being little more than inconsequential, lightweight fare. Most are romantic comedies, "fluff," according to many, even when Nora is recognized for her considerable ability as a writer. Nora has had three Oscar nominations for her film work. However, it is not the mainstream predictability of Nora's films which makes them unique or even interesting but how she has used the filmic form to build layers of meaning which extend far beyond the film's plot.

As with any discussion, to be able to engage with a subject in any meaningful way it is imperative to be familiar with the topic. Analysis of Nora Ephron has, with few exceptions, not extended beyond the superficial. Her work, as is evident from the included bibliography, is mostly the subject of popular magazine articles. Some writers, in particular McCreadie and Levy, have devoted space to a consideration of aspects of Nora's work. McCreadie, however, offers little by way of insight, while Levy's work begins to explore one of the central roles of Nora's work when she recognizes the use of wit as a mechanism of control.

It is often said that Ephron's work is about her, a statement which, in fact, means nothing. Nor is it enough to say that Nora wrote and directed romantic comedies. It is that which marks Nora Ephron's work as different that is important. It is how she fills the narrative space; it is how her characters respond to the events of their lives; it is how they view their lives; and it is how they understand their world which identifies and differentiates Nora's work from that of other artists. Nora's work is different because it is personal; it resonates with the particular circumstances of her life.

Recognizing Nora Ephron's work as personal, and attributing that uniqueness to the circumstances of her upbringing, does not deny the impact of the social and industrial contexts within which Nora lived and worked. Particularly given that Nora was a woman at the height of her career as a journalist and writer during the 1970s, when the second wave of the women's movement was at its strongest, and women's issues were foregrounded. Nor is it forgotten that, in relation to her success as a writer, the New Journalism movement was undoubtedly influential and an opportune time for her work. However, the same argument—that Nora's work is a reflection and product of the time—can also be used to demonstrate that Nora's fundamental influences were more than the social context within which she worked. If Nora's work was simply a product of the time and social movements specific to an historical moment it could reasonably be expected that her success would wane with the passing of said moment. To the contrary, both her writing and film work continues to be relevant. Similarly, her last two anthologies were on the *New York Times* best-seller list. Her films are neither dated nor arcane, despite the three decades that have passed since her first successful screenplay, *Silkwood*, was produced. That Nora did work as a very successful journalist and essayist and was then able to transition to another medium and context and remain successful is a testament to her adaptability. There is a demonstrated consistency of world view and subject matter across Nora's work which transcends historical contexts, influences and medium.

There is a stronger argument in support of an overarching ethos at work in relation to Nora's creative output when the context into which she moved with her transition to film is known for its collaborative nature. She once said of *When Harry Met Sally*: "This screenplay has my name on it, but it is very much a collaboration."[16] She further compares the process of script development to building a pizza.[17] Nora has collaborated with fellow writer Alice Arlen, writer and director Rob Reiner and, on a number of occasions, her sister Delia. However, all the shared works have the trademarks of a Nora Ephron work. It is because Nora could produce a work that was personal, that had a connection to her life.

Nora's uniqueness of voice is identified through her characterization, world view, dialogue, repeated motifs and biographical references. Nora's fictional women are based on her; their lives resonate with the echo of her life. Her films speak of her life while they speak of the lives of others. They are works that have a cultural anchor and relevance while they remain personal. They are informed by her world view. They operate as a space in which Nora can address the concerns of her life.

Borrowing from E.L. Doctorow, Nora believed that there is only narrative. Patrick McGilligan, who interviewed Nora regarding her screenplay for *Silkwood*, observes, "There are very few real 'facts,' but she agrees there are factual moments."[18] She held steadfast to this belief throughout her life. It informs *Lucky Guy* as much as it did *Silkwood*.

Nora's world view is fixed within the context of her family—parents who have a career based on creating stories, a family expectation of everyone turning the events of their life into a funny story, and the experience of having her life fictionalized by her parents. The belief that there is only narrative informs all of her work and, in essence, much of her work is concerned with the narratives of her culture, particularly In relation to expectations of love—*When Harry Met Sally, Sleepless in Seat-*

tle and *You've Got Mail* as well as the combination of things which comprise life, the imagined and the actual—*Heartburn*, *Julie and Julia*, *Michael*, *Lucky Numbers*, or simply the absurdity of life—*Mixed Nuts*.

Nora Ephron's films are often described as "old-fashioned," and there is some truth in that statement. When old-fashioned implies a romantic fantasy that is part of cultural conditioning, Nora's films are certainly that—but Nora exposes the fantasy; she does not propagate it. Her films are not sentimental, even when that is what is meant by the reviewers. Nora's films are old-fashioned Hollywood films in a very specific way. Nora Ephron was an incredibly smart filmmaker and, like her predecessors of Hollywood's Golden Age, she hid her secrets in her films. She used a very commercial, much prescribed form of artistic creative method to make films which are highly personal. She hid her secrets, her life, in her work, while convincing everyone she was making typical Hollywood films.

In an interview with Emma Brockes Nora Ephron describes her family thus:

> A lion that has killed a zebra and all the lions are feeding on it and the coyotes and the jackals and these rings of people. That is sometimes how I think of us.[19]

Nora's statement sits very closely and comfortably alongside the line written by her parents seventy-odd years prior, when they wrote of the mother guppy devouring her babies. In the same interview with Brockes, Nora also is quoted as saying, "Whoever you are as an adult is way more than simply that your parents were *x* or *y*." Nora would not want to be viewed as being merely the child of her parents. Her life was much more than a copy of her parents' life; Nora Ephron was much more than a copy of Phoebe, despite the similarities. Nora Ephron's life was definitely a life examined. Her life is the basis for her work and, at a deep level, Nora's work is about her. She learned the most essential of the defining characteristics of her work from her parents, who also used their life and the lives of their children in their work. Intimately aware of the potential consequences of having her life purloined by another, Nora never used the lives of her children Jacob and Max as material for her own work.

By addressing her death in her work (and *only* in her work), Nora validates the contention "Everything is copy" in a way that none of her other actions could. It established beyond doubt that Nora Ephron's work is identifiable as unique and belonging to her alone. Her art is the space she used to record and consider her life and the world around her. It is where she told the stories of her life. She did this because it was what she was taught to do.

Above all else in her life, the experience of being the child of screenwriters Henry and Phoebe Ephron was fundamental to the shaping of Nora Ephron's creative voice. Nora took the advice of her mother and used it to her own advantage and as her protection. By telling her own stories she maintained ownership of her life in a way that was not possible when she was a child. She determined to never again let someone else tell her stories. As she wrote in *Heartburn*: "If I tell the story, I control the version." Even in her death she controls the version, she set the parameters of what would follow. *Lucky Guy* provides the frame of reference. Nora *still* has control over her story. She wrote her own disclaimer—for this and every other piece that will ever be about her: "You are born, you die. Everything in between is subject to interpretation."[20]

Chapter Notes

Introduction

1. Tallmer.
2. Collins, 60–63.
3. Ephron, *Drexel*.
4. Hanson and Herman, 19.
5. Nonkin, 146.
6. The background and detail to the writing of *Three's a Family* will be addressed in Chapter 1.
7. Delia Ephron quoted in Pfefferman.
8. Turner Classic Movies.
9. Quinn.
10. Dinitia Smith.
11. Helmore.
12. Brooks.
13. D. Rooney, "Why Nora Ephron's Film Made Such An Impact: A Critic's Take," *The Hollywood Reporter*, June 27, 2012. http://www.hollywoodreporter.com/news/nora-ephron-death-when-harry-met-sally-342629.
14. Shone.
15. Straus.
16. *Anything*, 3.
17. *Anything*, 71.
18. A. Levy, 65.
19. A. Levy, 60.
20. See Wolfe for an overview of New Journalism.
21. Martin in Ephron, *Salad*, viii.
22. B. Levy, 40.
23. Levy cites the incident of Phoebe, close to the time of her death, telling Nora to "Take Notes" as the moment when Phoebe taught her daughter the controlling power of humor however as this book will show the notion of humor as control was well in place in the Ephron family long before Phoebe's death (41).
24. Beale.
25. Ephron has never taken credit for the line or the scene; she has always credited the suggestion for the "faking of the orgasm in the delicatessen scene" to Meg Ryan and the line to Billy Crystal. See the introduction to *When Harry Met Sally*.
26. A. Levy, 62.
27. The process of writing the screenplay has been recorded by Ephron, as the Introduction to the published version of the screenplay (Ephron, *Harry*) and reappears in part in (Mernit, 97–104). It has been used as case studies for university screenwriting courses, for example Advanced Screenwriting, La Trobe University Cinema Studies Program, Australia, 2007.
28. Krutnik in Neale, 139.
29. Pribram and Hall.
30. Mernit, 99.
31. Straus.
32. Tallmer.
33. Lopez-Guzman.
34. King, 85–115.
35. King, 89.
36. King, 89.
37. This statement is qualified by acknowledging the term "auteur" may not be commonly understood or used. By implication, however, "auteur" has validity because "film director" is understood in the contemporary context not only as a term denoting a particular profession but it is recognized as a term used to denote a distinctive creative voice. This is despite film scholars being fully aware of conditions of production and the other considerations impacting on the autonomy of the director.
38 King, 85.
39. Caughie, 9.
40. Cook, 175.
41. Stam, 6.
42. Caughie, 9.
43. Cook, 175.
44. Hutchings, 24.
45. This phrase "growing up Ephron" is the title of Hallie Ephron's article on growing

up as a member of the Ephron family. "Growing Up Ephron" was printed in *O, The Oprah Magazine* in March 2013.

Chapter 1

1. The quote is taken from a question posed to Nora Ephron by Patrick McGilligan (40). The suit to which he is referring is the romantic comedy film genre, with particular reference to *When Harry Met Sally*. Nora does not acknowledge his reference and comparison to her parents in her response to his question.

2. N. Ephron, *Academy*.

3. N. Ephron, *Drexel*.

4. N. Ephron, "The Company of Women," *Premiere*, 1992, 110.

5. After the breakup of her second marriage Nora had to support herself and her two young sons. She was looking for a way that would allow her to work and earn money as well as care for her children (*Premiere*, 111).

6. H. Ephron, *Anything*, 37.

7. See Sterling.

8. Sterling.

9. P. Cook, 175.

10. N. Ephron, *Nothing*, 32.

11. N. Ephron, *Neck*, 98.

12. Nora has said "I write about my friends. I write about my ex-exes but I don't write about my kids" (quoted in Nonkin, 146).

13. Biskind, 26.

14. "A Few Words About Breasts" first appeared in *Esquire* magazine in May 1972.

15. Henry Ephron claims he did not complete his degree at Cornell because six weeks before he was due to graduate he was caught stealing books from the campus bookstore and consequently expelled (12).

16. H. Ephron, *Anything*, 3.

17. "You Can't Take It with You," https://sites.google.com/site/utyoucanttakeitwithyou/kaufman-and-hart---the-collaboration.

18. H. Ephron, *Anything*, 36.

19. Wills, 62.

20. Grove.

21. "Algonquin Round Table."

22. B. Crowther, 71.

23. H. Ephron, *Anything*, 40–43.

24. The information relating to Dorothy Parker is taken from *Dorothy Parker* in *Nora Ephron Collected*.

25. H. Ephron, *Anything*, 6.

26. N. Ephron, *Nothing*, 34.

27. H. Ephron, *Anything*, 6.

28. *Ibid.*

29. H. Ephron, *Anything*, 79–80.

30. H. Ephron, *Anything*, 93.

31. *Ibid.*, 135.

32. A. Levy, 62.

33. A. Levy, 60.

34. N. Ephron, *Sally*, xi.

35. N. Collins, 63.

36. N. Ephron, *Sally*, xiv.

37. N. Ephron, *Nothing*, 38.

38. L. Bennetts, 86.

39. *Premier, The Company of Women*, 1992, 98.

40. Nora quoted in *Academy*.

41. N. Ephron, *Nothing*, 16.

42. N. Collins, 63.

43. N. Ephron, *Nothing*, 35.

44. H. Ephron, *Anything*, 162.

45. *Ibid.*, 39.

46. N. Ephron, *Heartburn*, 134.

47. *Ibid.*, 131.

48. N. Ephron, *Scribble*, 162.

49. L. Bennetts, 82.

50. *Ibid.*, 80.

51. Morris.

52. R. Maltby, 43.

53. A. Levy, 60.

54. See *Scribble Scribble, Wallflower at the Orgy* and *Crazy Salad*. Each of these collections contains Nora's most vivid and high profile essays.

55. Ephron and Ephron, 5.

56. Ephron and Ephron, 9.

57. Parallels found in *Desk Set* and *You've Got Mail* are discussed more fully in Chapter 3.

58. N. Ephron, *Author*.

59. By "biography" I do not mean a written account of Nora's life, but rather as the term is understood to denote "a life"—its shape and form.

60. Nora's belief that there is only narrative will be the subject of Chapter 4.

61. L. Bennetts, 82.

62. N. Ephron, *Nothing*, 208.

63. L. Bennetts, 82.

64. L. Bennetts, 82.

65. N. Ephron, *Collected*, 116.

66. L. Bennetts, 82.

67. N. Ephron, *Neck*, 112.

68. A. Levy, 68.

69. D. Ephron, *Sisters*, 191.

70. H. Ephron, *Anything*, 60.

71. Ephron and Ephron, 35.

72. Ephron and Ephron, 49.

73. Ephron and Ephron, 1962.

74. N. Ephron, *Heartburn*, 19.

75. H. Ephron, *Anything*, 7.

76. N. Ephron, 24–5.
77. N. Ephron, *Nothing*, 33.
78. H. Ephron, *Anything*, 1.
79. N. Collins, 63.
80. H. Ephron, *Anything*, 104.
81. H. Ephron, *Anything*, 105.
82. H. Ephron, *Anything*, 50.
83. D. Ephron, *Sister*, 188.
84. D. Ephron, *Sister*, 167.
85. N. Ephron, *Heartburn*, 30.
86. N. Ephron, *Nothing*, 209.
87. N. Ephron, *Nothing*, 209.
88. Zolotow.
89. N. Ephron, *Premier*, 98.
90. A. Levy, 46–47.
91. Ephron and Ephron, 19.
92. L. Bennetts, 82.
93. "Advice For Women."
94. Zolotow.
95. Biskind, 23.
96. Biskind, 23.
97. "Advice For Women."
98. Nonkin, 146.
99. D. Ephron, *Sister*, 165.
100. Henry quotes Darryl Zanuck who reportedly said of Phoebe: "She doesn't like to fight; she walks away from it" (141).
101. Pfefferman.
102. N. Ephron, *Heartburn*, 7.
103. N. Ephron, *Nothing*, 137.
104. L. Bennetts, 82.
105. H. Ephron, *Anything*, 33.
106. H. Ephron, *Anything*, 62.
107. H. Ephron, *Anything*, 96.
108. D. Ephron, *Sister*, 178.
109. D. Ephron, *Sister*, 169.
110. P. Ephron, 7.
111. N. Ephron, *Nothing*, 37.
112. "New Plays in Manhattan."
113. H. Ephron, *Anything*, 10.
114. H. Ephron, *Anything*, 51.
115. H. Ephron, *Anything*, 32.
116. H. Ephron, *Anything*, 40–43.
117. H. Ephron, *Anything*, 151.
118. Nora indicates that the impact of alcohol was less significant with Henry than Phoebe although the effects of his abuse of alcohol impacted much more strongly on Delia who was forced as a teenager to care for her father when he was drinking; a responsibility she continued until his death.
119. N. Ephron, *Nothing*, 36. Although Nora describes her father's alcoholism as benign there is considerable evidence that in fact Henry was at times violent and that his actions was exacerbated by his drinking. Henry's violent behavior is examined in Chapter 2.
120. N. Ephron, "Advice For Women."
121. Frank Rich, "Nora's Secret," *New York Magazine*, News and Features, August 19, 2012, n.p. Web. 27 Aug. 2012. http://nymag.com/news/frank-rich/nora-ephron-2012-8/.
122. N. Collins, 60, 63.
123. N. Collins, 63.
124. L. Bennetts, 82.
125. L. Bennetts, 82.
126. X. Brooks, 126.
127. N. Collins, 63.
128. L. Bennetts, 82.
129. L. Bennetts, 82.
130. N. Ephron, *Nothing*, 38.

Chapter 2

1. Moss, 20.
2. Tallmer.
3. H. Ephron and P. Ephron, *Three's a Family*, 11.
4. H. Ephron, *Anything*, 6.
5. H. Ephron and P. Ephron, *Three's a Family*, 67.
6. H. Ephron, *Anything*, 6.
7. H. Ephron, *Anything*, 6.
8. Bennetts, 82.
9. D. Ephron, *Hanging Up*, 250–1.
10. A. Ephron, *Cool Shades*, 34.
11. H. Ephron, *Anything*, 7, 8, 28, 53.
12. H. Ephron and P. Ephron, *Three's a Family*, 27.
13. H. Ephron and P. Ephron, *Three's a Family*, 39.
14. H. Ephron, *Anything*, 57.
15. H. Ephron, *Anything*, 111.
16. H. Ephron, *Anything*, 6.
17. H. Ephron, *Anything*, 40.
18. H. Ephron, *Anything*, 46.
19. H. Ephron, *Anything*, 65.
20. H. Ephron, *Anything*, 175.
21. H. Ephron, *Anything*, 50.
22. H. Ephron and P. Ephron, *Take Her, She's Mine*, 5.
23. H. Ephron and P. Ephron, *Take Her, She's Mine*, 18.
24. N. Ephron, *Wellesley*, 2.
25. H. Ephron and P. Ephron, *Take Her, She's Mine*, 32.
26. H. Ephron and P. Ephron, *Take Her, She's Mine*, 21.
27. N. Ephron, *Wellesley*, 2.
28. H. Ephron and P. Ephron, *Take Her, She's Mine*, 19.

29. H. Ephron and P. Ephron, *Take Her, She's Mine*, 30.

30. H. Ephron and P. Ephron, *Take Her, She's Mine*, 38.

31. N. Ephron, *Wellesley*, 3.

32. H. Ephron and P. Ephron, *Take Her, She's Mine*, 118.

33. H. Ephron and P. Ephron, *Take Her, She's Mine*, 67.

34. H. Ephron and P. Ephron, *Take Her, She's Mine*, 106.

35. For a detailed study of the movement, see Wolfe.

36. Ephron, *Nothing*, 29.

37. G. Wills, 2.

38. Levy, 60.

39. Ephron, *Salad*, xxiv.

40. Nonkin, 146.

41. Bennetts, 78.

42. Bennetts, 78.

43. Heartburn, 7.

44. H. Ephron and P. Ephron, *Take Her, She's Mine*, 67.

45. N. Collins, 60, 63, 93.

46. Ephron, *Deep*.

47. Ephron, *Collected*, 215.

48. N. Ephron, *Heartburn*, 19.

49. N. Ephron, *Heartburn*, 14.

50. N. Ephron, *Heartburn*, 153.

51. N. Ephron, *Heartburn*, 106.

52. Huffington.

53. L. Bennetts, 86.

54. N. Ephron, *Heartburn*, 154.

55. Levy, *New Yorker*, 66.

56. L. Bennetts, 80.

57. N. Ephron, *Heartburn*, 23.

58. N. Ephron, *Heartburn*, 23.

59. Ephron, *Premiere*, 98.

60. N. Ephron, *Nothing*, 38.

61. N. Ephron, *Heartburn*, 23.

62. Zolotow.

63. N. Ephron, *Nothing*, 33.

64. N. Ephron, *Heartburn*, 27; H. Ephron, *Anything*, 52.

65. N. Ephron, *Heartburn*, 27.

66. N. Ephron, *Heartburn*, 30.

67. N. Ephron, *Heartburn*, 30.

68. A. Levy, *New Yorker*, 66.

69. N. Ephron, *Nothing*, 38.

70. N. Ephron, *Heartburn*, 40.

71. N. Collins, 60, 63, 93.

72. N. Ephron, *Heartburn*, 41.

73. H. Ephron, *Anything*, 142.

74. N. Ephron, *Heartburn*, 18.

75. N. Ephron, *Heartburn*, 8.

76. N. Ephron, *Heartburn*, 65.

77. X. Brooks.

78. N. Ephron, *Heartburn*, 81.

79. Described in *Time* magazine "Portnoy's Complaint" as "a book that, while it charts the wild arc of Portnoy's sexual and romantic misadventures—all of this being recounted by him to his therapist—discovers exactly the most painful question about relations between children and parents" (Lacayo).

80. As described on Amazon the film of the book by Grace Metalious "Nominated for nine Academy Awards in 1957, Peyton Place has become synonymous with torrid soap opera. Though the novel by Grace Metalious is even more sensational" (Amazon.com).

81. Wills, 62.

82. Bennetts, 78.

83. Bennetts, 84.

84. The photograph of Henry with Phoebe and Eleanor Roosevelt taken on the night the First Lady visited their play *Three's a Family* which appears in *We Thought We Could Do Anything* beautifully captures Henry's iconic pose which when compared to the shots of Steven Hill as Harry as he waits for the bride, his daughter, to appear in *Heartburn* clearly captures the shared resemblance of Henry and the screen character Harry.

85. N. Ephron, *AFI*.

86. This couple, Mark's best friends, is based on the celebrity journalist, power couple Ben Bradlee and Amanda Urban.

87. Berkman, 1.

88. Biskind, 23.

89. *Sisters*, 194–195.

90. Moss, 20.

91. Moss, 20.

92. Moss, 20.

93. Moss, 20.

94. Moss, 20.

95. Berkman, 2.

96. Nonkin, 146.

97. Nonkin, 146.

98. Nonkin, 146.

99. Moss, 21.

100. Moss, 21.

101. Moss, 21.

102. Moss, 21.

103. Ephron, *Anything*, 208.

104. Nora's work does not often acknowledge her two younger sisters Hallie and Amy. *Hanging Up*, Delia's work, has three sisters but not four. Without it ever being stated it is almost as if there is a divide between the first two daughters Nora and Delia and the third and fourth daughters Hallie and Amy. It may be due to the before and after "alcoholism" nature of the Ephrons' young lives: "I thought I grew up in a sit com, and my youngest sister Amy, thinks she grew up in a looney

bin." (Bennetts, 82) Or it may be due to the fact that Hallie distanced herself from the family business for many years. She has only recently begun a career in writing. Certainly for the most part it is Nora and Delia who have the public prominence and the close public association.

105. Ephron, *Nothing*, 38.

106. Ephron, *Author*.

Chapter 3

1. N. Ephron, *Heartburn*, 114.

2. N. Ephron, *Collected*, 19.

3. "Nora Ephron and Delia Ephron wrote the screenplay, suggested by the classic Ernst Lubitsch comedy *The Shop Around the Corner*, screenplay by Samson Raphaelson, in turn, was based on the play *Parfumerie* by Miklos Laszlo" ("you've got mail"); Maslin hanks&ryan@romance.com; and Ebert.

4. N. Collins, 90.

5. N. Collins, 60 – 63, 90.

6. N. Collins, 63, 90.

7. Kimmel, 13.

8. Maltby and Craven, 112.

9. The use of the genre to chronicle and comment on social issues is common. *My Man Godfrey* (1936: La Cava) is an often cited example where within the framework of the screwball/romantic comedy the plight of the depression era "forgotten man" is highlighted.

10. Marks.

11. At the time of writing the Barnes and Noble book store on 66th Street in New York has recently announced its closure which in turn has prompted a number of articles such as the one cited. This particular piece gives an overview of the changes that have taken place in the book store retail business on the Upper West Side since Barnes and Noble opened there in 1996. This piece also notes that it is believed that Meg Ryan's children's book store was based on "Eeyore's Books for Children" on 79th which closed in the wake of the onslaught of the mega book stores. See ("West Side Rag"). See also Marks and Edinger.

12. Birdie Conrad is played by Jean Stapleton in *You've Got Mail*. The name of the character is the reversal of the name of the main character, Conrad Birdie from the stage play and 1963 film *Bye Bye Birdie*, in which Jean Stapleton did not appear. Maureen Stapleton (not a relative), who appeared as Vera in *Heartburn* was in the 1963 film *Bye, Bye Birdie*.

13. N. Collins, 60, 63, 93.

14. N. Collins, 60, 63, 93.

15. H. Ephron, *Anything*, 24–25.

16. N. Ephron, *Social*, 86.

17. N. Ephron, *Collected*, 150–151.

18. N. Ephron, *Collected*, 150–151.

19. Leo Tolstoy, *Anna Karenina*. The novel appeared in serial form between 1873 and 1877. First published as a novel in 1877, it is the story of an aristocratic woman who brings ruin upon herself.

20. N. Ephron, *Collected*, 151.

21. N. Ephron, *Collected*, 151.

22. Maltby, and Craven, 9.

23. Smith, D. "She's a Director with an Edge: She's a Writer," *New York Times*, Dec. 13, 1998. n.p. Web. 8 Oct. 2011. http://www.nytimes.com/1998/12/13/movies/film-she-s-a-director-with-an-edge-she-s-a-writer.html.

24. See Krutnik for the discussion he conducts around the new romantic comedies. I believe that a closer analysis of the Nora Ephron's romantic comedies will reveal that while they do "invoke keynote romantic texts of the past" (139); they do not simply riff off these texts as Krutnik claims but rather examine the validity of these romantic Fantasies. (Krutnik in Neale, 133).

25. In his essay in discussing depictions of romantic love in popular cinema, Ira Israel identifies *Sleepless in* Seattle as a "most interesting" variation of the *Tristan and Isolde* myth. While it is has little relevance to the discussion here what is worthy of note is Israel's identification of the film as being different and unusual. While he ascribes the difference a result of the issue of AIDS it is possible the difference marks Nora's view on the subject as much as on the societal factors which influence behavior. (Israel).

26. Riffin, 57.

27. Ephron, *Lucky Numbers*.

28. "Over the Rainbow." Written for the 1939 film *The Wizard of Oz*. Performed most famously by Judy Garland. Music by Harold Arlen, Lyrics by Yip Harburg. The song is ranked number one on the American AFI list of the greatest feature film songs of the past 100 years (American Film Institute). Judy Garland's rendition of the song is about dreams and fantasies; dreams you dare to dream. It is about a place that is not home; it is "a place of refuge from the everyday, the place where dreams come true, time after time after time" (Maltby, 4).

29. Played by Ida Moore in the film version.

30. W. Marchant, *The Desk Set*, 52.

31. Ephron and Ephron, *Desk Set* scene, 17.

32. H. Ephron, *Anything*, 24.

33. H. Ephron, *Anything*, 110.

34. H. Ephron, *Anything*, 196.

35. H. Ephron, *Anything*, 210.

36. H. Ephron, *Anything*, 210.

37. Nora and Delia wrote the screenplay for *You've Got Mail*.

38. This essay was first published in the *New York Times* on July 1, 2007. See Ephron, *Six*, and later published as part of her anthology *I Remember Nothing*.

39. N. Ephron, *Nothing*, 102.

40. N. Ephron, *Nothing*, 102.

41. N. Ephron, *Nothing*, 102.

42. N. Ephron, *Nothing*, 102.

43. N. Ephron, *Nothing*, 103.

44. See Harris and Olsen.

45. Mernit, 5.

46. Brockes.

47. Waxman.

48. Smith.

49. Frank, *You've Got Mail*. Frank is quoting information that was the subject of a 1995 article written by Levinson. In the article she writes how employers are removing games from work computers because of the time wasted by employees playing games such as Solitaire. Levinson writes "Now Virginia's state workforce of 110,000 can't play games on its 103,000 computers."

50. W. Marchant, *The Desk Set*.

51. Romantic comedy is usually the domain of the young unless the film can be identified as belonging to the sub-genre of romantic comedy coined by Stanley Cavell as the "comedy of remarriage." *Desk Set* fits that criteria by virtue of dialogue, age of the characters and because both Bunny and Richard have had previous relationships. *You've Got Mail* is also part of that sub-genre—the playful banter, the fact that both Kathleen and Jo are in relationships at the beginning of their association, and that they are in their thirties. For further detail see Cavell.

52. *Silkwood* (1983) Karen Silkwood was formerly married and has children; *Heartburn* (1986) Rachel has been previously married; *Cookie* (1989) Cookie's parents are lovers, her father married to another woman; *When Harry Met Sally* (1989) both Harry and Sally have a history of failed relationships; *My Blue Heaven* (1990) Barney and Hannah both have failed marriages; *This Is My Life* (1992) Dottie Ingels is divorced; *Sleepless in Seattle* (1993) Sam's wife has died and Annie leaves her long standing relationship; *Mixed Nuts* (1994) Phil-

lip has a failed relationship and Catherine is an older woman, living with her mother; *Michael* (1996) Frank's wife has died and Dorothy has a number of failed relationships; *Hanging Up* (2000) Eve is married with children; *Bewitched* (2005) Jack is separated from his wife; *Julie and Julia* (2009) Julia Child married Paul Child when she was 36.

53. Nora was involved in the 1970s Second Wave of Feminism. She was not a celebrity of the movement as was Betty Freidan, Gloria Steinem and bell hooks but she was influenced by the opportunity it afforded her to write about herself as a woman. However her stinging assessment of the internal struggles of the movement alienated her from many in the movement. See Ephron Introduction (xx) and the essay "Miami" in *Crazy Salad* (44).

54. Groves.

55. Nora, in her 1972 essay *Fantasies*, writes that as much as she is committed to the Women's Movement and as much as she is one of the women who hoots down men's questions such as "what happens to sex after the revolution (women's liberation)" she says that these men should not be dismissed. Nora at the height of the feminist movement allowed men to have a voice and she acknowledged their voice as legitimate. Nora has a history of setting herself apart in her stance on relationships between men and women (*Salad*, 14).

56. H. Ephron, *Anything*, 10.

57. N. Ephron, *Salad* 43.

58. Straus.

59. *Premiere*, 26.

60. It has to be acknowledged that the screenplay was written by both Nora and Delia Ephron but as the film clearly marks itself as a Nora Ephron film the work is discussed in relation to Nora only but with an awareness that it a collaborative effort involving the two sisters.

61. N. Collins, 63.

62. Hallie Ephron, "Coming of Age with the Ephron Sisters—and Their Mother," *O, The Oprah Magazine*. Oprah.com, March 2013.

63. H. Ephron, *Anything*, 209.

64. Eloise is the ultimate New York child. She of course is fictional. She lived at the Plaza Hotel where she was taken care of by her nanny while her mother lived a glamorous life, mostly away from Eloise. The parallels to be drawn between Nora Ephron who was never at home anywhere but New York and Eloise who was the child of New York are obvious. Both were the scrappy daughters of dis-

tant mothers with glamorous careers. Both dearly loved their respective mothers and was loved back but only on her respective mother's terms (Thompson).

65. I am speaking only in terms of women who worked behind the scenes in Hollywood. Many actresses had both careers and families but it must be said not many managed both successfully.

66. See B. Levy, 46–8; McCreadie.

67. I have not been able to find any evidence of this exact book. I cannot discern the authors name on the book as it appears in the film and major booksellers and the *New York Times Book Review* does not indicate such a title.

68. Ephron in Collins, 60.

69. Hallie Ephron.

70. As already discussed, see N. Ephron, *Heartburn*.

71. The notion of media manipulation, in line with Nora's philosophical position that there is only narrative will be addressed in the next chapter.

72. N. Ephron, *Nothing*, 30.

73. N. Ephron, *Collected*, 19.

Chapter 4

1. N. Ephron, *Neck*, 108–09.

2. Mollie-Ephron and Ephron, 106.

3. N. Ephron, *Neck*, 108–9.

4. N. Ephron, *Neck*, 109.

5. N. Ephron, *Lucky Guy* script, 25.

6. N. Ephron, *Nothing*, 63.

7. N. Ephron, *Nothing*, 30.

8. N. Ephron, *Heartburn*, 23.

9. Cookie is watching *The Brady Bunch* on television in her room when her father arrives. The fantasy is on television while the ersatz family meet in the lounge. *The Brady Bunch* was a popular television series spanning the years 1969–1974. It was the story of a blended family where everyone got along; there were no problems the harmonious group could not resolve. The Bradys were the fantasy outcome of the joining of two families.

10. The Witness Protection Program was introduced in the United States of America under the Organized Crime Control Act of 1970. Under the guidelines of the program, which is managed co-jointly by the United States Marshall Service, the United States Department of Justice and the Federal Bureau of Prisons, witness protection is offered to people who it is deemed have information es-

sential to the prosecution of criminal cases and where it is felt the witness or members of the immediate family may be threatened. The witness and family is provided with a new identity, a job opportunity, subsistence payments, housing, and counseling if this is needed. See Bonsor and links provided for more detail. The program effectively allows someone to live another life; a life and identity that is completely fabricated.

11. Henry Hill is the real person on whom both Vinnie Antonelli and Henry Hill, the character played by Ray Liotta in the 1990 Martin Scorsese film *Goodfellas* is based. *Goodfellas* in turn is based on the Nicholas Pileggi's book *Wiseguys*.

12. James of the *New York Times* describes it as "a disappointment on the screen." and the *Time Out* review says it is a "truly mind-numbingly awful movie"; "Box Office Mojo" reports a total gross domestic total since its release in 1990 as \$U.S. 23,591,472.

13. G. Wills.

14. The FBI mission statement provides a clear sense of the purported high level of importance of its functions: The overall mission of the FBI is to uphold the law through the investigation of violations of federal criminal statutes; to protect the United States from hostile intelligence efforts; to provide assistance to other federal, state, and local law enforcement agencies; and to perform these responsibilities in a manner that is faithful to the Constitution and laws of the United States (FBI).

15. As has been consistently evident in this consideration of the work of Nora Ephron, she uses her stories, the plot, as a vehicle to discuss other subjects: her romantic comedies to discuss how film and literature inform social expectations of love (*When Harry Met Sally, Sleepless in Seattle, You've Got Mail*); to document social change and advances in technology (*You've Got Mail*); to process the events of her life (*Heartburn, This Is My Life*) and as will be seen in the next chapter when *Julie and Julia* is examined, to write about things that interest her such as food and unusual women and again her life in relation to those things.

16. B. Markovits, *Jewish*.

17. Erica Engels, as discussed in Chapter 2, is one of the central characters in *This Is My Life*. Erica operates within that film as Nora's voice.

18. N. Ephron, *Nothing*, 37.

19. B. McCreadie, 206.

20. H. Ephron, "Growing Up Ephron," *O,*

The Oprah Magazine, March 2013. Web. Accessed 20 March 2014. http://www.oprah. com/spirit/Nora-Ephrons-Mother-Hallie-Ephron-Essay.

21. Huffington.

22. Coburn, 58.

23. *Heartburn* total domestic gross is recorded as $25,314,189 and *This Is My Life* $2,922,094 as of September 25, 2011 ("Box Office Mojo," *Life*).

24. Bennetts, 80.

25. Morris.

26. N. Ephron, *Salad*, 14–19.

27. N. Ephron, *Salad*, 16.

28. N. Ephron, *Salad*, 16.

29. Ref. in Eisenstein, Ch. 1.

30. Ref. in Eisenstein, Ch. 5.

31. Ephron, *Sally*, 7.

32. Pobjie, 51.

33. N. Ephron, *Salad*, 15.

34. McGilligan, 40.

35. McGilligan, 15.

36. This quote is taken from Nora's novel *Heartburn* (75) but Annie's brother Dennis (David Hyde Pierce) says the same thing to Annie in the film.

37. Maltby, 9.

38. "I'll have what she's having," Adele Reiner (the director Rob Reiner's mother) says these words after Sally does her fake orgasm in the restaurant. The quote is number 33 on the AFI list of top movie quotes of all times ("American Film Institute," *Quotes*).

39. N. Ephron, *Harry*, commentary.

40. This is the subject of the writer's master's thesis and as such will not be developed in any detail here.

41. William Shakespeare, The precise date of the writing of *The Taming of the Shrew* is unknown but is believed to be in the 1590s.

42. N. Ephron, *Salad*, 14–19.

43. N. Ephron, *Neck*, 109.

44. Ephron, *Anything*, 1; Cornell University does not have a record of Henry Ephron as a graduate indicating that in fact this story is probably true.

45. H. Ephron, *Anything*, 13.

46. H. Ephron, *Anything*, 27.

47. H. Ephron, *Anything*, 66.

48. A quote attributed to Somerset Maugham, although in relation to his autobiographical novel *Of Human Bondage*, it is applicable here.

49. H. Ephron, *Anything*, 37.

50. H. Ephron and P. Ephron, *Three's a Family*, 12.

51. Henry tells the story of meeting Mary Chase the playwright and screenwriter who created Harvey. She was staying at the Algonquin and was very upset as the producer of her play would not allow the play to go on as she intended. She wanted to use a real rabbit. Henry suggested that at the Boston previews they try both methods which did happen and Harvey as everyone knows remained imaginary and was a great hit. (Ephron, *Anything*, 43–44).

52. H. Ephron, *Anything*, 44.

53. Thornton Wilder, *Our Town*. First performed on stage in 1938 and released as a film 1940. Wilder won the Pulitzer Prize for the play.

54. Within the text of the film fictional characters are discussing "living" people, Jean Dixon and Johnny Carson. In relation to Jean Dixon the conversation is about a living person who also believes life is a combination of things and Johnnie Carson is a personality with a constructed persona.

55. In 1967 Nora Ephron wrote a series of articles on Johnny Carson for the *New York Post* which were later published as *And Now Here's Johnny!* (New York: Avon Books, 1968).

56. Canby.

57. Grimes, 141.

58. "The film's screenwriters conjured up a very clever gimmick when they decided to revamp a favourite 1960s television show. Too bad they forgot that a gimmick is no substitute for a screenplay, never mind a real movie" (Dargis).

59. N. Ephron, *Bewitched*, commentary.

60. N. Ephron, *Bewitched*, commentary.

61. Nora Ephron uses this phrase to describe the multiple layers operating in *Bewitched* on the director's commentary. She acknowledges the phrase as one used by the director Mike Nichols.

62. In casting Shirley MacLaine for the role of Iris another level of the notion "life is a combination of things" is introduced. MacLaine has written a number of books which deal with her belief in the metaphysical and spiritual world.

63. Maltby and Craven, 46.

64. Maltby and Craven, 46.

65. N. Ephron, *Heartburn*, 20.

66. N. Ephron, *Heartburn*, 62.

67. N. Ephron, *Heartburn*, 76.

68. N. Ephron, *Heartburn*, 79.

69. N. Ephron, *Heartburn*, 131.

70. Also Annie Reed (*Sleepless in Seattle*) another of Nora's characters understood the tearing of the sleeve of her mother's wedding dress when she tried it on as a sign that her impending marriage was not to be.

71. N. Ephron, *Heartburn*, 134.
72. N. Ephron, *When Harry Met Sally*, 6.

Chapter 5

1. Barnes.
2. Ephron, *Heartburn*, 19.
3. *Julie and Julia* returned a gross worldwide box office result of almost $U.S. 130 million ($U.S. 9.4 million domestic gross) on a $U.S. 40 million production budget. ("Box Office Mojo," *Julia*) and was nominated for a number of awards including the Golden Globe Best Motion Picture Musical or Comedy category and Nora Ephron was nominated for the best adapted screenplay 2010 Writer's Guild of America award for *Julie and Julia*. Meryl Streep was nominated for an Oscar for her portrayal of Julia Child and it was the *New York Times* Critics' Pick August 6, 2009 (Scott). *The Telegraph* said "'Julie and Julia' with Meryl Streep is easily Nora Ephron's best film since 'When Harry Met Sally'" (Sandhu).
4. For the purposes of accuracy, dialogue from the film quoted within this chapter has been sourced from the published final shooting script. Page citations refer to those within this screenplay.
5. Barnes.
6. The names Julie Powell and Julia Child are now linked. Julie Powell became known as the person who cooked her way through Julia Child's cookbook and wrote a blog about it. Julie Powell is thought of in relation to Julia Child, the association is what gives her notoriety. Julia Child is part of Julie Powell's biography.
7. N. Ephron, *Julie and Julia*, commentary.
8. N. Ephron, *Julie and Julia*, script, 62.
9. N. Ephron, *Neck*, 21.
10. Towards the end of the late 1960s and through the 1970s New Journalism, the Second Wave of the Women's Movement and the debate around the auteur were prominent discourses. Nora, in her early twenties and beginning her career as a journalist was directly impacted by the new journalism movement with its emphasis on "I" centered writing— the identification of the author in the work and the use of prose style reportorial journalism—and the women's movement of which she was a supporter. The Women's Movement with its demand for equality for women, politically, in terms of career and the home appealed to Nora who grew up in a home where the rights of women had always been acknowledged. See Eisenstein for a detailed overview of the theoretical discourse of the movement and Wolfe. Along with these movements the idea of the auteur director, who could make films which were personal in some way, found support in the changing conditions of Hollywood and in the introduction of film departments in universities and the college trained director. See Biskind, *Riders*, and King.
11. Sterling, 4.
12. Consider *Life Is Beautiful* (Benigni: 1997). Without the comedy the film would be almost unbearable to watch because of the overwhelming subject, the story of a Jewish father who uses comedy to help his son cope during internment in a concentration camp.
13. "Narrative comedy often deals with serious issues through mechanisms of relative knowledge or irony" (Neale, 158) and provides a safe place in which to contemplate the serious because "comedy frequently calls attention to its status as fiction the spectator is more aware that he/she is watching a film rather than looking in to a "realistically" constructed world" (Neale, 149) It is the contention here that in the same way that the artifice of comedy provides a safe place for the audience to contemplate the serious, comedy provides a safe place for the writer to do the same in relation to their own experience. For further discussion of comedy see Neale and Krutnik.
14. N. Ephron, *Wallflower at the Orgy*, xi.
15. N. Ephron, *Wallflower at the Orgy*, xi.
16. N. Ephron, *Wallflower at the Orgy*, xii.
17. A. Levy, 64.
18. United States Information Agency, Office of Security USIA was established by President Eisenhower in August 1953 and operated under that name until April 1978, when its functions were consolidated with those of the Bureau of Educational and Cultural Affairs of the Department of State and the agency was called the International Communication Agency (USICA). The agency's name was restored as USIA in August 1982. ("U.S. Department of State Web Page Archives"). See Conant (esp. 12–23). In April 1955, Paul Child was interrogated in Washington, D.C. He was questioned about his political beliefs and the political beliefs of his co-workers. Specifically, he was questioned about Jane Foster, a friend of the Childs during World War II.

19. N. Ephron, *Julie and Julia*, script, 35.

20. N. Ephron, *Neck*, 95.

21. N. Ephron, *Julie and Julia*, script, 3.

22. See also "Pruitt Igoe Housing Problems."

23. Although in the instance of the quote the reference is to the collision of urban life and technology versus the environment, the description is equally relevant to the collision of two worlds which took place on September 11, 2001 ("Qatsi Trilogy").

24. The Lower Manhattan Development Corporation was created in the aftermath of September 11, 2001, by then-Governor Pataki and then-Mayor Giuliani to help plan and coordinate the rebuilding and revitalization of Lower Manhattan, defined as everything south of Houston Street (RENEW NYC, "About Us," http://www.renewnyc.com/overlay/AboutUs/).

25. N. Ephron, *Julie and Julia*, script, 5.

26. N. Ephron, *Julie and Julia*, script, 5–6.

27. A. Levy, 68.

28. N. Ephron, *Heartburn*, 119.

29. N. Ephron, *Social*.

30. A. Levy, 64.

31. A. Levy, 68.

32. N. Ephron, *Neck*, 112.

33. N. Ephron, *Salad*, 177.

34. N. Ephron, *Wallflower at the Orgy*, 1.

35. N. Ephron, *Scribble*, 121.

36. N. Ephron, *Neck*, 17.

37. N. Ephron, *Salad*, 113.

38. N. Ephron, *Nothing*, 91.

39. N. Ephron, *Heartburn*, 17.

40. N. Ephron, *Nothing*, 134–5.

41. While the *Desk Set* version of "Floating Island" could not be Julia Child's version —*Desk Set* was made before the publication of Child's book—that Nora chose that particular dessert indicates a conscious reference to her parents work she has built into her film. The inclusion of the dessert and attendant reference is an aside to the main discussion-this is the technique Nora has frequently used in her work—a side reference to the personal which immediately alerts the reader to the work as being informed by her own experience. In this instance the dinner scene in *Desk Set* was written by Henry and Phoebe, it is not part of Marchant's original play. Food is an identifier of Henry and Phoebe's work and a motif of their work as it is with Nora.

42. N. Ephron, *Julie and Julia*, script, 19.

43. N. Ephron, *Julie and Julia*, script, 20.

44. N. Ephron, *Julie and Julia*, script, 32.

45. N. Ephron, *Julie and Julia*, script, 43.

46. N. Ephron, *Julie and Julia*, script, 85.

47. N. Ephron, *Julie and Julia*, script, 8.

48. N. Ephron, *Heartburn*, 116.

49. N. Ephron, *Collected*, 105.

50. N. Ephron, *Julie and Julia*, commentary.

51. N. Ephron, *Nothing*, 33.

52. N. Ephron, *Nothing*, 33.

53. N. Ephron, *Nothing*, 33.

54. N. Pileggi quoted in A. Levy, 68.

55. N. Ephron, *Heartburn*, 119.

56. Poole, 222.

57. N. Ephron, *Julie and Julia*, script, 44.

58. N. Ephron, *Julie and Julia*, script, 87.

59. H. Ephron, *Anything*, 104.

60. A. Levy, 68.

61. A. Levy, 68.

62. N. Ephron, *Julie and Julia*, script, 84.

63. A. Levy, 60.

64. A. Levy, 68.

65. L. Bennetts, 90.

66. N. Ephron, *Neck*, 20.

67. N. Ephron, *Neck*, 20.

68. N. Ephron, *Julie and Julia*, commentary.

69. N. Ephron, *Neck*, 21.

70. N. Ephron, *Neck*, 21.

71. N. Ephron, *Julie and Julia*, commentary.

72. N. Ephron, *Heartburn*, 21.

73. N. Ephron, *Heartburn*, 115.

74. N. Ephron, *Heartburn*, 69.

75. N. Ephron, *Wallflower*, 10.

76. Hesser, 6.

77. N. Ephron, *Julie and Julia*, commentary, 102.

78. See Nora's essay "Dorothy Parker" (*Salad*, 130–34).

79. N. Ephron, *Collected*, 150.

80. N. Ephron, *Collected*, 152–3.

81. J. Jones.

82. N. Ephron, *Julie and Julia*, script, 104.

83. N. Ephron, *Julie and Julia*, script, 62.

84. Voice-over is a device Nora has previously utilized for the same purpose. In *Heartburn*, the novel, Rachel's thoughts, her personal and private musings, are related through the use of a monologue—the written form of voice-over.

85. N. Ephron, *Heartburn*, 19.

86. N. Ephron, *Collected*, 215.

87. On the director's commentary of the DVD version of *Julie and Julia*, Nora acknowledges Amy Robinson, one of the film's producers, as suggesting the subject of *Julie and Julia* and suggesting the parallel construction of the narrative.

88. Although, as Amy Ephron writes in *Cool Shades* (68) and Nora writes in "The

Story of My Life in 3,500 Words or Less," "the immediate cause of her death was an overdose of sleeping pills administered by my father" (*I Feel Bad About My Neck*, 103). This is an interesting detail of Nora's account of her life in that it was one of the events of her life that she did not think of as falling under the "rubic of Everything is Copy" until the writing of this essay, although Nora notes "it did to my sister Amy, and she put it into a novel" (*I Feel Bad About My Neck*, 103).

89. N. Ephron, *Nothing*, 43.
90. N. Ephron, *Heartburn*, 31.
91. Julia Child was renowned for her use of butter and is credited with the quote; "If you're afraid of butter, use cream." See Behrens.
92. N. Ephron, *Heartburn*, 28.
93. N. Ephron, *Heartburn*, 31.
94. N. Ephron, *Heartburn*, 24.
95. N. Ephron, *Julie and Julia*, commentary.
96. See Stein. He refers to her as "a bad-ass" and of her and her television show he writes; "She never edited out any of her mistakes, showing you how to fix them, live with them or bluff. She dropped stuff on the floor, wiped it off and said, 'Remember, you're all alone in the kitchen, and no one can see you.' She was the Lee Marvin of cooking" ("About Julia Child"). This biography quotes from Child's early diary: "She confided in her diary: 'I am sadly an ordinary person ... with talents I do not use.' Yet she continued to yearn for adventure and the chance to escape from her comfortable upper middle class existence" and outlines a woman who was not content with the ordinary life or the life expected of her as the daughter of a comfortable middle class republican family.
97. N. Ephron, *Julie and Julia*, script, 19.
98. N. Ephron, *Julie and Julia*, script, 55.
99. N. Collins, 60.
100. N. Ephron, *Salad*, 13.
101. L. Bennetts, 82.
102. N. Ephron, *Heartburn*, 19.
103. L. Bennetts, 84.
104. Both "On Maintenance" and "I Feel Bad About My Neck" appear in Ephron's *I Feel Bad About My Neck*.
105. J. Bernstein, *Nora Ephron's Final Act*.
106. N. Ephron, *Julie and Julia*, script, 15.
107. N. Ephron, *Julie and Julia*, script, 56.
108. N. Ephron, *Collected*, 25.
109. N. Ephron, *Julie and Julia*, script, 32.
110. T. Brokaw, 197.
111. B. Markovits.
112. A. Levy, 60.
113. A. Levy, 69.
114. N. Ephron, *Julie and Julia*, script, 14.
115. Nora Ephron quoted in Tallmer. Nora was speaking about her essay "Serial Monogamy: A Memoir," which appears in her collection of essays *I Feel Bad About My Neck*.
116. N. Ephron, *Author*.

Conclusion

1. Nora Ephron in reply to Greenstreet.
2. H. Ephron, "Growing Up Ephron."
3. D. Ephron, *Sister*, 19.
4. H. Ephron, "Growing Up Ephron."
5. D. Ephron, *Sister*, 165.
6. D. Ephron, *Sister*, 186.
7. H. Ephron, "Growing Up Ephron."
8. H. Ephron, "Growing Up Ephron."
9. H. Ephron, "Growing Up Ephron."
10. N. Ephron, *Neck*, 134–135.
11. Ephron, "The Story of My Life in 3,500 Words or Less," *I Feel Bad About My Neck*, 103–104.
12. J. Bernstein.
13. L. Komisar, The imaginary cursing woman in Nora Ephron's "Lucky Guy."
14. N. Ephron, *Nothing*, 23.
15. John Cotter in N. Ephron, *Lucky Guy*, 26.
16. N. Ephron, *When Harry Met Sally* Screenplay, vii.
17. N. Ephron, *When Harry Met Sally* Screenplay, xiv.
18. P. McGillgan, 38.
19. E. Brockes.
20. N. Ephron, *Lucky Guy*. 25.

Bibliography

"About Julia Child." *American Masters*. PBS, 15 Jun. 2005. Radio. http://www.pbs.org/wnet/ americanmasters/episodes/julia-child/about-julia-child/555/.

An Affair to Remember. Dir. Leo McCarey. Fox, 1957. Film.

"AFI's 100 Years ... 100 Movie Quotes." *American Film Institute*. American Film Institute, n.d. Web. 27 Oct. 2011. http://www.afi.com/100years/quotes.asp&xgt.

"AFI's 100 Years ... 100 Songs." *American Film Institute*. American Film Institute, 2004. Web. 8 Oct. 2011. http://www.afi.com/100years/songs.asp&xgt.

"The Algonquin Round Table." *The Algonquin Round Table: An Online History of the Vicious Circle*. Kevin C. Fitzpatrick, 2008. Web. http://www.algonquinroundtable. org/.

Always Together. Dir. Frederick de Cordova. Warner Bros., 1947. Film.

Atkinson, Michael. "Oh, the Nora, the Nora: Every Little Thing She Does Is Tragic." *Village Voice*, 14 Jun. 2005: n.p. Web. http://villagevoice.com/film/0525,atkinson 2,65164,20.html.

Avedon, Richard, and Stanley Donen. "Introducing 'Funny Face.'" *Grand Classics*, Interview by Nora Ephron. 2 Feb. 2003. Web. 17 Jul. 2011. http://www.grandclassics.com/ nyc_ephron.shtml.

Barnes, Brooks. "Full Stomachs, and Full Marriages Too." *New York Times*, 31 Jul. 2009. n.p. Web. 28 Oct. 2011. http://www.nytimes.com/2009/08/02/movies/02barn.html? pagewanted=all.

Beale, Lewis. "Nora Ephron's Love Letter: The Queen of Romantic Comedy Films Delivers Again with 'You've Got Mail.'" *New York Daily News*, 20 Dec. 1998. n.p. Web. 9 Oct. 2011. http://articles.nydailynews.com/1998–12–20/entertainment/ 18085515_1_harry-nilsson-nora-ephron-pen-pals.

Beck, Simone, Louisette Bertholle, and Julia Child. *Mastering the Art of French Cooking*. New York: Alfred A. Knopf, 1961. Print.

Beckerman, Ilene. *Love, Loss and What I Wore*. Chapel Hill, NC: Algonquin, 2005. Print.

Behrens, Steve. "Julia Child Quenched Our Hunger for Learning—and Living." *Current*, 23 Aug. 2004. Web. 29 Oct. 2011. http://www.current.org/people/peop0415child. shtml.

Bennetts, Leslie. "Nora's Arc." *Vanity Fair*, Feb. 1992: 8. Print.

Berkman, Meredith. "Life Lessons." *Entertainment Weekly*, 6 Mar. 1992: n.p. Web. 14 Jan. 2011. http://www.ew.com/ew/article/0,,309747,00.html.

Bernstein, Jacob. "Nora Ephron's Final Act." *New York Times Magazine*, 10 March 2013. http://www.nytimes.com/2013/03/10/magazine/nora-ephrons-final-act.html ?pagewanted=all&_r=0.

Berry, Jo, and Angie Errigoe. *Chick Flicks*. London: Orion, 2004. Print.

Beuttler, Bill. "What Happened to the New Journalism? (Part 1)." Master's project, Columbia University Graduate School of Journalism, 1984. Bill Beuttler.com. Bill Beuttler, n.d. Web. http://www.billbeuttler.com/work50.htm.

Bewitched. Dir. Nora Ephron. Columbia, 2005. Film.

Biskind, Peter. *Easy Riders, Raging Bulls*. London: Bloomsbury, 1998. Print.
_____. "The World According to Nora." *Premiere*, Mar. 1992: 26. Print.
Blonde Crazy. Dir. Roy Del Ruth. Warner Bros., 1931. Film.
Bonsor, Kevin. "How Witness Protection Works." *How Stuff Works*, Discovery, n.d. Web. http://people.howstuffworks.com/witness-protection3.htm.
Bower, Anne L., ed. *Reel Food: Essays on Food and Film*. New York: Routledge, 2004. Print.
Bride by Mistake. Dir. Richard Wallace. RKO Radio Pictures, 1944. Film.
Brockes, Emma. "Everything Is Copy." *Guardian*, n.p. Web. 3 Mar. 2007. http://www.guardian.co.uk/books/2007/mar/03/fiction.
Brokaw, Tom. *BOOM! Voices of the Sixties: Personal Reflections on the '60s and Today*. New York: Random House, 2008. Print.
Brooks, Xan. "Flaming Nora." *The Guardian*, 19 Feb. 1999: 47.
Canby, Vincent. "Silkwood (1983) Film: Karen Silkwood's Story." *New York Times*, 14 Dec. 1983. n.p. Web. 27 Oct. 2011. http://movies.nytimes.com/movie/review?res=9C07EFD61638F937A25751C1A965948260.
Casablanca. Dir. Michael Curtiz. Warner Bros., 1942. Film.
Caughie, John. *Theories of Authorship*. London: Routledge & Kegan Paul, 1981.
Cavell, Stanley. *The Pursuit of Happiness: The Hollywood Comedy of Remarriage*. Cambridge: Harvard University Press, 1981. Print.
Child, Julia, and Prud'Homme, Alex. *My Life in France*. New York: First Anchor, 2007. Print.
Christensen, Jerome. "Critical Response: Taking It to the Next Level *You've Got Mail*, Havholm and Sandifer." *Critical Inquiry* 30.1 (2003): n.p. Web. http://criticalinquiry.uchicago.edu/issues/v30/30n1.Christensen.html.
Christmas in Connecticut. Dir. Peter Godfrey. Warner Bros., 1945. Film.
Coburn, Randy Sue. "An Affair to Inspire." *Premiere*, July 1993: 58. Print.
Collins, Nancy. "The US Interview." *US*, Feb. 1999: 60–63. Print.
Conant, Jennet. *A Covert Affair: Julia Child and Paul Child in the OSS*. New York: Simon & Schuster, 2011.
Cook, Pam. *The Cinema Book*. New York: Panthenon, 1985.
Cookie. Dir. Susan Seidelman. Lorimar, 1989. Film.
Crowther, Bosley. "The Screen." Rev. of *Always Together*, written by I.A.L. Diamond, Phoebe and Henry Ephron; Directed by Frederick de Cordova. *New York Times*, n.p. Web. 11 Dec. 1947. http://movies.nytimes.com/movie/review?res=9A04E1D6113BEF3ABC4952DFB467838C659EDE.
_____. "The Screen: Captain Newman M.D. Gregory Peck Plays a Healer of Army Minds." Rev. of *Captain Newman M.D.*, written by Richard L. Breen, Phoebe and Henry Ephron; Directed by David Miller. *New York Times*, n.p. Web. 21 Feb. 1964. http://movies.nytimes.com/movie/review?res=9E07E6DF1230E033A25752C2A9649C946591D6CF.
_____. "The Screen: 'Desk Set'; Murder and Mayhem in Garment Jungle." Rev. of *Desk Set*, written by Phoebe and Henry Ephron; Directed by Walter Lang. *New York Times*, n.p. Web. 16 May 1957. http://movies.nytimes.com/movie/review?res=9D03E3D91631E63ABC4E52DFB366838C649EDE.
_____. "The Screen: 'Jackpot' Opens at Roxy Theatre.'" Rev. of *Jackpot*, written by Phoebe and Henry Ephron; Directed by Walter Lang. *New York Times*, n.p. Web. 23 Nov. 1950. http://movies.nytimes.com/movie/review?res=9A02E7DD113FE23BBC4B51DFB767838B649EDE.
Daddy Long Legs. Dir. Jean Negulesco. Twentieth Century–Fox, 1955. Film.
Dance, Elizabeth. *Tiramisu: Layers of Meaning in Nora Ephron's Sleepless in Seattle*. Melbourne: Latrobe University, 2001.
Dargis, Manohla. "Bewitched (2005) Review Summary." *New York Times*, n.d. n.p. Web. http://movies.nytimes.com/movie/295630/Bewitched/overview.
Desk Set. Dir. Walter Lang. Twentieth Century–Fox, 1957. Film.

Bibliography

"The Desk Set." *Internet Broadway Database*. The Broadway League, n.d. Web. 3 Oct. 2011. http://www.ibdb.com/production.php?id=2544.

Desperately Seeking Susan. Dir. Susan Seidelman. Orion, 1985. Film.

De Vries, Hilary. "Darling, Listen to Me." *New York Times*, n.p. Web. 26 Jan. 1992. http://www.nytimes.com/1992/01/26/magazine/darling-listen-tome.html.

Dreams on Spec. Dir. Daniel Snyder. Indie Rights, 2007. Film.

Ebert, Roger. "You've Got Mail." *Chicago Sun-Times*, 19 Dec. 1998. n.p. Web. 9 Oct. 2011. ttp://rogerebert.suntimes.com/apps/pbcs.dll/article?AID=/19981218/REVIEWS/812180304/1023.

Edinger, Monica. "Eeyore's (the Best Children's Bookstore Ever) Is Remembered." *Educating Alice*, 4 Oct. 2008. Web. 8 Oct. 2011. http://medinger.wordpress.com/2008/10/04/eeyores-the-best-childrens- bookstore-ever-is-remembered/.

Eisenstein, Hester, ed. *Contemporary Feminist Thought*. London: Unwin and Allen, 1984. Print.

"The End of the Era of the Upper West Side Store, Again." *West Side Rag*, 21 Jul. 2011: n. page. Web. 8 Oct. 2011. http://www.westsiderag.com/2011/07/21/the-end-of-the-era-of-the-upper-west- side-bookstore-again.

Ephron, Amy. *Cool Shades*. New York: Dell Publishing, 1984. Print.

_____. *One Sunday Morning*. New York: William Morrow, 2005. Print.

Ephron, Delia. *Book Browse: Your Guide to Exceptional*. Interview. Print. http://www.bookbrowse.com/author_interviews/full/index.cfm/author_number/346/delia-ephron.

_____. *Sister Mother Husband Dog (etc)*. New York: Blue Rider Press, 2013. Print.

_____. *Hanging Up*. New York: Ballantine, 1995. Print.

Ephron, Hallie. "Growing Up Ephron." *O, The Oprah Magazine*, March 2013. Uploaded Thursday, March 20, 2014. http://www.oprah.com/spirit/Nora-Ephrons-Mother-Hallie-Ephron-Essay.

_____. *There Was an Old Woman*. New York: William Morrow, 2013. Print.

Ephron, Henry. *We Thought We Could Do Anything*. New York: W. W. Norton, 1977. Print.

Ephron, Henry, and Phoebe Ephron. *Three's a Family: A Comedy in Three Acts*. 1st. ed. New York: Samuel French, 1944. Print.

Ephron, Nora. *"Academy of Achievement* Interview." 21 Jun. 2007. American Academy of Achievement. Print. 18 Jul. 2011. http://www.achievement.org/autodoc/page/eph0int-1.

_____. "After the Love Is Gone." *New York Times*, 29 Sep 2005: n.p. Web. http://www.nytimes.com/2005/09/29/opinion/29ephron.html.

_____. *And Now...Here's Johnny!* New York: Avon, 1968. Print.

_____. Audio Commentary. *Julie & Julia*. Dir. Nora Ephron, Columbia DVD, 2008.

_____. Audio Commentary. *When Harry Met Sally*. Dir. Rob Reiner, MGM DVD, 2000.

_____. *Author*. December 2010. Interview. Web. 11 Jul. 2011. http://www.authormagazine.org/interviews/interview_page_ephron.htm.

_____. "The Company of Women: An Oral History." *Premiere: Women In Hollywood Special Issue*. 1993: Print.

_____. *Crazy Salad: Some Things About Women*. New York: The Modern Library, 2000. Print.

_____. "Deep Throat and Me: Now It Can Be Told, and Not for the First Time Either." *The Huffington Post*, 31 May 2005. Web. 29 Oct. 2011.

_____. *Heartburn*. London: Heinemann, 1983. Print.

_____. *I Feel Bad About My Neck: And Other Thoughts on Being a Woman*. New York: Knopf, 2006. Print.

_____. "I Feel Bad About My Neck: And Other Thoughts on Being a Woman." *Jewish Book Week*, Interview by Benjamin Markovits. 3 Mar. 2007. Web. http://www.jewishbookweek.com/festivalblog/2007/03/nora-ephron.html.

_____. *I Remember Nothing: And Other Reflections*. New York: Knopf, 2010. Print.

_____. Interview by Boris Kachka. *New York Magazine*, 6 Aug. 2006. Print. 18 Jul. 2011. http://nymag.com/arts/books/profiles/18854/.

_____. *Julie & Julia*. Screenplay Written and Directed By Nora Ephron (Based on *Julie and Julia* by Julie Powell and *My Life in France* by Julie Child). New York: Columbia Pictures, 2008.

_____. "The Last Picture Show." *New York Times*, 7 Apr. 2006: n.p. Web. http://www.nytimes.com/2006/04/07/opinion/07ephron.html?ex=1302062400&en=f2ee8c929f637af7&ei=5090&partner=rssuserland&emc=rss.

_____. *Lucky Guy*. Script. The Schubert Organization, 2013.

_____. "Lucky Numbers." 27 Oct. 2000. Online Posting to *Yahoo! Chat Event*. Web. 8 Oct. 2011.

_____. "Meet the Writers—Nora Ephron." Interview. Barnes and Noble, 10 Nov. 2010. Web. http://www.youtube.com/watch?v=eP2T6ibTnmM.

_____. "The 9/11 Itch." *Slate*, 3 Jun. 2002: n.p. Web. 17 Jul. 2011. http://www.slate.com/id/2066417/entry/2066486/.

_____. *Nora Ephron Collected*. New York: Avon, 1991. Print.

_____. "Nora Ephron: The Drexel Interview." Interview by Paula Marantz Cohen. 30 Jun. 2011. Drexel University. Web. http://www.youtube.com/watch?v=AZjBjOtqCes.

_____. "On Being Named Person of the Year." *Huffington Post*, 17 Dec. 2006: n.p. Web. http://www.huffingtonpost.com/nora-ephron/on-being-named-person-of-_b_36546.html.

_____. "Remarks to Wellesley College Class of 1996." Wellesley College Commencement. Wellesley College. Boston, MA. 1996. Address.

_____. "The Remix; If You Feel Bad About Your Neck." *New York Times*, n.p. Web 22 Oct. 2006. http://select.nytimes.com/gst/abstract.html?res=F4071EFC34540C718EDDA90994DE404482&showabstract=1.

_____. *Scribble, Scribble: Notes on the Media*. New York: Knopf, 1978. Print.

_____. "The Six Stages of E-Mail." *New York Times*, 1 Jul. 2007. n.p. Web. 29 Oct. 2011. http://www.nytimes.com/2007/07/01/opinion/01ephron.html.

_____. "Social Study." *Vanity Fair*, Dec. 1996: 86. Print.

_____. *Today*. Interview by Campbell Brown. 2 Aug. 2006. MSNBC. TV. 18 Jul. 2011. http://today.msnbc.msn.com/id/14027479.

_____. "A Tribute to Meryl Streep." 32nd AFI Life Achievement Award. American Film Institute. Kodak Theatre, Los Angeles. 10 Jun. 2004. Address. n.p. Web 3 April 2009. http://www.youtube.com/watch?v=M4Moh-Sw7xE.

_____. *Wallflower at the Orgy*. New York: Viking Press, 1970. Print.

_____. *When Harry Met Sally*. New York: Knopf, 1990. Print.

Ephron, Phoebe. *Howie: A Comedy in Three Acts*. Rev. acting ed. New York: Samuel French, 1959. Print.

Ephron, Phoebe, and Henry Ephron. *Take Her, She's Mine*. New York: Samuel French, 2011. Print.

"Farce: Definition." *Cambridge Dictionaries Online*. London: Cambridge University Press, Web. 29 Oct. 2011. http://dictionary.cambridge.org/dictionary/british/farce_1?q=farce.

FBI Mission Statement. Web http://www.textfiles.com/law/fbi-miss.txt.

Fox, Margalit. "Betty Friedan, Who Ignited Cause in 'Feminine Mystique,' Dies at 85." *New York Times*, n.p. Web. 5 Feb. 2006. http://www.nytimes.com/2006/02/05/national/05friedan.html?_r=1&scp=1&sq=betty%20friedan%20obituary&st=cse.

"Gale Reference Team." *Biography—Ephron, Henry (1911–1992): An Article From: Contemporary Authors [HTML] [Digital]*. Thomson-Gale, 2001. Web. http://media-server.amazon.com/exec/drm/amzproxy.cgi/mjk2icsinmqizkcs3hao3x7. (Retrieved: 02/05/2006).

Garner, Dwight. "Inside the List." *New York Times*, n.p. Web. 20 Aug. 2006. http://www.nytimes.com/2006/08/20/books/review/20tbr.html?ex=1179806400&en=3fed8af1650485a3&ei=5070.

Gilligan, Beth. "When Meg Met Nora." *Not Coming to a Theatre Near You*. notcoming.com, 17 Jul. 2006. Web. http://www.notcoming.com/features/when-meg-met-nora/.

Bibliography

Grimes, William. "What Debt Does Hollywood Owe to Truth?" *New York Times*, 5 Mar. 1992. 141. Print.

Greenstreet, Rosanna. "Q&A: Nora Ephron." *Guardian*, 5 Sep 2009. n.p. Web. 29 Oct. 2011. http://www.guardian.co.uk/lifeandstyle/2009/sep/05/nora-ephron-interview.

Groves, Valerie. "Writer with an Acid Pen...Nora Ephron." *Sunday Times*, 3 Dec. 1989. n.p. Print.

Gullette, Margaret M. "What's the Matter with Nora Ephron's Neck?" *Women's Enews*, n.p. Web. 6 Sept. 2006. http://www.womensenews.org/story/aging/060906/whats-the-matter-nora-ephrons-neck.

Hanging Up. Dir. Diane Keaton. Columbia, 2000. Film.

Hanson, Peter, and Paul Robert Herman, eds. *Tales from the Script: 50 Hollywood Screenwriters Share Their Stories*. New York: Itbooks, 2010. Print.

Harayda, Janice. "Ms. Ephron Regrets." Rev. of *I Feel Bad About My Neck* by Nora Ephron; *One-Minute Book Reviews*, n.p., Aug. 2006. Web. http://oneminutebookreviews.word press.com/2006/10/14/ms-ephron-regrets/.

Harris, John. "The Last Post." *Guardian*, 13 Oct. 2007. n.p. Web. 8 Oct. 2011. http://www.guardian.co.uk/uk/2007/oct/13/post.

Harvey. Dir. Henry Koster. Universal, 1950. Film.

Hayward, Susan. *Cinema Studies: The Key Concepts*. London: Routledge, 2006. Print.

Helmore, Edward. "Nora Ephron: Woman's Wit." *Independent on Sunday*, 15 Aug. 2009. n.p. Web. 9 Oct. 2011. http://www.independent.co.uk/news/people/profiles/nora-ephron-womans-wit-1772584.html.

Hesser, Amanda. "A Race to Master the Art of French Cooking." *New York Times*, 13 Aug. 2003. n.p. Web. 29 Oct. 2011. http://www.nytimes.com/2003/08/13/dining/a-race-to-master-the-art-of-french-cooking.html?src=pm.

His Girl Friday. Dir. Howard Hawks. Columbia, 1940. Film.

Huffington, Ariana, and Nora Ephron. "Advice for Women." 92Y. New York, 26 Sept. 2006. Address.

Hughes, Kathryn. "Crocodile Tears in Hollywood."

Hutchings, Peter. *Terence Fisher*. Manchester: Manchester University Press, 2001. Print.

Indiscreet. Dir. Stanley Donen. Warner Bros., 1958. Film.

Inverne, James. "Faking It Onstage." *Time Magazine*, 22 Feb. 2004: n.p. Web. 17 Jul. 2011. http://www.time.com/time/magazine/article/0,9171,593486,00.html.

Israel, Ira. "The Myth of Romantic Love in Western Culture, Its Recent Portrayal in Popular American Cinema, and Its Relation to Finitude." *L'Universite d'Ira*. Ira Israel, Dec. 1999. Web. 8 Oct. 2011. http://iraisrael.com/pdf/myth.pdf.

The Jackpot. Dir. Walter Lang. Twentieth Century–Fox, 1950. Film.

Jaffe, Rona. *The Best of Everything*. New York: Penguin, 1958. Print.

James, Caryn. "My Blue Heaven: When Heaven Turns Out Not to Be." *New York Times*, 18 Aug. 1990. n.p. Web. 26 Oct. 2011. http://movies.nytimes.com/movie/review?res=9C0CE5D81339F93BA2575BC0A966958260.

Jones, Judith. *Authors @ Google*. Interview. 25 Feb. 2009. Web. http://www.youtube.com/watch?v=WSLWwfBKF0A.

Julie and Julia. Dir. Nora Ephron. Columbia, 2008. Film.

"Julie and Julia" Box Office Mojo. IMDb, n.d. Web. http://boxofficemojo.com/movies/?id=julieandjulia.htm.

"Kaufman and Hart—The Collaboration." *You Can't Take It with You*. University of Wisconsin, n.d. Web. https://sites.google.com/site/utyoucanttakeitwithyou/kaufman-and-hart---the-collaboration.

Kimmell, Daniel M. *I'll Have What She's Having*. Chicago: Ivan R. Dee, 2008. Print.

King, Geoff. *New Hollywood Cinema*. London: I.B. Taurus, 2002. Print.

Komisar, L. "The Imaginary Cursing Woman in Nora Ephron's 'Lucky Guy.'" *The Komisar Scoop*, 1 July 2014. http://www.thekomisarscoop.com/2013/05/the-imaginary-cursing-woman-in-nora-ephrons-lucky-guy-2/.

Koyaanisqatsi. Dir. Godfrey Reggio. Island Alive, 1982. Film.

"Koyaanisqatsi." *The Qatsi Trilogy*. IRE, 1995. Web. http://www.koyaanisqatsi.org/films/koyaanisqatsi.php.

Kreamer, Anne. "Women as Heroines of Their Own Lives." *Fast*, 15 Feb. 2007: n.p. Web. http://www.fastcompany.com/magazine/70/kreamer.html.

Lacayo, Richard. "Portnoy's Complaint." *Time Magazine*, 16 Oct. 2005:n. page. Web. 26 Oct. 2011. http://www.time.com/time/specials/packages/article/0,28804,1951793_1951944_1952615,00.html.

Levinson, Arlene. "Employers Giving Boot to Games on Computers." *Reading Eagle/Reading Times*, 13 Jan. 1995. A9. Print.

Levy, Ariel. "Nora Knows What To Do: The Filmmaker Foodie Pays Homage to Julia Child." *New Yorker*, 6 Jul. 2009: Print.

Levy, Barbara. *Ladies Laughing: Wit as Control in Contemporary American Women Writers*. Amsterdam: Gordon & Breach, 1997. Print.

Life Is Beautiful. Dir. Roberto Benigni. Miramax, 1997. Film.

Look for the Silver Lining. Dir. David Butler. Warner Bros., 1949. Film.

López-Guzmán, Patricio. "Collaborators and Partners in Crime: François Truffaut." *Alfred Hitchcock, the Master Of Suspense*. N.p., n.d. Web. 25 Oct. 2011. http://hitchcock.tv/people/truffaut.html.

Maltby, Richard, and Ian Craven, eds. *Hollywood Cinema: An Introduction*. Oxford: Blackwell, 1995. Print.

Marchant, William. *The Desk Set*. London: Samuel French, 1952. Print.

Marks, Peter. "Citing Chains, Eeyore's Books Calls It Quits." *New York Times*, 1 Aug. 1993. n.p. Web. 8 Oct. 2011. http://www.nytimes.com/1993/08/01/nyregion/citing-chains-eeyore-s-books-calls-it-quits.html.

Maslin, Janet. "hanks&ryan@romance.com." *New York Times*, 18 Dec. 1998. n.p. Web. 9 Oct. 2011. http://movies.nytimes.com/movie/review?res=9505EEDE113DF93BA25751C1A96E958260.

_____. "Oh, the Indignity: Nora Ephron Confronts Aging and Other New York Battles." Rev. of *I Feel Bad About My Neck*, by Nora Ephron; *New York Times*, n.p. Web. 27 Jul. 2006. http://www.nytimes.com/2006/07/27/books/27masl.html?ex=1179806400&en=d9d5ebd5a6efdd3&ei=5070.

McCreadie, Marsha. *The Women Who Write the Movies: From Frances Marion to Nora Ephron*. New York: Birch Lane, 1994. Print.

McGilligan, Patrick. *Backstory 5: Interviews with Screenwriters of the 1990s*. Berkeley: University of California Press, 2009. Print.

Mernit, Billy. *Writing the Romantic Comedy*. New York: HarperCollins, 2000. Print.

Michael. Dir. Nora Ephron. Turner, 1995. Film.

Mixed Nuts. Dir. Nora Ephron. Tri-Star, 1994. Film.

Morris, Bonnie Rothman. "Interview with Nora Ephron." *Hollywood Lit Sales*, n.p., Apr. 1998. Web. http://www.hollywoodlitsales.com/archives/ephron.shtml.

Moss, Marilyn. "Whose Life Is This, Anyway?" *Box Office*, Feb. 1992: 20–21.

My Blue Heaven. Dir. Herbert Ross. Warner Bros., 1990. Film.

"My Blue Heaven." Box Office Mojo. IMDb, n.d. Web. http://boxofficemojo.com/movies/?id=myblueheaven.htm.

My Man Godfrey. Dir. Gregory La Cava. Universal, 1936. Film.

Neale, Steve. *Genre and Contemporary Hollywood*. London: BFI, 2002. Print.

Neale, Steve, and Frank Krutnik. *Popular Film and Television Comedy*. London: Routledge, 1990. Print.

"New Plays in Manhattan." *Time Magazine*, 7 May 1943. n.p. Web. 7 Jul. 2011. http://www.time.com/time/magazine/article/0,9171,851667.html.

"Nora Ephron." *Box Office Mojo*. IMDb.com, n.d. Web. 18 Jul. 2011. http://www.boxofficemojo.com/people/chart/?view=Writer&id=noraephron.htm.

"Nora Ephron: Box Office Data." *The Numbers: Box Office Data, Movie Stars, Idle Speculation*. Nash Information Services, n.d. Web. 17 Jul 2011. http://www.thenumbers.com/people/directors/NEPHR.php.

181

Bibliography

"Nora Ephron—Ephron's Alcoholism Torture." Contactmusic.com, 9 Aug. 2005: n.p. Web. http://www.contactmusic.com/new/xmlfeed.nsf/story/ephrons-alcoholism-torture.

Nonkin, Lesley Jane. "Take One." *Vogue*, Jan. 1992: 144–147.

O'Keefe, Claudia, ed. *Mother: Famous Writers Celebrate Motherhood with a Treasury of Short Stories, Essays and Poems*. New York: Pocket Books, 1996. Print.

Olson, Elizabeth. "Write Grandma a What?" *New York Times*, 16 Mar. 2006. n.p. Web. 8 Oct. 2011. http://www.nytimes.com/2006/03/16/fashion/thursdaystyles/16letters. Html.

"Overview for Nora Ephron." *Turner Classic Movies*, Turner Entertainment Networks, n.d. Web. 9 Oct. 2011. http://www.tcm.com/tcmdb/person/57813|0/Nora-Ephron/.

Parker, Dorothy. *The Portable Dorothy Parker*. Ed. Marion Meade. New York: Penguin, 2006. Print.

Le Père Noël est une ordure. Dir. Jean-Marie Poire. Trinacra, 1982. Film.

"Peyton Place (2004)." Amazon.com, Amazon Inc, n.d. Web. http://www.amazon.com/ Peyton-Place-Lana-Turner/dp/B0000DJZ8Q.

Pfefferman, Naomi. "Hanging On." *Jewish Journal of Greater Los Angeles*, 18 Feb. 2000: n.p. Web. 15 Feb. 2008. http://www.jewishjournal.com/old/ephron.2.18.0htm.

Pillow Talk. Dir. Michael Gordon. Universal, 1959. Film.

Pobjie, Ben. "In Defence of the Idiot Box." *Age*, 11 Jun. 2001. 51. Print.

Poole, Gaye. *Real Meals, Set Meals: Food in Film and Theatre*. Sydney: Currency Press, 1998. Print.

Powell, Julie. *Julie and Julia: My Year of Cooking Dangerously*. New York: Little, Brown, 2009. Print.

Pribram, Deidre, and Hall, Jeanne. "M.F.E.O.: Nora Ephron." *Creative Screenwriting* 1.1 n.p. Print.

"Pruitt Igoe Housing Problems." *News Report*. KMOX, St. Louis, Nov. 1968. Radio. 29 Oct. 2011. http://www.youtube.com/watch?v=t-cfjqh1sSY&feature=related.

Quinn, Christine. "Introduction." Gail Collins and Nora Ephron's "Women Come of Age" Conversation. 92nd Street Y, New York. 12 Jan. 2010. In Person. http://www. youtube.com/watch?V=JUp-VrDgZ8&featurerelmfu.

Rabkin, Gerald. "Imaginary Friends." Rev. of *Imaginary Friends* by Nora Ephron; *Culture Vulture*, 24 Jan. 2003: n.p. Web. http://www.culturevulture.net/Theater/Imaginary Friends.htm.

Raynsford, Jody. "Blogging: The New Journalism?" *Journalism.co.uk*, Mar. 25 2003: n.p. Web. 18 Jul. 2011. http://www.journalism.co.uk/news-features/blogging-the-new-journalism-/s5/a5604/.

Rich, Frank. "Nora's Secret." *New York Magazine*, News and Features. August 19, 2012, n. page. Web. Aug. 27, 2012. http://nymag.com/news/frank-rich/nora-ephron-2012–8/.

Riffin, Nancy. "That's the Way Love Goes." *Premiere*, Jul. 1993: 57. Print.

Rooney, D. "Why Nora Ephron's Film Made Such an Impact: A Critic's Take." *The Hollywood Reporter*, 27 Jun. 2012. n.p. Web. http://www.hollywoodreporter.com/news/ nora-ephron-death-when-harry-met-sally-342629.

S Gr. "My Blue Heaven." *Time Out London*, n.d. n. page. Web. 27 Oct. 2011. http://www. timeout.com/film/reviews/73694/my-blue-heaven.html.

Sandhu, Sukhdev. "Julie And Julia, review." *Telegraph*, 10 Sep 2009. n. page. Web. 28 Oct. 2011. http://www.telegraph.co.uk/culture/film/filmreviews/6169016/Julie-and-Julia-review.html.

Sarris, Andrew. "Notes on the Auteur Theory in 1962." *Film Culture* (Winter 1962-3): n.p. Print.

Schillinger, Liesl. "Wrinkles in Time." Rev. of *I Feel Bad About My Neck,* by Nora Ephron; *New York Times*, n.p. Web. 20 Aug. 2006. http://www.nytimes.com/2006/08/20/ books/review/20Schillinger.html?scp=29&sq=&st=nyt.

Schorow, Stephanie. "Hanging with ... Nora Ephron: The Author Strolls the Public Garden and Reminisces About Crab-Salad Sandwiches at the Ritz-Carlton." *Boston*

Globe, n.p. Web. 22 Sept. 2006. http://www.boston.com/ae/events/articles/2006/09/22/nora_ephron/.

Scott, A.O. "Two for the Stove." *New York Times*, 6 Aug. 2009. n.p. Web. http://movies.nytimes.com/2009/08/07/movies/07julie.html?pagewanted=allt.

Shone, Tom. "A Life in Pictures: Nora Ephron." *Sunday Times*, 1 Aug. 1993:4. Print.

Silkwood. Dir. Mike Nichols. ABC Motion Pictures, 1983. Film.

Singer, Natasha. "Is Looking Your Age Now Taboo?" *New York Times*, n.p. Web 1 Mar. 2007. http://www.nytimes.com/2007/03/01/fashion/01skin.html?ex=1179806400&en=beb09cc761210194&ei=5070.

Singin' in the Rain. Dir. Stanley Donen and Gene Kelly. MGM, 1952. Film.

Sleepless in Seattle. Dir. Nora Ephron. Tri-Star, 1993. Film.

Smith, Dinitia. "She's a Director with an Edge: She's a Writer." *New York Times*, 13 Dec. 1998. n.p. Web. 8 Oct. 2011. http://www.nytimes.com/1998/12/13/movies/film-she-s-a-director-with-an-edge-she-s-a-writer.html.

Staiger, Janet. *Perverse Spectators*. New York: New York University Press, 2000. Print.

Stam, Robert, and Miller, Toby. Ed. *Film and Theory: An Anthology*. Blackwell: Boston, 2000. Print.

Stein, Joel. "Living Through Better Cooking." *Time Magazine*, 15 Aug. 2004: n. page. Web. 26 Oct. 2011. http://www.time.com/time/magazine/article/0,9171,682275,00.html.

Sterling, Kristen. "Acclaimed Screenwriter Nora Ephron Offers Insights to School of the Arts Students." *Columbia University Record*, 30 Nov. 2001: 4. Print.

Straus, Tamara. "Nora Ephron: One Step Forward for Women in Hollywood, Two Leaps Back for the Rest of Us." *AlterNet*, 1 Apr. 2000. n.p. Web. 9 Oct. 2011. http://www.alternet.org/story/276.

Take Her, She's Mine. Dir. Henry Koster. Twentieth Century–Fox, 1963. Film.

Tallmer, Jerry. "Vital Force Profile: Nora Ephron." *Thrive: Life Begins at Sixty*. 1–31. May 2007: Print.

This Is My Life. Dir. Nora Ephron. Twentieth Century–Fox, 1992. Film.

"This Is My Life." Box Office Mojo. IMDb, n.d. Web. http://boxofficemojo.com/movies/?id=thisismylife.htm.

Thompson, Kay. *Eloise*. New York: Simon & Schuster, 1999. Print.

Truffaut, Francois. "A Certain Tendency of French Cinema." *Cahiers du Cinema* (Jan. 1954): n.p. Web. 25 Oct. 2011. http://nezumi.dumousseau.free.fr/trufcahier.htm.

Tu, Yvonne. "Dorothy Rothschild Parker 1893–1967: Celebrated Conversationalist Renowned for Her Literary Contributions and Founder/Member of the 'Algonquin Round Table.'" *New York City Women's Biography Hub*, The City University of New York. 17 Apr. 2000. Web. 17 Jul. 2011. http://www.library.csi.cuny.edu/dept/history/lavender/386/dparker.html.

"USIA factsheet." *U.S. Department of State Web Page Archives*. Department of State Foreign Affairs Network, Feb. 1999. Web. http://dosfan.lib.uic.edu/usia/usiahome/factshe.html.

Wallflower. Dir. Frederick de Cordova. Warner Bros., 1947. Film.

Waxman, Sarah. "The History of the Upper West Side." NY.com, Mediabridge, n.d. Web. 3 Oct. 2011. http://www.ny.com/articles/upperwest.html.

Weinstein, Joshua L. "Directors Guild to Honor Nora Ephron, Sen. Patrick Leahy." *Reuters*, 12 Aug. 2011: n. page. Web. 29 Oct. 2011. http://www.reuters.com/article/2011/08/12.

Wills, Garry. "How to Repossess a Life: Nora Ephron Takes Control by Telling Her Story Her Way." *Time*, 27 Jan. 1992: 62. Print.

When Harry Met Sally. Dir. Rob Reiner. Columbia, 1989. Film.

The Wizard of Oz. Dir. Victor Fleming. Metro-Goldwyn-Mayer, 1939. Film.

Wizzy. "Bewitched the Movie: Bewitched's Journey to the Silver Screen." Bewitched at Harpie's Bizarre, *Harpie's Bizarre*, 23 Oct. 2005. Web. 16 Jul. 2011. http://www.harpiesbizarre.com/movie.htm.

Bibliography

Wolfe, Tom, and Edward Warren Johnson, eds. *The New Journalism*. New York: Harper and Row, 1973. Print.

Wolitzer, Meg. *This Is Your Life*. New York: Crown, 1988. Print.

Yardley, Jonathan. "Nora Ephron's 'Crazy Salad': Still Crisp." Rev. of *Crazy Salad* by Nora Ephron. *Washington Post*, 2 Nov. 2004. Web. http://www.washingtonpost.com/wp-dyn/articles/A17418–2004Nov1.html.

You've Got Mail. Dir. Nora Ephron. Warner Bros., 1998. Film.

"You've Got Mail." *Warner Brothers Online*. Warner Bros., n.d. Web. 9 Oct. 2011. http://youvegotmail.warnerbros.com/cmp/1frameset.html.

Zolotow, Maurice. "New Lady Playwright at Home and Abroad." *New York Times*, 14 Sep. 1958. Print.

Index

185

Index